TOGA

Study Guide 2nd Edition

The Open Group Publications available from Van Haren Publishing

The TOGAF Series:
TOGAF® Version 9.1
TOGAF® Version 9.1 – A Pocket Guide
TOGAF® 9 Foundation Study Guide, 2nd Edition
TOGAF® 9 Certified Study Guide, 2nd Edition

The Open Group Series:
Cloud Computing for Business – The Open Group Guide
Archimate® 2.0 Specification (Publishes 2012)

The Open Group Security Series:
Open Information Security Management Maturity Model (O-ISM3)
Open Enterprise Security Architecture (O-ESA)
Risk Management – The Open Group Guide

All titles are available to purchase from:
www.opengroup.org
www.vanharen.net
and also many international and online distributors.

TOGAF® 9 Certified

Certified

Study Guide

2nd Edition

Prepared by Rachel Harrison of Oxford Brookes University

Title:	TOGAF® 9 Certified Study Guide 2nd Edition
Series:	TOGAF Series
A Publication of:	The Open Group
Author:	Prof. Rachel Harrison
Publisher:	Van Haren Publishing, Zaltbommel, www.vanharen.net
ISBN:	978 90 8753 680 0
Edition:	Second edition, first impression, December 2011
Layout and Cover design:	CO2 Premedia, Amersfoort –NL
Print:	Wilco, Amersfoort – NL
Copyright:	© 2010-2011 The Open Group All rights reserved

In the event of any discrepancy between text in this Study Guide and the official TOGAF documentation, the TOGAF documentation remains the authoritative version for certification, testing by examination, and other purposes. The official TOGAF documentation can be obtained online at www.opengroup.org/togaf.

TOGAF®9 Certified Study Guide, 2nd Edition

Document Number: B112

Comments relating to the material contained in this document may be submitted to:

The Open Group
Apex Plaza
Forbury Road
Reading
Berkshire, RG1 1AX
United Kingdom

or by electronic mail to: ogspecs@opengroup.org

For any further enquiries about Van Haren Publishing, please send an email to: info@vanharen.net.

Contents

PART 3 THE ARCHITECTURE CONTENT FRAMEWORK

PART 4 THE ENTERPRISE CONTINUUM

PART 5 TOGAF REFERENCE MODELS

Chapter 20 The Technical Reference Model (TRM) 225

Chapter 21 Integrated Information Infrastructure
Reference Model (III-RM) 235

PART 6 ARCHITECTURE CAPABILITY

Chapter 22 Architecture Governance 245

PART 7 BRIDGING FROM TOGAF 8 CERTIFIED TO TOGAF 9 CERTIFIED

Preface

This Document

This document is a Study Guide for TOGAF® 9 Certified. This second edition is based on Version 2 of the TOGAF Certification for People Conformance Requirements, published in December 2011. This edition is aligned to TOGAF Version 9.1, which was published in December 2011.

It gives an overview of every learning objective for the TOGAF 9 Certified Syllabus beyond the Foundation level, and is specifically designed to help individuals prepare for certification.

The audience for this Study Guide is:
- Individuals who require a deeper understanding of TOGAF 9
- Professionals who are working in an organization where TOGAF 9 has been adopted and who need to participate in architecture projects and initiatives
- Architects who will be responsible for developing architecture artifacts
- Architects who wish to introduce TOGAF 9 into an architecture practice
- Architects who want to achieve a recognized qualification to demonstrate their detailed knowledge of TOGAF 9
- Architects who have achieved certification to TOGAF 8 Certified and who wish to upgrade their certification

This Study Guide assumes a prior knowledge equivalent to TOGAF 9 Foundation.

While reading this Study Guide, the reader should also refer to the TOGAF documentation[1] available online at www.opengroup.org/architecture/togaf9-doc/arch and also available as a hardcopy book.

The Study Guide is structured as follows:
- Chapter 1 (Introduction) provides a brief introduction to TOGAF certification and the TOGAF 9 examinations that lead to TOGAF 9 Certified, as well as how to use this Study Guide.

---

1   TOGAF Version 9.1 (ISBN:978 90 8753 679 4, G116), available at www.opengroup.org/bookstore/catalog/g116.htm.

- Part 1: TOGAF 9 Architecture Development Method (ADM) comprises Chapters 2 through 13 and consists of a tour of the ADM phases:

  - Chapter 2 describes the Preliminary Phase within the ADM. This chapter covers the preparation and initiation activities required to create an Architecture Capability.
  - Chapter 3 describes Phase A: Architecture Vision. This chapter covers the initial phase of an Architecture Development Cycle. It includes information about defining the scope, identifying the stakeholders, creating the Architecture Vision, and obtaining approvals.
  - Chapter 4 describes Phase B: Business Architecture. This chapter covers the development of a Business Architecture to support an agreed Architecture Vision.
  - Chapter 5 provides an introduction to Phase C: Information Systems Architectures. The next two chapters describe the details of the two parts of Phase C.
  - Chapter 6 describes the development of the Data Architecture within Phase C.
  - Chapter 7 describes the development of the Application Architecture within Phase C.
  - Chapter 8 describes Phase D: Technology Architecture. The Technology Architecture is used as the basis of the following implementation work.
  - Chapter 9 describes Phase E: Opportunities and Solutions. This phase identifies major implementation projects and groups them into work packages that deliver the Target Architecture defined in the previous phases.
  - Chapter 10 describes Phase F: Migration Planning. This phase develops a detailed Implementation and Migration Plan addressing how to move from the Baseline to the Target Architecture.
  - Chapter 11 describes Phase G: Implementation Governance. This phase ensures that the implementation projects conform to the architecture.
  - Chapter 12 describes Phase H: Architecture Change Management. This phase ensures that the architecture capability can respond to the needs of the enterprise as changes arise.
  - Chapter 13 describes ADM Architecture Requirements Management, a process that applies throughout the ADM.

- Part 2: Guidelines for Adapting the ADM consists of three chapters:
  - Chapter 14 describes how to apply iteration to the ADM, and how to apply the ADM at different enterprise levels.
  - Chapter 15 describes security considerations during the application of the ADM.
  - Chapter 16 describes SOA as an architectural style.
- Part 3: The Architecture Content Framework consists of a single chapter:
  - Chapter 17 describes the Architecture Content Framework and the TOGAF Content Metamodel.
- Part 4: The Enterprise Continuum consists of two chapters:
  - Chapter 18 describes Architecture Partitioning.
  - Chapter 19 describes the Architecture Repository, which is a model for a physical instance of the Enterprise Continuum.
- Part 5: TOGAF Reference Models consists of two chapters:
  - Chapter 20 describes the Technical Reference Model (TRM).
  - Chapter 21 describes the Integrated Information Infrastructure Reference Model (III-RM).
- Part 6: Architecture Capability consists of three chapters:
  - Chapter 22 describes the relationship between Architecture Governance and the ADM. It also describes how to establish and operate an Architecture Board.
  - Chapter 23 describes Architecture Maturity Models.
  - Chapter 24 describes the Architecture Skills Framework.
- Part 7: Bridging from TOGAF 8 Certified to TOGAF 9 Certified consists of a single chapter:
  - Chapter 25 describes the differences between TOGAF 8 and TOGAF 9. This chapter is primarily for individuals who have achieved the TOGAF 8 Certified qualification, and who intend taking the TOGAF 8 – 9 Advanced Bridge Examination.
- Appendix A provides a Practice Test for Section 1 of the TOGAF 8 – 9 Advanced Bridge Examination.
- Appendix B provides a Practice Test for TOGAF 9 Part 2/Section 2 of the TOGAF 8 – 9 Advanced Bridge Examination.
- Appendix C provides the answers to the examination in Appendix A.
- Appendix D provides the answers to the examination in Appendix B.
- Appendix E provides the TOGAF 9 Certified Syllabus.

How to Use this Study Guide

The chapters in this Study Guide should be read in order. However, you may wish to use this Study Guide to study topics with which you are already familiar, and it is certainly possible to select topics for review in any order. Where a topic requires further information from a later part in the syllabus, a cross-reference is provided.

Within each chapter are "Key Learning Points" and "Summary" sections that help you to easily identify what you need to know for each topic. Where applicable, a chapter has an "Exercises" section that will help you reinforce key learning points in the chapter.

Each chapter also has a "Recommended Reading" section that indicates relevant, additional sections of the TOGAF document and other sources that should be read to obtain a full understanding of the subject material.

Finally, at the end of this Study Guide are two "Test Yourself" examination papers that can be used to test your readiness to take the official TOGAF examination. Two papers are provided so that this guide covers both the TOGAF 9 Part 2 Examination as well as the TOGAF 8 – 9 Advanced Bridge Examination.

Conventions Used in this Study Guide

The following conventions are used throughout this Study Guide in order to help identify important information and avoid confusion over the intended meaning.

- Ellipsis (…)
  Indicates a continuation; such as an incomplete list of example items, or a continuation from preceding text.
- **Bold**
  Used to highlight specific terms.
- *Italics*
  Used for emphasis. May also refer to other external documents.
- *(Syllabus Reference Unit X, Learning Outcome Y: Statement)*
  Used at the start of a text block to identify the associated TOGAF 9 Certified Syllabus learning outcome.

In addition to typographical conventions, the following conventions are used to highlight segments of text:

A Note box is used to highlight useful or interesting information.

A Tip box is used to provide key information that can save you time or that may not be entirely obvious.

About TOGAF

TOGAF®, an Open Group Standard, is a proven enterprise architecture methodology and framework used by the world's leading organizations to improve business efficiency. It is the most prominent and reliable enterprise architecture standard, ensuring consistent standards, methods, and communication among enterprise architecture professionals. Enterprise architecture professionals fluent in TOGAF standards enjoy greater industry credibility, job effectiveness, and career opportunities. TOGAF helps practitioners avoid being locked into proprietary methods, utilize resources more efficiently and effectively, and realize a greater return on investment.

TOGAF is developed and maintained by The Open Group Architecture Forum. The first version of TOGAF, developed in 1995, was based on the US Department of Defense Technical Architecture Framework for Information Management (TAFIM). Starting from this sound foundation, The Open Group Architecture Forum has developed successive versions of TOGAF at regular intervals and published each one on The Open Group public web site.

This second edition of this document covers TOGAF Version 9.1, referred to as "TOGAF 9" within the text of this document. TOGAF 9.1 is a maintenance update to TOGAF 9, addressing comments raised since the introduction of TOGAF 9 in 2009.

TOGAF can be used for developing a broad range of different enterprise architectures. TOGAF complements, and can be used in conjunction with, other frameworks that are more focused on specific deliverables for particular vertical sectors such as Government, Telecommunications, Manufacturing, Defense, and Finance.

About The Open Group

The Open Group is a global consortium that enables the achievement of business objectives through IT standards. With more than 375 member organizations, The Open Group has a diverse membership that spans all sectors of the IT community – customers, systems and solutions suppliers, tool vendors, integrators, and consultants, as well as academics and researchers – to:

- Capture, understand, and address current and emerging requirements, and establish policies and share best practices
- Facilitate interoperability, develop consensus, and evolve and integrate specifications and open source technologies
- Offer a comprehensive set of services to enhance the operational efficiency of consortia
- Operate the industry's premier certification service

Further information on The Open Group is available at www.opengroup.org.

The Open Group publishes a wide range of technical documentation, most of which is focused on development of Open Group Standards and Guides, but which also includes white papers, technical studies, certification and testing documentation, and business titles. Full details and a catalog are available at www.opengroup.org/bookstore.

About the Author

Rachel Harrison is a Professor of Computer Science in the Department of Computing and Communication Technologies at Oxford Brookes University. Previously she was Professor of Computer Science, Head of the Department of Computer Science, and Director of Research for the School of Systems Engineering at the University of Reading. Her research interests include systems evolution, software metrics, requirements engineering, software architecture, usability, and software testing. She has published over 100 refereed papers and consulted widely with industry, working with organizations such as IBM, the DERA, Philips Research Labs, Praxis Critical Systems, and The Open Group. She is Editor-in-Chief of the Software Quality Journal, published by Springer.

Prof. Harrison holds an MA in Mathematics from Oxford University, an MSc in Computer Science from University College London, and a PhD in Computer Science from the University of Southampton. She is a Member of the British Computer Society, an Affiliate Member of the IEEE-CS, a Member of the Association of Computing Machinery, and is a Chartered Engineer.

Trademarks

Boundaryless Information Flow™ is a trademark and ArchiMate®, Jericho Forum®, Making Standards Work®, Motif®, OSF/1®, The Open Group®, TOGAF®, UNIX®, and the "X" device are registered trademarks of The Open Group in the United States and other countries.

BPMN™ and Business Process Modeling Notation™ are trademarks of the Object Management Group (OMG).

All other brand, company, and product names are used for identification purposes only and may be trademarks that are the sole property of their respective owners.

Acknowledgements

The Open Group gratefully acknowledges The Open Group Architecture Forum for developing TOGAF.

The Open Group gratefully acknowledges the following reviewers who participated in the review of this Study Guide:
- Beryl Bellman
- Geoff Burke
- Roger Cutts
- Jörgen Dahlberg
- Steve Else
- Bill Estrem
- Howard Gottlieb
- Joop Hoefnagels
- Paul Homan
- Andrew Josey
- Graham Neal
- Marleen Olde Hartman
- Simon Parker
- Mona Pomraning
- Felix Rausch
- Brian Selves
- Selvyn Wright

References

The following documents are referenced in this Study Guide:

- TOGAF Version 9.1, available online at www.opengroup.org/architecture/ togaf9-doc/arch, and also available as a book at (ISBN: 978 90 8753 679 4, G116) at www.opengroup.org/bookstore/catalog/g116.htm.
- TOGAF 9 Foundation Study Guide, 2nd Edition (ISBN: 978 90 8753 6817, B111) available at www.opengroup.org/bookstore/catalog/b111. htm.
- The Open Group Architecture Principles, Case Study by Darren Hawley on behalf of The Open Group Internal Architecture Board, October 2008 (Y082), published by The Open Group (www.opengroup.org/bookstore/ catalog/y082.htm).
- SOA Source Book, April 2009 (G093), published by The Open Group (www.opengroup.org/bookstore/catalog/g093.htm).
- ISO/IEC 42010:2007, Systems and Software Engineering – Recommended Practice for Architectural Description of Software-Intensive Systems, Edition 1 (technically identical to ANSI/IEEE Std 1471-2000).
- TOGAF Certification for People: Program Summary Datasheet, February 2009, published by The Open Group (www.opengroup.org/togaf9/cert/ docs/togaf9_cert_summary.pdf).
- TOGAF 9 Certified Datasheet, February 2009, published by The Open Group (www.opengroup.org/togaf9/cert/docs/togaf9_foundation.pdf).
- TOGAF 9 Certified Datasheet, February 2009, published by The Open Group (www.opengroup.org/togaf9/cert/docs/togaf9_cert.pdf)
- TOGAF Certification for People: Certification Policy, February 2009 (X091), published by The Open Group (www.opengroup.org/bookstore/ catalog/x091.htm).
- TOGAF Certification for People: Conformance Requirements (Multi-Level), Version 2, December 2011 (X111), published by The Open Group (www.opengroup.org/bookstore/catalog/x111.htm).
- Zachman Framework, Zachman Institute for Framework Advancement (ZIFA) (www.zifa.com).
- Bill Estrem, "TOGAF to the Rescue" (www.opengroup.org/downloads)

- Enterprise Architecture Planning (EAP): Developing a Blueprint for Data, Applications, and Technology, Steven H. Spewak & Steven C. Hill, ISBN: 0-47-159985-9, John Wiley & Sons, 1993.
- US Department of Commerce Enterprise Architecture Capability Maturity Model (ACMM), Version 1.2 (http://ocio.os.doc.gov/ ITPolicyandPrograms/Enterprise_Architecture/PROD01_004935).
- ArchiMate 1.0 Specification, Technical Standard, February 2009 (C091), published by The Open Group (www.opengroup.org/bookstore/catalog/ c091.htm).
- Mapping of TOGAF 8.1 With COBIT 4.0 by the IT Governance Institute (ITGI), White Paper, July 2007 (W072), published by The Open Group (www.opengroup.org/bookstore/catalog/w072.htm)
- Guide to Security Architecture in TOGAF ADM, White Paper developed by The Open Group Security Forum and Members of The Open Group Architecture Forum, December 2005 (W055), published by The Open Group (www.opengroup.org/bookstore/catalog/w055.htm)

The following web links are referenced in this Study Guide:
- The Open Group TOGAF 9 Certification web site: www.opengroup.org/ togaf9/cert
- The TOGAF information web site: www.togaf.info
- TOGAF 9 People Certification Overview presentation: www.togaf.info/ sg01
- Introduction to the ADM presentation: www.togaf.info/sg02
- Sample Catalogs, Matrices, and Diagrams presentation: www.togaf.info/ sg03
- TOGAF 9 Architecture Content Metamodel Overview presentation: www.togaf.info/sg04

xxx

Chapter 1

Introduction

1.1 Key Learning Points

This document is a Study Guide for TOGAF Version 9 for students planning
to qualify as TOGAF 9 Certified. This document is a companion document
to the TOGAF 9 Foundation Study Guide, and focuses on the learning
outcomes beyond the Foundation level.

Prerequisite Knowledge

This Study Guide assumes a prior knowledge equivalent to TOGAF 9 Foundation.
This can be obtained by reading the TOGAF 9 Foundation Study Guide (see
References).

This first chapter will familiarize you with the TOGAF 9 certification
program, as well as give you important information about the structure of the
TOGAF 9 examinations.

The objectives of this chapter are as follows:
- To provide an understanding of TOGAF certification
- To learn key facts about the TOGAF 9 examinations

1.2 The TOGAF Certification for People Program

Certification is available to individuals who wish to demonstrate they have
attained the required knowledge and understanding of TOGAF Version 9..

There are two levels defined for TOGAF 9 "people certification", denoted
TOGAF 9 Foundation and *TOGAF 9 Certified*, respectively. This Study Guide
covers the second of these – TOGAF 9 Certified. Studying for TOGAF 9
Certified includes all the learning outcomes for TOGAF 9 Foundation, which
are covered in a separate companion document (see References).

1.2.1 Certification Document Structure

The documents available to support the program are as shown in Figure 1:

Figure 1:   Certification Document Structure

Program description documents, such as this Study Guide, are intended
for an end-user audience including those interested in becoming certified.
The Program definition documents are intended for trainers, examination
developers, and the Certification Authority. All these documents are available
from The Open Group web site.[2]

1.2.2 TOGAF 9 Foundation

The purpose of certification to TOGAF 9 Foundation is to provide validation
that the Candidate has gained knowledge of the terminology, structure,

2   Available at the TOGAF 9 certification web site (www.opengroup.org/togaf9/cert), or The Open Group
     bookstore (www.opengroup.org/bookstore).

and basic concepts of TOGAF 9, and understands the core principles of Enterprise Architecture and TOGAF. The learning objectives at this level focus on knowledge and comprehension. More information is provided in the TOGAF 9 Foundation Study Guide (see References).

1.2.3 TOGAF 9 Certified

The purpose of certification to TOGAF 9 Certified is to provide validation that, in addition to the knowledge and comprehension of TOGAF 9 Foundation, the Candidate is able to analyze and apply this knowledge. The learning objectives at this level therefore focus on application and analysis in addition to knowledge and comprehension.

Individuals certified at this level, in addition to the knowledge required for TOGAF 9 Foundation, will have demonstrated their understanding of:

- How to apply the ADM phases in development of an enterprise architecture
- How to apply Architecture Governance in development of an enterprise architecture
- How to apply the TOGAF Architecture Content Framework
- How to apply the concept of building blocks
- How to apply the Stakeholder Management Technique
- How to apply the TOGAF Content Metamodel
- How to apply TOGAF recommended techniques when developing an enterprise architecture
- The TOGAF Technical Reference Model (TRM) and how to customize it to meet an organization's needs
- The Integrated Information Infrastructure Reference Model (III-RM)
- The content of the key deliverables of the ADM cycle
- How an enterprise architecture can be partitioned to meet the specific needs of an organization
- The purpose of the Architecture Repository
- How to apply iteration and different levels of architecture with the ADM
- How to adapt the ADM for security
- SOA as a style of architecture
- The role of architecture maturity models in developing an enterprise architecture
- The purpose of the Architecture Skills Framework and how to apply it within an organization

Self-Study Paths

The self-study paths[3] to achieve certification for TOGAF 9 Certified are summarized in Figure 2. The chosen path depends on existing qualifications, such as whether you are TOGAF 8 Certified, and whether you want to first become certified to TOGAF 9 Foundation or proceed direct to TOGAF 9 Certified.

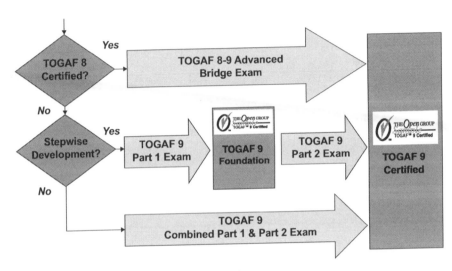

Figure 2:   Paths to Achieving TOGAF 9 Certified

What is the Relationship between TOGAF 9 Foundation and TOGAF 9 Certified?
Candidates are able to choose whether they wish to become certified in a stepwise manner by starting with TOGAF 9 Foundation and then at a later date TOGAF 9 Certified, or bypass TOGAF 9 Foundation and go directly to TOGAF 9 Certified. For those going directly to TOGAF 9 Certified there is a choice of taking the two examinations separately or a Combined examination. The advantage of taking the two examinations over the single Combined examination is that if you pass Part 1 but fail Part 2 you can still qualify for TOGAF 9 Foundation.

---

3   The latest information on the TOGAF 9 certification program can be obtained from the TOGAF 9 Certification web site at www/opengroup.org/togaf9/cert.

1.2.4 The Certification Process

The TOGAF 9 Certified Syllabus is contained in Appendix E.

Readers are assumed to be already familiar with the syllabus for TOGAF 9 Foundation and its accompanying TOGAF 9 Part 1 Examination. Detailed information is provided in the TOGAF 9 Foundation Study Guide (see References).

The TOGAF 9 Part 2 Examination

The syllabus for the TOGAF 9 Part 2 Examination consists of all the learning outcomes defined in both Level 1 and Level 2 of the Conformance Requirements document. At the time of writing this document, the examination topics are drawn from the learning outcomes with eight scenario-based questions.

The eight scenarios are drawn from the following major topic areas:
* ADM Phases: Project Establishment (Phases Preliminary, A, Requirements Management)
* ADM Phases: Architecture Definition (Phases B, C, D)
* ADM Phases: Transition Planning (Phases E and F)
* ADM Phases: Governance (Phases G and H)
* Adapting the ADM
* Architecture Content Framework
* TOGAF Reference Models
* Architecture Capability Framework

The TOGAF 8 – 9 Advanced Bridge Examination

Candidates who have previously qualified to TOGAF 8 Certified can take a single examination known as the TOGAF 8 – 9 Advanced Bridge Examination.

This contains two sections as follows:
* Section 1: Twenty simple multiple-choice questions drawn from the TOGAF 9 Level 1 Syllabus. This is a subset of the TOGAF 9 Part 1 Examination
* Section 2: Eight scenario-based questions as per the TOGAF 9 Part 2 Examination

1.2.4.1 *Format of the Examination Questions*

The questions for Section 1 of the Advanced Bridge Examination are simple multiple-choice questions as described in the TOGAF 9 Foundation Study Guide. Examples of these questions are provided in Appendix A.

The questions for the TOGAF 9 Part 2 Examination and Section 2 of the Advanced Bridge Examination consist of eight complex scenario questions. Candidates must read a scenario describing a situation where TOGAF is being applied. The question will then ask how TOGAF would be used to address a particular point, and provide four possible answers. The answers are graded. One answer is more correct than two of the others, and one is incorrect for the situation. The aim is to select the best answer according to TOGAF 9. The correct answer scores five points, the second best answer three points, and the third best answer one point. The incorrect answer (or distracter) scores zero points. You may need to refer to the TOGAF specification during the examination and a copy is provided with the examination (see below for more details).

The exact display format is test center-specific and will be made clear on the screens when taking the examination. Examples of these questions are provided in Appendix B.

1.2.4.2 *What do I need to bring with me to take the examination?*

You should consult with the test center regarding the forms of picture ID needed to verify your identification.

1.2.4.3 *If I fail, how soon can I retake the examination?*

You are expected to be familiar with the current policy on The Open Group web site. At the time of writing, the policy states that individuals who have failed the examination are not allowed to retake the examination within one month of the first sitting.

1.2.5 Preparing for the Examination

You can prepare for the examination by working through this Study Guide section-by-section. After completing each section you should complete the exercises and read the referenced sections from the TOGAF documentation. Once you have completed all the sections in this Study Guide, you can then attempt the appropriate Test Yourself examination paper(s) in the appendices.

This is designed as a thorough test of your knowledge. If you have completed all the prescribed preparation and can attain a pass mark for the Test Yourself examination paper(s), then you may be ready to sit the examination.

Open-Book Examinations

Both the TOGAF 9 Part 2 Examination and the TOGAF 8 – 9 Advanced Bridge Examinations are open-book. The test center will provide access to the TOGAF 9 specification. At Prometric test centers, the TOGAF specification is provided as part of the examination itself.

1.3 Summary

The TOGAF 9 People certification program is a knowledge-based certification program. It has two levels, leading to certification for TOGAF 9 Foundation and TOGAF 9 Certified, respectively.

The topic for this Study Guide is preparation for the TOGAF 9 Part 2 Examination or Section 2 of the TOGAF 8 – 9 Advanced Bridge Examination, leading to TOGAF 9 Certified. The TOGAF 9 Part 2 Examination comprises eight scenario-based questions to be completed in 90 minutes. The Bridge examination also includes twenty multiple-choice questions and has a time limit of two hours.[4]

Preparing for the examination includes the following steps:
- You should work through this Study Guide step-by-step.
- At the end of each chapter, you should complete the exercises (where provided) and read the sections of the TOGAF documentation listed under Recommended Reading.
- Once you have completed all the chapters in this Study Guide, you should attempt the applicable Test Yourself examination paper in the appendices.
- If you can attain the target score for the paper, then you have completed your preparation.

---

4   Additional time is allowed for candidates for whom English is a second language where the examination is not available in the local language. For further information see the advice to candidates sheet on The Open Group TOGAF 9 certification web site.

1.4 Recommended Reading

The following are recommended sources of further information for this chapter:

- TOGAF Certification for People: Program Summary Datasheet
- TOGAF 9 Certified Datasheet
- TOGAF Certification for People: Certification Policy)
- TOGAF Certification for People: Conformance Requirements (Multi-level)
- The Open Group TOGAF 9 Certification web site: www.opengroup.org/togaf9/cert
- The TOGAF information web site: www.togaf.info
- TOGAF 9 People Certification Overview presentation: www.togaf.info/sg01

PART 1

TOGAF 9 Architecture Development Method (ADM)

In this Part, we take a tour of the Architecture Development Method (ADM) which forms the core of TOGAF. The descriptions in this Part focus on the detail of the inputs, steps, and outputs of each phase and build upon rather than duplicate the TOGAF 9 Foundation Syllabus.

Recommended reading before commencing this part of the Study Guide includes:
- TOGAF 9 Foundation Study Guide, Chapter 5, Introduction to the Architecture Development Method
- Introduction to the ADM presentation: www.togaf.info/sg02

Chapter 2

Preliminary Phase

2.1 Key Learning Points

This chapter describes the Preliminary Phase within the TOGAF Architecture Development Method (ADM). This chapter will help you understand how to apply the Preliminary Phase to develop an enterprise architecture.

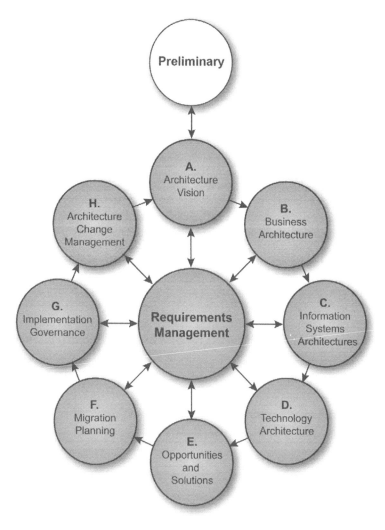

Figure 3:   Preliminary Phase

Key Points Explained

Upon completion of this chapter you should be able to:

1. Understand the inputs to the phase, and be able to explain the following key elements:

   - Architecture Frameworks
   - Business principles, business goals, and business drivers

2. Explain the influence of pre-existing architectural inputs on the phase

3. Understand the steps, and be able to:

   - Describe how to establish an enterprise architecture team and organization
   - Identify and establish a set of architecture principles for a given scenario
   - Discuss the appropriate considerations for tailoring the framework

4. Understand the outputs, and be able to explain the following key elements:

   - Architecture Principles
   - Architecture Governance Framework
   - Request for Architecture Work

2.2 Objectives

The objectives of the Preliminary Phase are to:

- Determine the Architecture Capability desired by the organization:
  - Review the organizational context for conducting enterprise architecture
  - Identify and scope the elements of the enterprise organizations affected by the Architecture Capability
  - Identify the established frameworks, methods, and processes that intersect with the Architecture Capability
  - Establish a Capability Maturity target
- Establish the Architecture Capability:
  - Define and establish the Organizational Model for Enterprise Architecture
  - Define and establish the detailed process and resources for architecture governance
  - Select and implement tools that support the Architecture Capability
  - Define the architecture principles

2.3 Inputs

(Syllabus Reference: Unit 1, Learning Outcome 1: You should understand the inputs to the phase.)

The Preliminary Phase takes as inputs:
- TOGAF
- Other Architecture Framework(s)
- Board strategies and board business plans, business strategy, IT strategy
- Business principles, business goals, and business drivers
- Governance and legal frameworks, including Architecture Governance strategy
- Existing Organizational Model for Enterprise Architecture
- Existing Architecture Framework, if any

2.3.1 Architecture Frameworks

(Syllabus Reference: Unit 1, Learning Outcome 1.1: You should be able to explain the key element: Architecture Frameworks.)

An Architecture Framework is a tool for assisting in the acceptance, production, use, and maintenance of architectures. TOGAF is an example of an Architecture Framework. It is based on an iterative process model supported by best practices and a re-usable set of existing architectural assets. Other popular architecture frameworks include Zachman, Gartner, DoDAF, FEAF, and TEAF.

2.3.2 Business Principles, Business Goals, and Business Drivers

(Syllabus Reference: Unit 1, Learning Outcome 1.2: You should be able to explain the key element: business principles, business goals, and business drivers.)

A statement of the business principles, goals, and drivers usually exists in an enterprise before the architecture activity starts (for example, the annual report). Architecture work is guided by business principles as well as architecture principles. The architecture principles themselves are also normally based in part on business principles.

See also Section 2.5.5.

2.3.3 Pre-Existing Architectural Inputs

(Syllabus Reference: Unit 1, Learning Outcome 2: You should be able to explain the influence of pre-existing architectural inputs on this phase.)

Pre-existing architectural inputs can influence the approach taken. For example, existing models for operating an enterprise architecture capability can be used as a baseline for the Preliminary Phase.

Typical inputs to consider include:
- The Organizational Model for Enterprise Architecture, including:
  - Scope of organizations impacted
  - Maturity assessment, gaps, and resolution approach
  - Roles and responsibilities for architecture team(s)
  - Budget requirements
  - Governance and support strategy
- Existing Architecture Framework, if any, including:
  - Architecture method
  - Architecture content
  - Configured and deployed tools
  - Architecture principles
  - Architecture Repository

2.4 Steps

(Syllabus Reference: Unit 1, Learning Outcome 3: You should understand the steps in this phase.)

The Preliminary Phase consists of the following steps:
1. Scope the enterprise organizations impacted
2. Confirm governance and support frameworks
3. Define and establish the enterprise architecture team and organization
4. Identify and establish architecture principles
5. Tailor TOGAF and, if any, other selected Architecture Frameworks
6. Implement architecture tools

The steps are described in more detail in the following subsections.

2.4.1 Scope the Enterprise Organizations Impacted

TOGAF recommends identification of various units of an enterprise scoped by the impact of the enterprise architecture activity:

- Identify those who will be the most affected and who stand to get the most value from the work: this is the *core* enterprise or unit(s).
- Identify those who will see change to their capability and work with core units, but are otherwise not directly affected: this is the *soft* enterprise or unit.
- Identify those units outside the scoped enterprise who will be affected in their own enterprise architecture: this is the *extended* enterprise.
- Identify those stakeholders who will be affected and who are in groups: this is known as *communities*.
- Finally in this step, we must determine the *governance* involved, including legal frameworks and geographies.

2.4.2 Confirm Governance and Support Frameworks

Part of the major output of this phase is a framework for Architecture Governance. Here we must decide how architectural material is brought under governance and the required characteristics for a governance repository.

It is likely that the existing governance and support models of an organization will need to change to support the newly adopted Architecture Framework. To manage the change required to adopt the new Architecture Framework, the current enterprise governance and support models will need to be assessed to understand their overall shape and content. Additionally, the sponsors and stakeholders for architecture will need to be consulted on potential impacts that could occur.

Upon completion of this step, the architecture touch-points and likely impacts should be understood and agreed by relevant stakeholder

TOGAF provides significant guidance on establishing effective Architecture Governance and coordinating with other governance processes within the organization. Effective governance ensures that problems are identified early and that subsequent changes to the environment occur in a controlled manner.
Bill Estrem, "TOGAF to the Rescue" (www.opengroup.org/downloads)

2.4.3 Define and Establish the Enterprise Architecture Team and Organization

(Syllabus Reference: Unit 1, Learning Outcome 3.1: You should be able to describe how to establish an enterprise architecture team and organization.)

TOGAF recommends the following to define and establish the enterprise architecture team/organization:

- Determine the existing enterprise and business capability
- Conduct an architecture/business change maturity assessment
- Identify gaps in existing work areas
- Allocate key roles and responsibilities for enterprise architecture capability management and governance
- Write requests for change for existing projects
- Determine constraints on enterprise architecture work
- Review and agree with sponsors and board
- Assess budget requirements

2.4.4 Identify and Establish Architecture Principles

(Syllabus Reference: Unit 1, Learning Outcome 3.2: You should be able to identify and establish a set of architecture principles for a given scenario.)

Principles are general rules and guidelines that inform the way in which an organization fulfills its mission. Principles are intended to be enduring and seldom amended.

Prerequisite Knowledge

This Study Guide assumes a prior knowledge equivalent to TOGAF 9 Foundation This includes understanding the need for principles and where they are used in TOGAF, the standard template for principles, as well as what makes a good principle. [TOGAF 9 Foundation Study Guide, Section 8.3]
For further information on principles, see TOGAF 9 Part III, Chapter 23 (Architecture Principles).

2.4.4.1 *Developing Architecture Principles*

Architecture principles are typically developed by the enterprise architects, in conjunction with the key stakeholders, and are approved by the Architecture Board.

The following typically influences the development of architecture principles:

- **Enterprise mission and plans**: The mission, plans, and organizational infrastructure of the enterprise.
- **Enterprise strategic initiatives**: The characteristics of the enterprise – its strengths, weaknesses, opportunities, and threats – and its current enterprise-wide initiatives (such as process improvement and quality management).
- **External constraints**: Market factors (e.g., time-to-market imperatives, customer expectations, etc.); existing and potential legislation.
- **Current systems and technology**: The set of information resources deployed within the enterprise, including systems documentation, equipment inventories, network configuration diagrams, policies, and procedures.
- **Computer industry trends**: Predictions about the usage, availability, and cost of computer and communication technologies, taken from credible sources along with associated best practices presently in use.

Principles and the Content Metamodel

Information related to principles can be modeled, if the right information is captured. The metamodel relates principles back to specific drivers, goals, and objectives and defines the principles catalog as an artifact produced in the Preliminary Phase.

2.4.4.2 Applying Architecture Principles

Architecture principles are used to capture the fundamental truths about how the enterprise will use and deploy IT resources and assets. The principles are used in a number of different ways:

- To provide a framework within which the enterprise can start to make conscious decisions about enterprise architecture and projects that implement the target enterprise architecture
- As a guide to establishing relevant evaluation criteria, thus exerting strong influence on the selection of products, solutions, or solution architectures in the later stages of managing compliance to the enterprise architecture
- As drivers for defining the functional requirements of the architecture
- As an input to assessing both existing implementations and the future strategic portfolio, for compliance with the defined architectures; these

assessments will provide valuable insights into the transition activities needed to implement an architecture, in support of business goals and priorities

- The Rationale statements in the TOGAF template for principles highlight the value of the architecture to the enterprise, and therefore provide a basis for justifying architecture activities
- The Implications statements in the TOGAF template for principles provide an outline of the key tasks, resources, and potential costs to the enterprise of following the principle; they also provide valuable inputs to future transition initiatives and planning activities
- To support the Architecture Governance activities in terms of:
  - Providing support for the standard Architecture Compliance assessments where some interpretation is allowed or required
  - Supporting a decision to initiate a dispensation request where the implications of a particular architecture amendment cannot be resolved within local operating procedures

Principles are inter-related and need to be applied as a set. Principles will sometimes compete; for example, the principles of "accessibility" and "security". Each principle must be considered in the context of "all other things being equal". At times a decision will be required as to which principle will take precedence on a particular issue. The rationale for such decisions should always be documented. The fact that a principle seems self-evident does not mean that the principle is actually observed or accepted in an organization, even when there are verbal acknowledgements of the principle. Although specific penalties are not prescribed in a declaration of principles, violations of principles generally cause operational problems and inhibit the ability of the organization to fulfill its mission.

Principles in Federated Architectures

In large organizations with federated architectures, requirements from a higher-level architecture often appear as "principles" in lower-level ones. This usually takes the form of a principle stating that the lower-level architecture must adhere to the principles of the higher-level architecture. Another example might be a technology principle that has been passed down, such as "all network assets must be IPV6-capable."

Example 1 is a set of principles[5] developed in the Preliminary Phase by The Open Group in one of its own architecture projects.

Example 1:   Preliminary Phase Principles

An Example Statement of Principles

Principles guide us in developing the architecture. They should neither undermine each other nor behave as a blockage to the achievement of others. Policies direct execution. We are unlikely to achieve the principles all of the time – but should aspire to get there.

The following set of principles have been approved by the Internal Architecture Board:

Business Principles

1. Primacy of Principles
2. Maximize Benefit to the Enterprise
3. Compliance with Law
4. Availability at Anytime from Anywhere
5. Business Continuity
6. Citizenship
7. Custodianship
8. De-Customization
9. Painless User Experience
10. Self-Serve

Architecture Principles

1. De-Skill
2. One Source
3. Content Management

Each of these principles is then expanded into a statement with rationale and implications, as shown in Example 2 and Example 3.

---

5   A Case Study covering the development of these architecture principles is published by The Open Group – see References.

Example 2:   Sample Principle 1

Primacy of Principles	
Statement	Principles apply throughout the enterprise and override all other considerations when decisions are made.
Rationale	The only way we can provide a recognized, consistent, and measurable level of operations is if all parts of the enterprise abide by the principles when making decisions.
Implications	Without this principle, short-term considerations, supposedly convenient exceptions, and inconsistencies would rapidly undermine the management of information. Information management initiatives will not be permitted to begin until they are examined for compliance with the principles. A conflict with a principle will be resolved by changing the conflicting initiative, which could delay or prevent the initiative.

Example 3:   Sample Principle 2

Self-Serve	
Statement	Customers should be able to serve themselves.
Rationale	Applying this principle will improve customer satisfaction, reduce administrative overhead, and potentially improve revenue.
Implications	There is an implication to improve ease-of-use and minimize training needs; for example, members should be able to update their contact details, etc., and be able to buy additional membership products online.

See also Exercise 2-1.

2.4.5   Tailor TOGAF and, if any, Other Selected Architecture Frameworks

(Syllabus Reference: Unit 1, Learning Outcome 3.3: You should be able to discuss the appropriate considerations for tailoring the framework.)

To use TOGAF most effectively, it should be tailored for the architecture project in the Preliminary Phase.

Firstly, it is necessary to tailor the TOGAF model for integration into the enterprise. This tailoring should include integration with project and process management frameworks, customization of terminology, development of presentational styles, selection, configuration, and deployment of architecture tools, etc. The formality and detail of any frameworks adopted should also be aligned with other contextual factors for the enterprise, such as culture, stakeholders, commercial models for enterprise architecture, and the existing level of architecture capability.

Why is it necessary to Adapt the ADM?

The ADM is a generic method for architecture development, which is designed to deal with most system and organizational requirements. However, it will often be necessary to modify or extend the ADM to suit specific needs. One of the tasks before applying the ADM is to review its components for applicability, and then tailor them as appropriate to the circumstances of the individual enterprise. This activity may well produce an "enterprise-specific" ADM.

[Source: TOGAF 9 Part II, Chapter 5 (Introduction)]

Once the framework has been tailored to the enterprise, further tailoring is necessary in order to fit the framework to the specific architecture project. Tailoring at this level will select appropriate deliverables and artifacts to meet project and stakeholder needs.

Considerations for tailoring include the following:

- **Terminology tailoring**: The terminology used should be that which is understood across the enterprise. Tailoring should produce an agreed terminology set for the description of architectural content. A glossary should be developed, if appropriate.
- **Process tailoring**: The ADM is a generic process. Process tailoring allows for the removal of tasks that are already carried out elsewhere in the organization, the addition of organization-specific tasks (such as specific checkpoints), and the alignment of the ADM processes to external process frameworks.
- **Content tailoring**: Using the Architecture Content Framework and the Enterprise Continuum as a basis, tailoring of the content structure and classification approach allows for adoption of third-party content frameworks and also customization of the framework to support organization-specific requirements.

The outcome of this step should be a description of how TOGAF is to be adapted for use in the enterprise.

Content Tailoring and the Architecture Content Framework

The TOGAF 9 Architecture Content Framework includes the concept of extensions enabling an architecture engagement to select precisely which parts of TOGAF 9, over and above the lightweight core, are needed.

See Chapter 17 for more information.

2.4.6 Implement Architecture Tools

As part of the Preliminary Phase, the architect should select and implement tools to support the architecture activity. TOGAF does not require or recommend any specific tool. Issues in tools standardization are described in TOGAF 9 Part V, Chapter 42 (Tools for Architecture Development). The implementation of the tools may range from a trivial task to a detailed activity utilizing the Architecture Content Metamodel. The value of any tool is dependent on the maturity of the organization and needs to be matched to the capability of the organization.

2.5 Outputs

(Syllabus Reference: Unit 1, Learning Outcome 4: You should understand the outputs and be able to explain the following key elements: Architecture Principles, Governance Framework, Request for Architecture Work.)

The outputs of this phase are:

- Organizational Model for Enterprise Architecture
- Tailored Architecture Framework, including architecture principles
- Initial Architecture Repository
- Restatement of, or reference to, business principles, business goals, and business drivers
- Request for Architecture Work
- Architecture Governance Framework

Descriptions of Phase Outputs

Where an output of a phase is first introduced in this Study Guide, a description of the contents appears in the Outputs section for the phase. This description is not duplicated in later phases.

The purpose of each deliverable is covered in Chapter 12 of the TOGAF 9 Foundation Study Guide.

2.5.1 Architecture Principles

(Syllabus Reference: Unit 1, Learning Outcome 4.1: You should be able to explain the key element: Architecture Principles.)

See also Section 2.4.4.

2.5.2 Organizational Model for Enterprise Architecture

An important deliverable produced in the Preliminary Phase is the Organizational Model for Enterprise Architecture.

In order for an Architecture Framework to be used successfully, it must be supported by the appropriate organization, roles, and responsibilities within the enterprise. Of particular importance is the definition of boundaries between different enterprise architecture practitioners and the governance relationships that span across these boundaries.

Typical contents of an Organizational Model for Enterprise Architecture are:
- Scope of organizations impacted
- Maturity assessment, gaps, and resolution approach
- Roles and responsibilities for architecture team(s)
- Constraints on the architecture work
- Budget requirements
- Governance and support strategy

2.5.3 Tailored Architecture Framework

The following contents are typical within a Tailored Architecture Framework:
- Tailored architecture method
- Tailored architecture content (deliverables and artifacts)
- Configured and deployed tools

- Interfaces with governance models and other frameworks; examples of other frameworks include Corporate Business Planning, Enterprise Architecture, Portfolio Management, Program Management, Project Management, System Development/Engineering, and Operations (Services).

2.5.4 Architecture Repository

The Architecture Repository acts as a content management system for all architecture-related projects within the enterprise. The repository allows projects to manage their deliverables, locate re-usable assets, and publish outputs to stakeholders and other interested parties.

The following contents are typical within an Architecture Repository:
- Architecture Framework
- Standards Information Base
- Architecture Landscape
- Reference Architectures
- Governance Log

The initial repository content in the Preliminary Phase includes the Architecture Framework.

See also Chapter 19.

2.5.5 Business Principles, Business Goals, and Business Drivers

A statement of the business principles, goals, and drivers has usually been defined elsewhere in the enterprise prior to the architecture activity. They are restated as an output of the Preliminary Phase and reviewed again as a part of Phase A: Architecture Vision. TOGAF 9 Part III: ADM Guidelines and Techniques contains an example set of business principles that is a useful starting point.

There is no defined content for this deliverable as its content and structure are likely to vary considerably from one organization to the next.

See also Section 2.3.2.

2.5.6 Architecture Governance Framework

(Syllabus Reference: Unit 1, Learning Outcome 4.2: You should be able to explain the key element: Architecture Governance Framework.)

An enterprise architecture is only as good as the decision-making framework that is established around it. This is known as an Architecture Governance Framework. Guidance on establishing Architecture Governance is provided in TOGAF 9 Part VII: Architecture Capability Framework.

See also Chapter 22.

2.5.7 Request for Architecture Work

(Syllabus Reference: Unit 1, Learning Outcome 4.3: You should be able to explain the key element: Request for Architecture Work.)

This is a document that is sent from the sponsoring organization to the architecture organization to trigger the start of an Architecture Development Cycle. It is produced with the assistance of the architecture organization as an output of the Preliminary Phase. Requests for Architecture Work will also be created as a result of approved architecture Change Requests, or terms of reference for architecture work originating from migration planning. In general, all the information in this document should be at a high level and free of implementation details.

The suggested contents of this document are as follows:
- Organization sponsors
- Organization's mission statement
- Business goals (and changes)
- Strategic plans of the business
- Time limits
- Changes in the business environment
- Organizational constraints
- Budget information, financial constraints
- External constraints, business constraints
- Current business system description
- Current architecture/IT system description
- Description of the organization developing the architecture
- Description of resources available to the organization developing the architecture

2.6 Summary

The objective of the Preliminary Phase is to prepare an organization for successful enterprise architecture projects by defining "how this enterprise does architecture". Key activities are as follows:

- Understand the business environment
- Obtain high-level management commitment
- Obtain agreement on scope
- Establish architecture principles
- Establishing governance structure
- Tailor the architecture method

The outputs should be an initial set of architecture principles, a statement of the tailored architecture method, and a restatement of the business principles, goals, and drivers.

2.7 Exercises

Exercise 2-1
Compare and contrast TOGAF with two other Architecture Frameworks.

Exercise 2-2
Select seven principles at random from the *Example Set of Architecture Principles* in TOGAF 9 Part III, Chapter 23 (Architecture Principles). For each selected principle, state whether it applies to your organization or not, and give your reasons.

Exercise 2-3
Select two business goals from the list below and for each develop an architecture principle:

- Minimize time when people are not doing productive, profitable work
- Maximize availability of executives for decision-making
- Maximize competitive advantage by the timely availability of information
- Improve the quality of enterprise information

Exercise 2-4
Identify three or more sources of information within your organization that can be used for creating a statement of the business principles, goals, and drivers.

2.8 Recommended Reading

The following are recommended sources of further information for this chapter:

- TOGAF 9 Part II, Chapter 6 (Preliminary Phase)
- TOGAF 9 Part III, Chapter 23 (Architecture Principles)
- TOGAF 9 Part IV, Chapter 36 (Architecture Deliverables)
- TOGAF 9 Part VII, Chapter 46 (Establishing an Architecture Capability)
- TOGAF 9 Part VII, Chapter 50 (Architecture Governance)
- TOGAF 9 Part VII, Chapter 47 (Architecture Board)
- TOGAF 9 Foundation Study Guide, Section 8.3, Architecture Principles
- TOGAF 9 Foundation Study Guide, Chapter 9, Architecture Governance
- The Open Group Architecture Principles, Case Study

Phase A: Architecture Vision

3.1 Key Learning Points

This chapter describes Phase A: Architecture Vision of the TOGAF
Architecture Development Method (ADM).

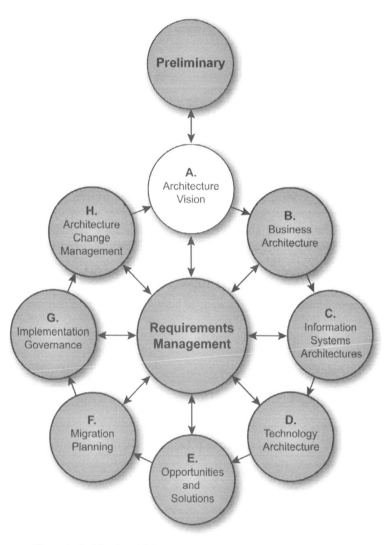

Figure 4:   Phase A: Architecture Vision

Key Points Explained

Upon completion of the chapter you should be able to:

1. Understand the inputs to the phase, and be able to:
   - Describe the typical contents of the Architecture Repository at this point
2. Understand the steps, and be able to:
   - Describe how to identify stakeholders, their concerns, and business requirements
   - Explain the purpose of a Business Transformation Readiness Assessment
   - Describe the risk assessment approach taken in this phase
3. Understand the outputs, and be able to explain the following key elements including their purpose:
   - Statement of Architecture Work
   - Capability Assessment
   - Architecture Vision
   - Communications Plan

In addition, you should be able to:

- Describe the steps in developing a Stakeholder Map
- Use a Stakeholder Map to identify stakeholders and their concerns
- Explain the benefits of creating views
- Explain how capability-based planning is applied in an enterprise architecture context
- Explain the factors that influence Business Transformation Readiness
- Describe the properties of a good Business Scenario
- Explain how to develop and validate a Business Scenario

3.2 Objectives

The objectives of Phase A: Architecture Vision are to:

- Develop a high-level aspirational vision of the capabilities and business value to be delivered as a result of the proposed enterprise architecture
- Obtain approval for a Statement of Architecture Work that defines a program of works to develop and deploy the architecture outlined in the Architecture Vision

3.3 Inputs

(Syllabus Reference: Unit 4, Learning Outcome 1: You should understand the inputs to the phase, and be able to describe the typical contents of the Architecture Repository at this point.)

The inputs to this phase are:

- Request for Architecture Work
- Business principles, business goals, and business drivers
- Organizational Model for Enterprise Architecture
- Tailored Architecture Framework, including architecture principles
- Populated Architecture Repository; that is, existing architecture documentation (framework description, architecture descriptions, existing baseline descriptions, etc.)

3.4 Steps

(Syllabus Reference: Unit 4, Learning Outcome 2: You should understand the steps in this phase.)

Phase A consists of the following steps:

1. Establish the architecture project
2. Identify stakeholders, concerns, and business requirements
3. Confirm and elaborate business goals, business drivers, and constraints
4. Evaluate business capabilities
5. Assess readiness for business transformation
6. Define scope
7. Confirm and elaborate architecture principles, including business principles
8. Develop Architecture Vision
9. Define the Target Architecture value propositions and KPIs
10. Identify the business transformation risks and mitigation activities
11. Develop Statement of Architecture Work; secure approval

The steps are described in more detail in the following subsections.

3.4.1 Establish the Architecture Project

In this step you must conduct the necessary procedures to obtain recognition of the project, endorsement by corporate management, and the support and commitment of line management. Reference must be made to the other management frameworks in use in the enterprise and an explanation provided of how this project relates to those frameworks.

3.4.2   Identify Stakeholders, Concerns, and Business Requirements

(Syllabus Reference: Unit 4, Learning Outcome 2.1: You should understand how to identify stakeholders, their concerns, and business requirements.)

In this step you must identify key stakeholders, their concerns, and define the key business requirements to be addressed in the architecture engagement. The key technique for Stakeholder Management is to generate a Stakeholder Map, which should then be used to support various outputs of the Architecture Vision phase. The concerns and viewpoints that are relevant to this project should be documented in the Architecture Vision. The stakeholders that are involved with the project and their positions should be used to form the starting point for a Communications Plan. The key roles and responsibilities within the project should be included within the Statement of Architecture Work.

3.4.2.1   *Stakeholder Management*

Stakeholder Management is an important discipline that successful architects can use to win support from others. It helps them ensure that their projects succeed where others fail. The technique should be used during Phase A to identify the key players in the engagement, and should also be updated throughout each phase.

The benefits of successful Stakeholder Management are that:
- The most powerful stakeholders can be identified early and their input can then be used to shape the architecture; this ensures their support and improves the quality of the models produced.
- Support from the more powerful stakeholders will help the engagement win more resources; thus making the architecture engagement more likely to succeed.
- By communicating with stakeholders early and frequently, the architecture team can ensure that they fully understand the architecture process, and the benefits of enterprise architecture; this means they can support the architecture team more actively when necessary.
- The architecture team can more effectively anticipate likely reactions to the architecture models and reports, and can build into the plan the actions that will be needed to capitalize on positive reaction whilst avoiding or addressing any negative reactions.

- The architecture team can identify conflicting or competing objectives among stakeholders early and develop a strategy to resolve the issues arising from them.

3.4.2.2 *The Stakeholder Management Process*
(Syllabus Reference: Unit 6, Learning Outcome 1: You should be able to describe the steps in developing a Stakeholder Map.)

TOGAF defines a process for creation of a Stakeholder Map as follows:

Identify Stakeholders
The first task is to determine who the main enterprise architecture stakeholders are. TOGAF provides a sample stakeholder analysis that distinguishes 22 types of stakeholder in five broad categories, as shown in Figure 5. Any particular architecture project may have more, fewer, or different stakeholders; and they may be grouped into more, fewer, or different categories.

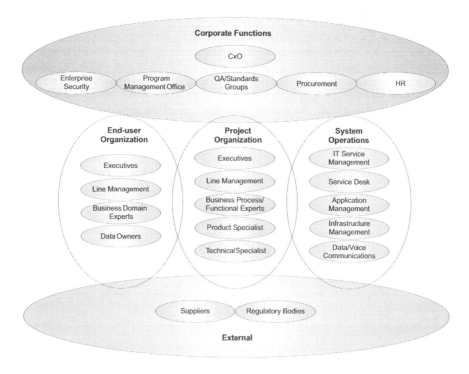

Figure 5:   Sample Stakeholders and Categories

Classify Stakeholder Positions

Develop a good understanding of the most important stakeholders and record this analysis (as shown in the example in Table 1) for reference during the project. It may be necessary to refresh the analysis periodically.

Table 1:   Example Stakeholder Analys

Stake-holder Group	Stake-holder	Ability to Disrupt the Change	Current Under-standing	Required Under-standing	Current Commit-ment	Required Commit-ment	Required Support
CIO	Smith	H	M	H	L	M	H
CFO	Brown	M	M	M	L	M	M

Key: H = High, M = Medium, L = Low

Determine Stakeholder Management Approach

This enables the team to easily see which stakeholders are expected to be blockers or critics, and which stakeholders are likely to be advocates and supporters of the initiative.

Work out stakeholder power, influence, and interest, so as to focus the enterprise architecture engagement on the key individuals. These can be mapped onto a power *versus* interest matrix, which also indicates the strategy to adopt for engaging with them.

Figure 6 shows an example power *versus* interest matrix.

Figure 6:   Power versus Interest Matrix

Tailor Engagement Deliverables

Identify the catalogs, matrices, and diagrams that the architecture engagement needs to produce and validate with each stakeholder group to deliver an effective architecture model. This enables the architecture to be communicated to, and understood by, all the stakeholders, and enables them to verify that the enterprise architecture initiative will address their concerns.

View Creation

(Syllabus Reference: Unit 6, Learning Outcome 2: You should be able to explain the benefits of creating views.)

Architecture Views are representations of the architecture in terms meaningful to stakeholders that make it simpler to comprehend. They enable stakeholders to verify that the resulting architecture will address their concerns.

It is often possible to create the required views for a particular architecture by referring to and selecting from an existing library of viewpoints.

This approach brings a number of benefits, such as reduced effort for the architects as the viewpoints have already been defined, improved comprehensibility for stakeholders since the viewpoints are familiar, and greater confidence in the validity of the views since they have been used before.

Example Stakeholder Map

A Stakeholder Map can be used to record the findings of Stakeholder Management. TOGAF provides an example, an extract of which is provided in Table 2.

Table 2:   Example Stakeholder Map (Extract)

STAKEHOLDER	KEY CONCERNS	CLASS	CATALOGS, MATRICES, AND DIAGRAMS
CxO (Corporate Functions) For example, CEO, CFO, CIO, COO	The high-level drivers, goals, and objectives of the organization, and how these are translated into an effective process and IT architecture to advance the business.	KEEP SATISFIED	Business Footprint Diagram Goal/Objective/Service Diagram Organization Decomposition Diagram

STAKEHOLDER	KEY CONCERNS	CLASS	CATALOGS, MATRICES, AND DIAGRAMS
Program Management Office (Corporate Functions) For example, Project Portfolio Managers	Prioritizing, funding, and aligning change activity. An understanding of project content and technical dependencies between projects adds a further dimension of richness to portfolio management decision-making.	KEEP SATISFIED	Requirements Catalog Project Context Diagram Benefits Diagram Business Footprint Diagram Application Communication Diagram Functional Decomposition Diagram
Procurement (Corporate Functions); For example, Acquirers	Understanding what building blocks of the architecture can be bought, and what constraints (or rules) exist that are relevant to the purchase. Acquirers will shop with multiple vendors looking for the best cost solution while adhering to the constraints (or rules) applied by the architecture, such as standards. The key concern is to make purchasing decisions that fit the architecture, and thereby to reduce the risk of added costs arising from non-compliant components.	KEY PLAYERS	Technology Portfolio Catalog Technology Standards Catalog
IT Service Management (Systems Operations) For example, Service Delivery Manager	Ensuring that IT services provided to the organization meet the service levels required by that organization to succeed in business.	KEEP INFORMED	Technology Standards Catalog Technology Portfolio Catalog Contract/Measure Catalog Process/Application Realization Diagram Enterprise Manageability Diagram

3.4.3 Confirm and Elaborate Business Goals, Business Drivers, and Constraints

Here you must identify business goals and strategic drivers of the organization. If these have already been defined elsewhere, ensure that the existing definitions are current and clarify any areas of ambiguity. Otherwise, go back to the originators of the Statement of Architecture Work, define these items again, and get their endorsement by management.

3.4.4 Evaluate Business Capabilities

The purpose of this step is to understand the capabilities within the enterprise. This refers to the capability of the enterprise to develop and consume the architecture, and also the baseline and target capability level of the enterprise. The results of this activity are documented in a Capability Assessment (see Section 3.5).

Any gaps identified in the Architecture Capability will require iteration between Architecture Vision and Preliminary Phase to ensure that the Architecture Capability is suitable to address the scope of the architecture project.

3.4.4.1 *Capability-Based Planning*

(Syllabus Reference: Unit 8, Learning Outcome 4: You should be able to explain how Capability-Based Planning is applied in an enterprise architecture context.)

Capability-based planning ensures that the corporate strategic plan drives the enterprise from a top-down approach. It focuses on delivery of business outcomes rather than technical deliverables; for example, an enterprise architecture project would be provision of electronic service delivery, rather than delivery of a web-based commerce solution.

In an enterprise architecture context the capabilities to be developed should be derived from the corporate strategic plan. All architectures should be expressed in terms of the business outcomes and business value they deliver, thereby ensuring IT alignment with the business. In Phase A, the Architecture Vision should be driven by the corporate strategic direction. The focus of the architecture development in Phases B, C, and D will be the specific capabilities. In Phase E work packages and projects are identified to deliver the capabilities.

It is recommended to break a capability into capability increments because a new capability can take an extended period of time to be developed and can involve many projects delivering numerous increments. This has the advantage of potentially providing real business value to stakeholders in the form of discrete, visible, and quantifiable outcomes that can provide focus for Transition Architectures.

The capability increments driving the Transition Architectures in Phase E lead to the identification of project increments, the actual delivery of which is coordinated through the Implementation and Migration Plan completed in Phase F.

3.4.5   Assess Readiness for Business Transformation
(Syllabus Reference: Unit 4, Learning Outcome 2.2: You can explain the purpose of a Business Transformation Readiness Assessment.)

A Business Transformation Readiness Assessment can be used to evaluate and quantify the organization's readiness to undergo a change. This assessment is based upon the determination of a series of readiness factor ratings.

Understanding the readiness of the organization to accept change, identifying the issues, and then dealing with them is a key part of successful architecture transformation. This assessment is recommended to be a joint effort between corporate staff, lines of business, and IT planners.

To do this, the readiness factors that will impact the organization must be determined and presented using maturity models. The risks for each readiness factor should be assessed and improvement actions to mitigate the risk identified. TOGAF recommends creation of a summary table to consolidate factors and provide a management overview. The findings are then documented into the Capability Assessment (see Section 3.5.2), and later incorporated into the Implementation and Migration Plan (see Section 10.5.1).

3.4.5.1   *Transformation Readiness Factors*
(Syllabus Reference: Unit 8, Learning Outcome 2: You should be able to explain the factors that influence Business Transformation Readiness.)

The following is an example list of readiness factors that can impact the business transformation when migrating from Baseline to Target Architectures. These have been drawn from the Canadian Government Business Transformation Enablement Program (BTEP):[6]

- **Vision**: The ability to clearly define and communicate what is to be achieved.
- **Desire, Willingness, and Resolve**: The presence of a desire to achieve the results, willingness to accept the impact of doing the work, and the resolve to follow through and complete the endeavor.
- **Need**: There is a compelling need to execute the endeavor.
- **Business Case Exists**: Creates a strong focus for the project, identifying benefits that must be achieved and thereby creating an imperative to succeed.
- **Funding**: In the form of a clear source of fiscal resources, funding exists that meets the endeavor's potential expenditures.
- **Sponsorship and Leadership**: Exists and is broadly shared, but not so broadly as to diffuse accountability.
- **Governance**: The ability to engage the involvement and support of all parties with an interest in or responsibility to the endeavor with the objective of ensuring that the corporate interests are served and the objectives achieved.
- **Accountability**: The assignment of specific and appropriate responsibility, the recognition of measurable expectations by all concerned parties, and the alignment of decision-making between areas of responsibility and where the impact of the decisions will be felt.
- **Workable Approach and Execution Model**: An approach that makes sense relative to the task, with a supporting environment modeled after a proven approach.
- **IT Capacity to Execute**: The ability to perform all the IT tasks required by the project, including the skills, tools, processes, and management capability.
- **Enterprise Capacity to Execute**: The ability of the enterprise to perform all the tasks required by the endeavor, in areas outside of IT, including the ability to make decisions within tight time constraints.
- **Enterprise Ability to Implement and Operate**: The transformation elements and their related business processes operationally absorb the changes arising from implementation.

---

6   See www.tbs-sct.gc.ca/btep-pto/index_e.asp.

3.4.6 Define Scope

Here you must define the scope of the architecture work (see TOGAF 9 Part II, Section 5.5 (Scoping the Architecture). In particular, define:

- Breadth of coverage
- Level of detail
- The partitioning characteristics of the architecture
- The specific architecture domains to be covered (Business, Data, Application, Technology)
- Schedule the project milestones, including intermediate milestones (termed by TOGAF as the extent of the time period)
- The architecture assets to be leveraged from the organization's Enterprise Architecture Continuum, including assets created in previous iterations of the ADM cycle, and assets available elsewhere in industry (other frameworks, systems models, vertical industry models, etc.)

3.4.7 Confirm and Elaborate Architecture Principles, including Business Principles

In this step you should review the principles, developed in the Preliminary Phase, under which the architecture is to be developed. Architecture principles are usually based on the principles developed in the Preliminary Phase. Ensure the existing definitions are current, and clarify any areas of ambiguity. Otherwise, go back to the body responsible and work with them to define these essential items.

3.4.8 Develop Architecture Vision

Based on the stakeholder concerns, business capability requirements, scope, constraints, and principles, create a high-level view of the Baseline and Target Architectures. Business Scenarios are an appropriate technique to discover and document business requirements, and to produce an Architecture Vision (see Section 3.5.3).

This step will generate the first, very high-level definitions of the baseline and target environments, from a business, information systems, and technology perspective.

Business Scenarios

The ADM has its own method, known as Business Scenarios, for identifying and articulating the business requirements implied in new business functionality. Business Scenarios are documented in TOGAF 9 Part III: ADM Guidelines and Techniques.

(Syllabus Reference: Unit 3, Learning Outcome 1: You should be able to describe the properties of a good Business Scenario.)

A good Business Scenario is representative of a significant business need or problem, enables vendors to understand the value of a developed solution for a customer, and is "SMART" – Specific (defines what needs to be done in the process), Measurable (has clear metrics for success), Actionable (clearly segments the problem and provides a basis to find the solution), Realistic (defines the bounds of the technology capability and cost constraints), and Time-bound (gives a clear understanding of when a solution expires).

(Syllabus Reference: Unit 3, Learning Outcome 2: You should be able to explain how to develop and validate a Business Scenario.)

The generic Business Scenario process is as follows:

- Identify, document, and rank the problem that is driving the project
- Document, as high-level architecture models, the business and technical environments where the problem situation is occurring
- Identify and document desired objectives; the results of handling the problems successfully
- Identify human actors and their place in the business model, the human participants, and their roles
- Identify computer actors and their place in the technology model, the computing elements, and their roles
- Identify and document roles, responsibilities, and measures of success per actor, the required scripts per actor, and the desired results of handling the situation properly
- Check for fitness-for-purpose of inspiring subsequent architecture work, and refine only if necessary

See also the exercises in Section 3.7.

3.4.9   Define the Target Architecture Value Propositions and KPIs

This step defines value propositions and Key Performance Indicators (KPIs) for the Target Architecture:

- Develop the business case for the architectures and changes required

- Produce the value proposition for each of the stakeholder groupings
- Assess and define the procurement requirements
- Review and agree on the value propositions with the sponsors and stakeholders concerned
- Define the performance metrics and measures to be built into the enterprise architecture to meet the business needs
- Assess the business risk

The outputs from this activity should be incorporated into the Statement of Architecture Work to allow performance to be tracked accordingly.

3.4.10   Identify the Business Transformation Risks and Mitigation Activities
(Syllabus Reference: Unit 4, Learning Outcome 2.3: You can describe the risk assessment approach taken in this phase.)

In this step, identify the risks associated with the Architecture Vision and assess the initial level of risk (e.g., catastrophic, critical, marginal, or negligible) and the potential frequency associated with it. Assign a mitigation strategy for each risk.

There are two levels of risk that should be considered, namely:
- **Initial Level of Risk**: Risk categorization prior to determining and implementing mitigating actions.
- **Residual Level of Risk**: Risk categorization after implementation of mitigating actions (if any).

Risk mitigation activities should be included in the Statement of Architecture Work. TOGAF provides risk identification and mitigation assessment worksheet examples that can be used as governance artifacts.

3.4.10.1 *Risk Assessment*
(Syllabus Reference: Unit 8, Learning Outcome 3: You can explain how to determine requirements for risk assessments.)

TOGAF provides guidance on techniques for risk management in TOGAF 9 Part III, Chapter 31 (Risk Management). This includes a risk classification scheme and sample worksheets for risk assessment. The process for risk management documented by TOGAF is:

- Risk classification
- Risk identification
- Initial risk assessment
- Risk mitigation and residual risk assessment
- Risk monitoring

As well as identifying risks in Phase A, TOGAF states that risk monitoring should occur in Phase G. This may then lead to change requests related to risk management being handled in Phase H.

3.4.11 Develop Statement of Architecture Work; Secure Approval

The Statement of Architecture Work should then be produced (see Section 3.5.1), and approval of this document obtained from the governing body (usually the Architecture Board).

3.5 Outputs

(Syllabus Reference: Unit 4, Learning Outcome 3: You should understand the outputs.)

The outputs of this phase are:
- Statement of Architecture Work
- Refined statements of business principles, business goals, and business drivers
- Architecture principles
- Capability assessment
- Tailored Architecture Framework
- Architecture Vision, including:
  - Problem description
  - Objective of the Statement of Architecture Work
  - Summary views
  - Business scenario (optional)
  - Refined key high-level stakeholder requirements
- Draft Architecture Definition Document (see Section 4.5.1), including (when in scope):
  - Baseline Business Architecture (high-level)
  - Baseline Data Architecture (high-level)
  - Baseline Application Architecture (high-level)

- – Baseline Technology Architecture (high-level)
- – Target Business Architecture (high-level)
- – Target Data Architecture (high-level)
- – Target Application Architecture (high-level)
- – Target Technology Architecture (high-level)
- Communications Plan
- Additional content populating the Architecture Repository

The outputs may also include the Principles catalog.

3.5.1 Statement of Architecture Work

(Syllabus Reference: Unit 4, Learning Outcome 3.1: You should be able to explain the Statement of Architecture Work.)

The Statement of Architecture Work is created as a deliverable of Phase A and is effectively a contract between the architecting organization and the sponsor of the architecture project. This document is a response to the Request for Architecture Work input document (see Section 2.5.7). It should describe an overall plan to address the request for work and propose how solutions to the problems that have been identified will be addressed through the architecture process. The suggested contents of this document are as follows:

- Title
- Architecture project request and background
- Architecture project description and scope
- Overview of Architecture Vision
- Specific change of scope procedures
- Roles, responsibilities, and deliverables
- Acceptance criteria and procedures
- Architecture project plan and schedule
- Approvals

3.5.2 Capability Assessment

(Syllabus Reference: Unit 4, Learning Outcome 3.2: You should be able to explain the Capability Assessment.)

Before embarking upon a detailed Architecture Definition, it is valuable to understand the baseline and target capability level of the enterprise. This Capability Assessment is first carried out in Phase A, and updated in Phase E. It can be examined on several levels:

- What is the capability level of the enterprise as a whole? Where does the enterprise wish to increase or optimize capability? What are the architectural focus areas that will support the desired development of the enterprise?
- What is the capability or maturity level of the IT function within the enterprise? What are the likely implications of conducting the architecture project in terms of design governance, operational governance, skills, and organization structure? What is an appropriate style, level of formality, and amount of detail for the architecture project to fit with the culture and capability of the IT organization?
- What are the capability and maturity of the architecture function within the enterprise? What architectural assets are currently in existence? Are they maintained and accurate? What standards and reference models need to be considered? Are there likely to be opportunities to create re-usable assets during the architecture project?
- Where capability gaps exist, to what extent is the business ready to transform in order to reach the target capability? What are the cultural barriers, risks to transformation, and other considerations to be addressed beyond the basic capability gap?

The following contents are typical within a Capability Assessment deliverable:
- Business Capability Assessment, including:
  - Capabilities of the business
  - Baseline state assessment of the performance level of each capability
  - Future state aspiration for the performance level of each capability
  - Baseline state assessment of how each capability is realized
  - Future state aspiration for how each capability should be realized
  - Assessment of likely impacts to the business organization resulting from the successful deployment of the Target Architecture
- IT Capability Assessment, including:
  - Baseline and target maturity level of the change process
  - Baseline and target maturity level of operational processes
  - Baseline capability and capacity assessment
  - Assessment of likely impacts to the IT organization resulting from the successful deployment of the Target Architecture
- Architecture Maturity Assessment, including:
  - Architecture Governance processes, organization, roles, and responsibilities

- Architecture skills assessment
- Breadth, depth, and quality of landscape definition, standards definition, and reference model definition within the Architecture Repository
- Assessment of re-use potential
- Business Transformation Readiness Assessment, including:
  - Readiness factors
  - Vision for each readiness factor
  - Current and target readiness ratings
  - Readiness risks

3.5.3 Architecture Vision

(Syllabus Reference: Unit 4, Learning Outcome 3.3: You should be able to explain the Architecture Vision.)

The Architecture Vision is created in Phase A and provides a high-level summary of the changes to the enterprise that will follow from successful deployment of the Target Architecture. The purpose of the vision is to agree at the outset what the desired outcome should be for the architecture, so that architects can then focus on the detail necessary to validate feasibility. Providing an Architecture Vision also supports stakeholder communication by providing a summary version of the full Architecture Definition.

Business Scenarios are an appropriate and important technique that can be used as part of the process of developing an Architecture Vision document.

The suggested contents are as follows:
- Problem description, including the stakeholders and their concerns, and the list of issues/scenarios to be addressed
- Objective of the Statement of Architecture Work
- Summary views necessary for the Request for Architecture Work and the high-level Business, Application, Data, and Technology Architectures
- Mapped requirements
- Reference to the Draft Architecture Definition Document

3.5.4 Communications Plan

(Syllabus Reference: Unit 4, Learning Outcome 3.4: You should be able to explain the key element including its purpose: Communications Plan.)

Enterprise architectures contain large volumes of complex and inter-dependent information. Effective communication of targeted information to the right stakeholders at the right time is a Critical Success Factor (CSF) for enterprise architecture. Development of a Communications Plan in Phase A allows for this communication to be carried out within a planned and managed process.

Typically, a Communications Plan includes the identification of:
- Stakeholders grouped by communication requirements
- The communication needs, key messages in relation to the Architecture Vision, communication risks, and CSFs
- Methods that will be used to communicate with stakeholders and allow access to architecture information, such as meetings, newsletters, repositories, etc.
- A communications timetable, showing which communications will occur with which stakeholder groups at what time and in what location

3.6 Summary

Phase A: Architecture Vision is about project establishment and initiates an iteration of the architecture process. It sets the scope, constraints, and expectations for this iteration of the ADM. It is required at the start of every architecture cycle, in order to validate the business context and create the Statement of Architecture Work.

3.7 Exercises

Exercise 3-1
Write a Business Scenario describing how you would choose a new car. Include the following in your answer: (a) Problem description; (b) Detailed objectives; (c) Views of environments and processes; (d) Actors, their roles, and responsibilities; (e) Principles and constraints; (f) Requirements; (g) Next steps.

Make the objectives SMART.

Exercise 3-2

Consider the following objective: "The system's security could be improved. This will reduce the loss of revenue when our system is accessed by unauthorized users".

How could this be re-phrased to make it into a SMART objective?

Exercise 3-3

Match the most applicable Roles below to the following Computer actors:
1. Business applications
2. Enterprise computers
3. Information services
4. Network devices
5. User devices

Roles:
A: User access to core technical activities; local application execution; local information store
B: Operated by enterprises and service providers; supplies information to users
C: Information transport; switching and routing of information in transit; security of information in transit; control of access to networks and systems; network quality of service; sessions management; bandwidth management
D: Run on users' devices and/or on servers; information processing and display
E: Operated by enterprises and service providers; central application · processing and information store; platform for information services; user identification, authentication, and access control

Exercise 3-4

Consider the Vehicle Licensing Bureau (or equivalent in your country), that handles car registrations, driving licenses, car taxes, and insurance records. Identify the stakeholders (human actors) and their place in the business model, the human participants and their roles. Identify computer actors and their place in the technology model. Also, identify the computing elements, and their roles. For each stakeholder, identify the stakeholder concerns.

Exercise 3-5

Select a business problem from your own organization. Identify the stakeholders and categorize them. Classify the stakeholder positions and determine the Stakeholder Management approach. Identify the engagement deliverables for each stakeholder. Finally, create a Stakeholder Map to summarize your findings.

Exercise 3-6

(Syllabus Reference: Unit 6, Learning Outcome 3)

Select three example views from TOGAF 9 Part IV, Section 35.7, Recommended Architecture Views to be Developed. For each selected view, use the example Stakeholder Map from TOGAF 9 Part III, Section 24.4 (Template Stakeholder Map) as a guideline to identify stakeholders and their concerns.

Exercise 3-7

Select a business problem from your own organization where there is a need for significant change. Rate your organization's readiness for change using the Business Factor Assessment Summary table from TOGAF 9 Part III, Section 30.4.2 (Readiness Factor Rating).

Exercise 3-8

Suppose your role is the Lead Architect for a program rolling out a potentially disruptive upgrade of new equipment to all your customers. How would you manage the risk?

3.8 Recommended Reading

The following are recommended sources of further information for this chapter:

- TOGAF 9 Part II, Chapter 5 (Introduction)
- TOGAF 9 Part II, Chapter 7 (Phase A: Architecture Vision)
- TOGAF 9 Part III, Chapter 23 (Architecture Principles)
- TOGAF 9 Part III, Chapter 24 (Stakeholder Management)
- TOGAF 9 Part III, Chapter 26 (Business Scenarios)
- TOGAF 9 Part III, Chapter 30 (Business Transformation Readiness Assessment)

- TOGAF 9 Part III, Chapter 31 (Risk Management)
- TOGAF 9 Part III, Chapter 32 (Capability-Based Planning)
- TOGAF 9 Part IV, Chapter 36 (Architecture Deliverables)

Chapter 4

Phase B: Business Architecture

4.1 Key Learning Points

This chapter describes Phase B: Business Architecture of the TOGAF
Architecture Development Method (ADM).

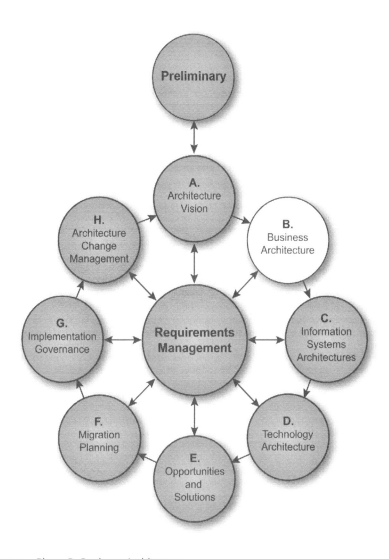

Figure 7: Phase B: Business Architecture

Key Points Explained

Upon completion of this chapter you should be able to:

1. Understand the inputs to the phase, and explain the following key elements:
   - Business principles, business goals, and business drivers
2. Understand the steps, and be able to:
   - Describe three techniques for business modeling
   - Explain the considerations for selecting reference models, viewpoints, and tools
   - Explain the technique of Gap Analysis
   - Explain how building blocks are used in the development of the Business Architecture
3. Understand the outputs, and be able to explain the following key elements:
   - Business Architecture components of the Architecture Definition Document
   - Business Architecture components of the Architecture Requirements Specification

4.2 Objectives

The objectives of Phase B: Business Architecture are to:

- Develop the Target Business Architecture that describes how the enterprise needs to operate to achieve the business goals, and respond to the strategic drivers set out in the Architecture Vision, in a way that addresses the Request for Architecture Work and stakeholder concerns
- Identify candidate Architecture Roadmap components based upon gaps between the Baseline and Target Business Architectures

4.3 Inputs

(Syllabus Reference: Unit 9, Learning Outcome 1: You should understand the inputs to the phase, and also be able to explain the key elements: business principles, business goals, and business drivers.)

The inputs to this phase are:

- Request for Architecture Work
- Business principles, business goals, and business drivers (see Section 2.5.5)
- Capability Assessment
- Communications Plan

- Organizational Model for Enterprise Architecture
- Tailored Architecture Framework
- Approved Statement of Architecture Work
- Architecture principles, including business principles, when pre-existing
- Enterprise Continuum
- Architecture Repository
- Architecture Vision, including:
  - Problem
  - Objective of the Statement of Architecture Work
  - Summary views
  - Business scenario (optional)
  - Refined key high-level stakeholder requirements
- Draft Architecture Definition Document, including (when in scope):
  - Baseline Business Architecture (high-level)
  - Baseline Data Architecture (high-level)
  - Baseline Application Architecture (high-level)
  - Baseline Technology Architecture (high-level)
  - Target Business Architecture (high-level)
  - Target Data Architecture (high-level)
  - Target Application Architecture (high-level)
  - Target Technology Architecture (high-level)

4.3.1 Business Principles

Business principles form part of the overarching set of architecture principles, initially developed in the Preliminary Phase. Example business principles drawn from TOGAF 9 Part III, Chapter 23 (Architecture Principles) are summarized in Table 3.

Table 3: Example Business Principles

Principle	Summary
Primacy of Principles	These principles of information management apply to all organizations within the enterprise.
Maximize Benefit to the Enterprise	Information management decisions are made to provide maximum benefit to the enterprise as a whole.
Information Management is Everybody's Business	All organizations in the enterprise participate in information management decisions needed to accomplish business objectives.

Principle	Summary
Business Continuity	Enterprise operations are maintained in spite of system interruptions.
Common Use Applications	Development of applications used across the enterprise is preferred over the development of similar or duplicate applications which are only provided to a particular organization.
Service Orientation	The architecture is based on a design of services which mirrors real-world business activities comprising the enterprise (or inter-enterprise) business processes.
Compliance with Law	Enterprise information management processes comply with all relevant laws, policies, and regulations.
IT Responsibility	The IT organization is responsible for owning and implementing IT processes and infrastructure that enable solutions to meet user-defined requirements for functionality, service levels, cost, and delivery timing.
Protection of Intellectual Property	The enterprise's Intellectual Property (IP) must be protected. This protection must be reflected in the IT architecture, implementation, and governance processes.

4.4 Steps

(Syllabus Reference: Unit 9, Learning Outcome 2: You understand the steps in this phase.)

Phase B consists of the following steps:

1. Select reference models, viewpoints, and tools
2. Develop Baseline Business Architecture Description
3. Develop Target Business Architecture Description
4. Perform Gap Analysis
5. Define candidate roadmap components
6. Resolve impacts across the Architecture Landscape
7. Conduct formal stakeholder review
8. Finalize the Business Architecture
9. Create the Architecture Definition Document

The order of the steps should be adapted to the situation: in particular, you should determine whether it is appropriate to do the Baseline Business Architecture or the Target Business Architecture development first.

The level of detail addressed in Phase B will depend on the scope and goals of the overall architecture effort. New business processes being introduced as part of this effort will need to be defined in detail during Phase B. Existing business processes to be carried over and supported in the target environment may already have been adequately defined in previous architectural work; but, if not, they too will need to be defined in Phase B. The steps are described in more detail in the following sections.

4.4.1 Select Reference Models, Viewpoints, and Tools

(Syllabus Reference: Unit 9, Learning Outcome 2.2: You should be able to explain the considerations for selecting reference models, viewpoints, and tools.)

In this step, select relevant Business Architecture resources (reference models, patterns, etc.) from the Architecture Repository, on the basis of the business drivers, and the stakeholders and their concerns. Also, select relevant Business Architecture viewpoints (e.g., operations, management, financial); that is, those that demonstrate how the stakeholder concerns are being addressed in the Business Architecture. Then, identify appropriate tools and techniques to be used for the capture, modeling, and the analysis of the selected viewpoints.

4.4.1.1 *Determine Overall Modeling Process*

For each viewpoint, select the models needed to support the specific view required, using the selected tool or method. Confirm that all stakeholders' concerns are addressed. If they are not, use Business Scenarios to discover business requirements.

4.4.1.2 *Identify Required Service Granularity Level, Boundaries, and Contracts*

Identify which components of the architecture are functions and which are services. Specify the required service levels. This can lead to the generation of formal Service Level Agreements (SLAs).

4.4.1.3   Identify Required Catalogs, Matrices, and Diagrams

TOGAF provides definitions of catalogs, matrices, and diagrams for use in the development of a Business Architecture. *Catalogs* capture inventories of the core assets of the business. *Matrices* show the core relationships between model entities. *Diagrams* represent the Business Architecture information from a set of different perspectives (viewpoints).

TOGAF recommends that the catalogs, matrices, and diagrams shown in Table 4 be considered in Phase B and provides guidance on their structure in TOGAF 9 Part IV, Chapter 34 (Content Metamodel).

Table 4:   Phase B Catalogs, Diagrams, and Matrice

Catalogs	Matrices	Diagrams
Organization/Actor catalog	Business Interaction matrix	Business Footprint diagram
Driver/Goal/Objective catalog	Actor/Role matrix	Business Service/ Information diagram
Role catalog		Functional Decomposition diagram
Business Service/Function catalog		Product Lifecycle diagram
Location catalog		Goal/Objective/Service diagram
Process/Event/Control/ Product catalog		Use-Case diagram
Contract/Measure catalog		Organization Decomposition diagram
		Process Flow diagram
		Event diagram

4.4.1.4   Identify Types of Requirement to be Collected

Once the catalogs, matrices, and diagrams have been developed, modeling should be completed by formalizing the business requirements for the Target Architecture. The architect should identify types of requirements to be met by the architecture. These requirements may relate to the business domain, may provide requirements input into the Data, Application, and Technology Architectures, or may provide detailed guidance to be reflected during design and implementation.

4.4.2 Develop Baseline Business Architecture Description

Develop a Baseline Description of the existing Business Architecture, to
the extent necessary to support the Target Business Architecture. The scope
and level of detail to be defined will depend on the extent to which existing
business elements are likely to be carried over into the Target Business
Architecture, and on whether architecture descriptions exist. Where possible,
identify the relevant Business Architecture building blocks, drawing on
the Architecture Repository. Where new architecture models need to be
developed to satisfy stakeholder concerns, use the models identified within
Step 1 as a guideline for creating new architecture content to describe the
Baseline Architecture.

4.4.3 Develop Target Business Architecture Description

Develop a Target Description for the Business Architecture, to the extent
necessary to support the Architecture Vision. The scope and level of detail to
be defined will depend on the relevance of the business elements to attaining
the Target Architecture Vision, and on whether architectural descriptions
exist. Where possible, identify the relevant Business Architecture building
blocks, drawing on the Architecture Repository. Where new architecture
models need to be developed to satisfy stakeholder concerns, use the models
identified within Step 1 as a guideline for creating new architecture content to
describe the Target Architecture.

Business Modeling

*(Syllabus Reference: Unit 9, Learning Outcome 2.1: You should be able to describe
three techniques for business modeling.)*

Business models should be logical extensions of the Business Scenarios from
the Architecture Vision, so that the architecture can be mapped from high-level
business requirements to more detailed ones. A variety of modeling tools and
techniques may be employed, if considered appropriate. For example:

Activity Models (also called Business Process Models) describe the functions
associated with the enterprise's business activities, the data and/or information
exchanged between activities (internal exchanges), and the data and/or
information exchanged with other activities that are outside the scope of the
model (external exchanges). Activity models are hierarchical in nature. They
capture the activities performed in a business process, and the ICOMs (inputs,
controls, outputs, and mechanisms/resources used) of those activities. Activity

models can be annotated with explicit statements of business rules, which represent relationships among the ICOMs. For example, a business rule can specify who can do what under specified conditions, the combination of inputs and controls needed, and the resulting outputs. One technique for creating activity models is the IDEF (Integrated Computer Aided Manufacturing (ICAM) DEFinition) modeling technique.

The Object Management Group (OMG) has developed the Business Process Modeling Notation (BPMN), a standard for business process modeling that includes a language with which to specify business processes, their tasks/steps, and the documents produced.

Use-Case Models can describe either business processes or systems functions, depending on the focus of the modeling effort. A use-case model describes the business processes of an enterprise in terms of use-cases and actors corresponding to business processes and organizational participants (people, organizations, etc.). The use-case model is described in use-case diagrams and use-case specifications.

Class Models are similar to logical data models. A class model describes static information and relationships between information. A class model also describes informational behaviors. Like many of the other models, it can also be used to model various levels of granularity. Depending on the intent of the model, a class model can represent business domain entities or systems implementation classes. Specifications further elaborate and detail information that cannot be represented in the class diagram.

Gap Analysis

(Syllabus Reference: Unit 9, Learning Outcome 2.3: You should be able to explain the Gap Analysis technique.)

The technique known as Gap Analysis is widely used in the TOGAF ADM to validate an architecture that is being developed. The technique involves drawing up a matrix to highlight any shortfalls between a Baseline Architecture and a Target Architecture. See TOGAF 9 Part III: ADM Guidelines and Techniques for full details of the Gap Analysis technique, including an example.

4.4.4 Perform Gap Analysis

Verify the architecture models for internal consistency and accuracy. Perform trade-off analysis to resolve conflicts (if any) among the different views.

Check that the models support the principles, objectives, and constraints. Note changes to the viewpoint(s) represented in the selected models from the Architecture Repository, and document them. Test architecture models for completeness against requirements. Finally, identify gaps between the baseline and target using the Gap Analysis technique.

4.4.5 Define Candidate Roadmap Components

Following creation of a Baseline Architecture, a Target Architecture, and Gap Analysis results, a Business Roadmap is required to prioritize activities over the coming phases. This initial Business Architecture Roadmap (see Section 4.5.3) will be used as raw material to support a more detailed definition of a consolidated, cross-discipline roadmap within Phase E: Opportunities & Solutions.

4.4.6 Resolve Impacts across the Architecture Landscape

Once the Business Architecture is finalized, it is necessary to understand any wider impacts or implications. At this stage, other architecture artifacts in the Architecture Landscape should be examined to address the following:

- Does this Business Architecture impact any pre-existing architectures?
- Have recent changes been made that impact the Business Architecture?
- Are there any opportunities to re-use work from this Business Architecture in other areas of the organization?
- Does this Business Architecture impact other projects (those planned, as well as those in progress)?
- Will this Business Architecture be impacted by other projects (those planned, as well as those in progress)?

4.4.7 Conduct Formal Stakeholder Review

Check the original motivation for the architecture project and the Statement of Architecture Work against the proposed Business Architecture, asking if it is fit for the purpose of supporting subsequent work in the other architecture domains. Refine the proposed Business Architecture only if necessary.

4.4.8 Finalize the Business Architecture

Select standards for each of the building blocks, re-using as much as possible from the reference models selected from the Architecture Repository. Fully document each building block, then conduct a final cross-check of overall architecture against business goals; document the rationale for building block decisions in the architecture document. Document the final requirements traceability report. Document the final mapping of the architecture within the Architecture Repository. From the selected building blocks, identify those that might be re-used (working practices, roles, business relationships, job descriptions, etc.) and publish via the Architecture Repository. Finalize all the work products.

4.4.9 Create the Architecture Definition Document

Document the rationale for building block decisions in the Architecture Definition Document. Prepare the business sections of the Architecture Definition Document (see Section 4.5.1.1). Send the document for review by relevant stakeholders, and incorporate any feedback.

Building Blocks

(Syllabus Reference: Unit 9, Learning Outcome 3: You should be able to explain how building blocks are used in the development of a Business Architecture.)

Building blocks are used widely within TOGAF for building architectures, where they are known as Architecture Building Blocks (ABBs) and for building solutions, where they are known as Solution Building Blocks (SBBs).

The way in which functionality, products, and custom developments are assembled into building blocks varies widely between individual architectures. Every organization must decide for itself what arrangement of building blocks works best for it. A good choice of building blocks can lead to improvements in legacy system integration, interoperability, and flexibility in the creation of new systems and applications.

In Phase B, when creating the Baseline and Target Architecture descriptions, the architect should identify relevant Business Architecture building blocks, drawing on the Architecture Repository if possible. A number of catalogs are provided to help to model the decomposition of a building block and also decompositions across related building blocks. Once the initial Baseline and Target Architectures are complete, a Gap Analysis is then used to identify building blocks to carry over to the target; eliminated building blocks; and new, required building blocks. When finalizing the Business Architecture, standards are selected for each building block, each building block is documented, and those which look likely to be re-usable are published in the Architecture Repository.

4.5 Outputs

(Syllabus Reference: Unit 9, Learning Outcome 4: You should understand the outputs.)

The outputs of this phase are:
- Statement of Architecture Work, updated if necessary
- Validated business principles, business goals, and business drivers
- Elaborated Business Architecture principles
- Draft Architecture Definition Document (see Section 4.5.1) containing content updates (see Section 4.5.1.1)
- Draft Architecture Requirements Specification (see Section 4.5.2), including content updates (see Section 4.5.2.1)
- Business Architecture components of an Architecture Roadmap (see Section 4.5.3)

The outputs may also include some or all of the catalogs, matrices, and diagrams listed in Table 4.

4.5.1 Architecture Definition Document

(Syllabus Reference: Unit 9, Learning Outcome 4.1: You should be able to explain the key element: Business Architecture components of the Architecture Definition Document.)

The Architecture Definition Document is the deliverable container for the core architectural artifacts created during a project and for important related information. The Architecture Definition Document spans all four architecture domains (Business, Data, Application, and Technology) and also examines all relevant states of the architecture (baseline, transition, and target). It is first created in Phase A, where it is populated with artifacts created to support the Architecture Vision. It is updated in Phase B, with Business Architecture-related material, and subsequently updated with Information Systems Architecture material in Phase C, and then with Technology Architecture material in Phase D. Where the scope of change to implement the Target Architecture requires an incremental approach, the Architecture Definition Document will be updated to include one or more Transition Architectures in Phase E (see Section 10.5.2).

The Architecture Definition Document is a companion to the Architecture Requirements Specification, with a complementary objective to provide a qualitative view of the solution. The aim is to communicate the intent of the architects. The Architecture Requirements Specification, on the other hand, provides a quantitative view of the solution, stating measurable criteria that must be met during the implementation of the architecture.

The following contents are typically found within an Architecture Definition Document:

- Scope
- Goals, objectives, and constraints
- Architecture principles
- Baseline Architecture
- Architecture models (for each state to be modeled); such as models for Business Architecture, Data Architecture, Application Architecture, and Technology Architecture
- Rationale and justification for architectural approach
- Mapping to Architecture Repository, including mappings to the Architecture Landscape, the reference models, the standards, as well as a re-use assessment
- Gap Analysis
- Impact assessment
- Transition Architecture (see Section 10.5.2)

4.5.1.1 *Business Architecture Components*

The topics that should be addressed in the Architecture Definition Document related to Business Architecture are as follows:

- Baseline Business Architecture, if appropriate; this is a description of the existing Business Architecture
- Target Business Architecture, including:
  - Organization structure identifying business locations and relating them to organizational units
  - Business goals and objectives for the enterprise and each organizational unit
  - Business functions identified using a detailed, recursive step involving successive decomposition of major functional areas into sub-functions
  - Business services that the enterprise and each enterprise unit provides to its customers, both internally and externally
  - Business processes, including measures and deliverables

- Business roles, including development and modification of skills requirements
- Business data model
- A correlation of organization and functions which relate business functions to organizational units in the form of a matrix report
- Views corresponding to the selected viewpoints addressing key stakeholder concerns

4.5.2 Architecture Requirements Specification

(Syllabus Reference: Unit 9, Learning Outcome 4.2: You should be able to explain the key element: Business Architecture components of the Architecture Requirements Specification.)

The Architecture Requirements Specification provides a set of quantitative statements that outline what an implementation project must do in order to comply with the architecture. An Architecture Requirements Specification will typically form a major component of an implementation contract or contract for more detailed architecture definition. As mentioned in Section 4.5.1, the Architecture Requirements Specification is a companion to the Architecture Definition Document, and provides a quantitative view.

The following contents are typical within an Architecture Requirements Specification:
- Success measures
- Architecture requirements
- Business service contracts
- Application service contracts
- Implementation guidelines
- Implementation specifications
- Implementation standards
- Interoperability requirements
- IT service management requirements
- Constraints
- Assumptions

4.5.2.1 *Business Architecture Requirements*

Business Architecture requirements populating the Architecture Requirements Specification in Phase B include:

- Gap Analysis results
- Technical requirements: An initial set of technical requirements should be generated as the output of Phase B: Business Architecture. These are the drivers for the Technology Architecture work that follows, and should identify, categorize, and prioritize the implications for work in the remaining architecture domains; for example, by a dependency/priority matrix (e.g., guiding trade-offs between speed of transaction processing and security); a list of the specific models that are expected to be produced (e.g., expressed as primitives of the Zachman Framework).
- Updated business requirements, identified by use of the Business Scenarios technique

4.5.3 Architecture Roadmap

The Architecture Roadmap lists individual work packages that will realize the Target Architecture and lays them out on a timeline to show progression from the Baseline Architecture to the Target Architecture. The Architecture Roadmap highlights individual work packages' business value at each stage. Transition Architectures necessary to effectively realize the Target Architecture are identified as intermediate steps. The Architecture Roadmap is incrementally developed throughout Phases E and F, and informed by the roadmap components developed in Phases B, C, and D.

The following contents are typically found within an Architecture Roadmap:

- Work package portfolio:
    - Work package description (name, description, objectives, deliverables)
    - Functional requirements
    - Dependencies
    - Relationship to opportunity
    - Relationship to Architecture Definition Document and Architecture Requirements Specification
    - Business Value
- Implementation Factor Assessment and Deduction matrix, including:
    - Risks
    - Issues

- – Assumptions
- – Dependencies
- – Actions
- – Impact
- Consolidated Gaps, Solutions, and Dependencies Matrix, including:
  - – Architecture domain
  - – Gap
  - – Potential solutions
  - – Dependencies
- Transition Architectures, if any
- Implementation recommendations:
  - – Criteria/measures of effectiveness of projects
  - – Risks and issues
  - – Solution Building Blocks (SBBs)

4.6 Summary

The objective of Phase B: Business Architecture is to document the fundamental organization of a business, embodied in its business processes and people, their relationships to each other and the environment, and the principles governing its design and evolution. It should show how the organization meets its business goals.

4.7 Exercises

Exercise 4-1

Identify five sources of information within your organization that could be used to draw up a Baseline Business Architecture Description.

Exercise 4-2

Which of the Phase B catalogs, matrices, and diagrams would be most suitable for addressing the following concerns?
- Identifying where the enterprise carries out its business operations
- Identifying all agreed service contracts
- Identifying relationships between organizations and business functions in the enterprise

Exercise 4-3

Which of the Phase B catalogs, matrices, and diagrams would be most suitable for addressing the following stakeholders?

- Human Resource Managers
- Chief Financial Officer

4.8 Recommended Reading

The following are recommended sources of further information for this chapter:

- TOGAF 9 Part II, Chapter 8 (Phase B: Business Architecture)
- TOGAF 9 Part IV, Chapter 36 (Architecture Deliverables)
- Sample Catalogs, Matrices, and Diagrams presentation: www.togaf.info/ sg03

Chapter 5

Phase C: Information Systems Architectures

5.1 Key Learning Points

This chapter describes Phase C: Information Systems Architectures of the TOGAF Architecture Development Method (ADM).

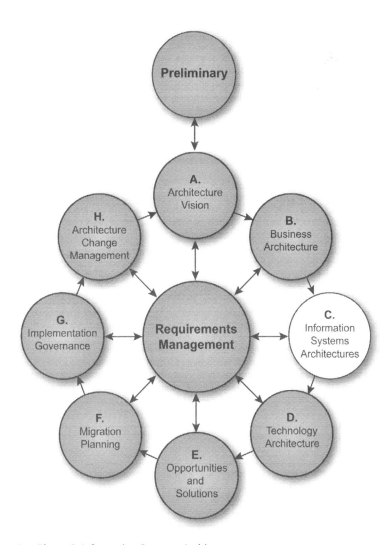

Figure 8:   Phase C: Information Systems Architectures

> **Key Points Explained**
>
> Upon completion of this chapter you should be able to:
>
> 1. Explain the considerations for the implementation order and approach of the Data and Application Architectures

5.2 Objectives

The objectives of Phase C: Information Systems Architectures are to:

-   Develop the Target Information Systems (Data and Application) Architectures, describing how the enterprise's Information Systems Architecture will enable the Business Architecture and the Architecture Vision, in a way that addresses the Request for Architecture Work and stakeholder concerns
-   Identify candidate Architecture Roadmap components based upon gaps between the Baseline and Target Information Systems (Data and Application) Architectures

5.3 Considerations for the Implementation Order

(Syllabus Reference: Unit 10, Learning Outcome 1: You should be able to explain the considerations for the implementation order of the Data and Application Architectures.)

Phase C involves some combination of Data and Application Architecture. These may be developed in either order, or in parallel. There will need to be some iteration to ensure consistency.

5.4 Inputs

See Chapter 6 and Chapter 7.

5.5 Steps

There are two steps in this phase:

1. Data Architecture
2. Application Architecture

The details for these steps are covered in the following two chapters. The outline steps for both architectures in Phase C (and also the Technology Architecture in Phase D) are consistent with those in Phase B.

5.6 Outputs

See Chapter 6 and Chapter 7.

5.7 Summary

Phase C: Information Systems Architectures documents the fundamental organization of an organization's IT systems, embodied in the major types of information and the applications that process them, their relationships to each other and the environment, and the principles governing their design and evolution.

5.8 Exercises

See Chapter 6 and Chapter 7.

5.9 Recommended Reading

The following are recommended sources of further information for this chapter:

- TOGAF 9 Part II, Chapter 9 (Phase C: Information Systems Architectures)

Phase C: Data Architecture

6.1 Key Learning Points

This chapter describes the Data Architecture part of Phase C: Information Systems Architectures of the TOGAF Architecture Development Method (ADM).

Key Points Explained

Upon completion of this chapter you should be able to:

1. Understand the inputs to the phase, and explain Data Principles
2. Understand the steps, and be able to explain the considerations for selecting reference models, viewpoints, and tools
3. Understand the outputs, and be able to explain the following key elements:
   - Data Architecture components of the Architecture Definition Document
   - Data Architecture components of the Architecture Requirements Specification

---

6.2 Objectives

The objectives of the Data Architecture part of Phase C are to:

- Develop the Target Data Architecture that enables the Business Architecture and the Architecture Vision, while addressing the Request for Architecture Work and stakeholder concerns
- Identify candidate Architecture Roadmap components based upon gaps between the Baseline and Target Data Architectures

6.3 Inputs

(Syllabus Reference: Unit 10, Learning Outcome 2: You should understand the inputs to the phase.)

The inputs to this phase are:

- Request for Architecture Work

- Capability Assessment
- Communications Plan
- Organizational Model for Enterprise Architecture
- Tailored Architecture Framework
- Data principles, if existing
- Statement of Architecture Work
- Architecture Vision
- Architecture Repository
- Draft Architecture Definition Document:
  - Baseline Business Architecture (detailed)
  - Target Business Architecture (detailed)
  - Baseline Data Architecture (high-level)
  - Target Data Architecture (high-level)
  - Baseline Application Architecture (high-level or detailed)
  - Target Application Architecture (high-level or detailed)
  - Baseline Technology Architecture (high-level)
  - Target Technology Architecture (high-level)
- Draft Architecture Requirements Specification:
  - Gap Analysis results
  - Relevant technical requirements
- Business Architecture components of an Architecture Roadmap

6.3.1 Data Principles

(Syllabus Reference: Unit 10, Learning Outcome 2.1: You should be able to explain the following key element: Data Principles.)

Data principles should form part of the overarching set of architecture principles, initially developed in the Preliminary Phase. Example data principles drawn from TOGAF 9 Part III, Chapter 23 (Architecture Principles) are summarized in Table 5.

Table 5:   Example Data Principles

Principle	Summary
Data is an Asset	Data is an asset that has value to the enterprise and is managed accordingly.
Data is Shared	Users have access to the data necessary to perform their duties; therefore, data is shared across enterprise functions and organizations.

Principle	Summary
Data is Accessible	Data is accessible for users to perform their functions.
Data Trustee	Each data element has a trustee accountable for data quality.
Common Vocabulary and Data Definitions	Data is defined consistently throughout the enterprise, and the definitions are understandable and available to all users.
Data Security	Data is protected from unauthorized use and disclosure. In addition to the traditional aspects of national security classification, this includes, but is not limited to, protection of pre-decisional, sensitive, source selection-sensitive, and proprietary information.

6.4 Steps

(Syllabus Reference: Unit 10, Learning Outcome 3: You should understand the steps in this phase.)

Phase C: Data Architecture consists of the following steps:

1. Select reference models, viewpoints, and tools
2. Develop Baseline Data Architecture Description
3. Develop Target Data Architecture Description
4. Perform Gap Analysis
5. Define candidate roadmap components
6. Resolve impacts across the Architecture Landscape
7. Conduct formal stakeholder review
8. Finalize the Data Architecture
9. Create Architecture Definition Document

The order of the steps should be adapted to the situation. In particular, you should determine whether it is appropriate to do the Baseline Data Architecture or the Target Data Architecture development first.

The steps are described in more detail in the following sections.

6.4.1 Select Reference Models, Viewpoints, and Tools

(Syllabus Reference: Unit 10, Learning Outcome 3.1: You should be able to explain the considerations for selecting reference models, viewpoints, and tools.)

After reviewing and validating the set of data principles, select relevant
Data Architecture resources (reference models, patterns, etc.) from the
Architecture Repository, on the basis of the business drivers, stakeholders,
concerns, and the Business Architecture. Also, select relevant Data
Architecture viewpoints; for example, stakeholders of the data (regulatory
bodies, users, generators, subjects, auditors, etc.), various time dimensions
(real-time, reporting period, event-driven, etc.), locations; business processes;
i.e., those that will enable the architect to demonstrate how the stakeholder
concerns are being addressed in the Data Architecture. Then, identify
appropriate tools and techniques to be used for data capture, modeling, and
analysis, in association with the selected viewpoints.

6.4.1.1 Determine Overall Modeling Process

For each viewpoint, select the models needed to support the specific view
required, using the selected tool or method. Examples of data models
include the DODAF Logical Data Model, the ARTS data model, the Pipeline
Open Data Standard (PODS) data model, the Professional Petroleum Data
Management (PPDM) Association data model, and the Energistics Epicenter
data model. Confirm that all stakeholder concerns have been addressed. If
they are not, create new models to address concerns not covered, or augment
the existing models.

The recommended process for developing a Data Architecture is as follows:
*   Collect data-related models from existing Business Architecture and
    Application Architecture materials
*   Rationalize data requirements and align with any existing enterprise data
    catalogs and models; this allows the development of a data inventory and
    entity relationship model
*   Update and develop matrices across the architecture by relating data to
    business services, business functions, access rights, and applications
*   Elaborate Data Architecture views by examining how data is created,
    distributed, migrated, secured, and archived

6.4.1.2 Identify Required Catalogs, Matrices, and Diagrams

TOGAF provides definitions of catalogs, matrices, and diagrams for use in
development of a Data Architecture. Catalogs capture inventories of the core
assets of the business. Matrices show the core relationships between model
entities. Diagrams represent the Data Architecture information from a set of
different perspectives (viewpoints).

TOGAF recommends that the catalogs, matrices, and diagrams shown in Table 6 be considered in Phase C: Data Architecture and provides guidance on their structure in TOGAF 9 Part IV, Chapter 34 (Content Metamodel).

Table 6:   Phase C: Data Architecture Catalogs, Matrices, and Diagrams

Catalogs	Matrices	Diagrams
Data Entity/Data Component catalog	Data Entity/Business Function matrix	Conceptual Data diagram
	Application/Data matrix	Logical Data diagram
		Data Dissemination diagram
		Data Lifecycle diagram
		Data Security diagram
		Data Migration diagram

6.4.1.3 *Identify Types of Requirement to be Collected*

Once the catalogs, matrices, and diagrams have been developed, modeling should be completed by formalizing the data-focused requirements for the Target Architecture. The architect should identify types of requirements to be met by the architecture. These requirements may relate to the data domain, may provide requirements input into the Application and Technology Architectures, or may provide detailed guidance to be reflected during design and implementation.

6.4.2 Develop Baseline Data Architecture Description

Develop a Baseline Description of the existing Data Architecture to the extent necessary to support the Target Data Architecture. The scope and level of detail to be defined will depend on the extent to which existing data elements are likely to be carried over into the Target Data Architecture, and on whether there are any existing architectural descriptions. Where possible, identify the relevant Data Architecture building blocks, drawing on the architecture. Where new architecture models need to be developed to satisfy stakeholder concerns, use the models identified within Step 1 as a guideline for creating new content to describe the Baseline Architecture.

6.4.3 Develop Target Data Architecture Description

Develop a Target Description for the Data Architecture to the extent necessary to support the Architecture Vision and Target Business

Architecture. The scope and level of detail to be defined will depend on the relevance of the data elements to the Target Architecture, and on whether architectural descriptions exist. Where possible, identify the relevant Data Architecture building blocks, drawing on the architecture. Where new architecture models need to be developed to satisfy stakeholder concerns, use the models identified within Step 1 as a guideline for creating new content to describe the Target Architecture.

6.4.4   Perform Gap Analysis

Verify the architecture models for internal consistency and accuracy. Document changes to the viewpoint(s) represented in the selected models from the Architecture Repository. Test the architecture models for completeness against requirements. Finally, identify gaps between the baseline and target using Gap Analysis.

6.4.5   Define Candidate Roadmap Components

Following creation of a Baseline Architecture, Target Architecture, and Gap Analysis, a Data Roadmap is required to prioritize activities over the coming phases. This initial Data Architecture Roadmap will be used to support more detailed definition of a consolidated, cross-discipline roadmap within Phase E: Opportunities & Solutions.

6.4.6   Resolve Impacts Across the Architecture Landscape

Once the Data Architecture is finalized, it is necessary to understand any wider impacts or implications. At this stage, other architecture artifacts in the Architecture Landscape should be examined to determine the following:

- Does this Data Architecture impact any pre-existing architectures?
- Have recent changes been made that impact the Data Architecture?
- Are there any opportunities to re-use work from this Data Architecture in other areas of the organization?
- Does this Data Architecture impact other projects (planned or in progress)?
- Will this Data Architecture be impacted by other projects (planned or in progress)?

6.4.7   Conduct Formal Stakeholder Review

Check the original motivation for the architecture project and the Statement of Architecture Work against the proposed Data Architecture. Conduct an impact analysis to identify any areas where the Business and Application

Architectures (e.g., business practices) may need to change in light of changes in the Data Architecture (for example, changes to forms or procedures, applications, or database systems). If the impact is significant, this may warrant the Business and Application Architectures being revisited.

Identify any areas where the Application Architecture (if it exists at this point) may need to change in light of changes in the Data Architecture or to identify constraints on the Application Architecture about to be designed. If the impact is significant, it may be appropriate to do a short iteration of the Application Architecture.

Identify any constraints on the Technology Architecture about to be designed, refining the proposed Data Architecture only if necessary.

6.4.8 Finalize the Data Architecture

Select standards for each of the building blocks, re-using as much as possible from the reference models selected from the Architecture Repository. Fully document each building block, then conduct a final cross-check of the overall architecture against business requirements; document rationale for building block decisions in the architecture document. Document the final requirements traceability report. Document the final mapping of the architecture within the Architecture Repository. From the selected building blocks, identify those that might be re-used, and publish them in the Architecture Repository. Finalize all the work products.

6.4.9 Create Architecture Definition Document

Document the rationale for building block decisions in the Architecture Definition Document. Prepare the Data Architecture sections of the Architecture Definition Document (see Section 6.5.1). Send the document for review by relevant stakeholders, and incorporate feedback.

6.5 Outputs

(Syllabus Reference: Unit 10, Learning Outcome 4: You should understand the outputs of this phase.)

The outputs of this phase are:
- Statement of Architecture Work, updated if necessary
- Validated data principles, or new data principles

- Draft Architecture Definition Document, containing content updates (see Section 6.5.1)
- Draft Architecture Requirements Specification, including content updates (see Section 6.5.2)
- Data Architecture components of an Architecture Roadmap

The outputs may also include some or all of the catalogs, matrices, and diagrams listed in Table 6.

6.5.1   Components of the Architecture Definition Document

(Syllabus Reference: Unit 10, Learning Outcome 4.1: You should be able to explain the following key element: Data Architecture Components of the Architecture Definition Document.)

The topics that should be addressed in the Architecture Definition Document that are related to the Data Architecture are as follows:
- Baseline Data Architecture, if appropriate
  - Target Data Architecture, including models for business data , logical data and the data management process, as well as a Data Entity/ Business Function matrix
- Data Architecture views corresponding to the selected viewpoints addressing key stakeholder concerns

6.5.2   Components of the Architecture Requirements Specification

(Syllabus Reference: Unit 10, Learning Outcome 4.2: You should be able to explain the following key element: Data Architecture Components of the Architecture Requirements Specification.)

Data Architecture requirements populating the Architecture Requirements Specification in Phase C include:
- Gap Analysis results
- Data interoperability requirements (e.g., XML schema, security policies)
- Areas where the Business Architecture may need to change in order to comply with changes in the Data Architecture
- Constraints on the Technology Architecture about to be designed
- Updated business requirements, if appropriate
- Updated application requirements, if appropriate

6.6 Summary

The Data Architecture part of Phase C defines the types and sources of data needed to support the business, and does so in a way that can be understood by stakeholders. The architecture team should consider existing relevant data models, such as the ARTS and POSC models.

6.7 Exercises

Exercise 6-1

Identify five sources of information within your organization that could be used to draw up a Baseline Data Architecture description.

Exercise 6-2

Which of the Phase C: Data Architecture catalogs, matrices, and diagrams would be most suitable to address the following concerns:

- Enabling development of data governance programs across the enterprise
- Identifying systems that access and update data
- Depicting critical relationships between data entities within the enterprise
- Determining who or what has access to enterprise data

6.8 Recommended Reading

The following are recommended sources of further information for this chapter:

- TOGAF 9 Part II, Chapter 10 (Phase C: Information Systems Architectures – Data Architecture)
- TOGAF 9 Part IV, Chapter 36 (Architecture Deliverables)
- Sample Catalogs, Matrices, and Diagrams presentation: www.togaf.info/sg03

Phase C: Application Architecture

7.1 Key Learning Points

This chapter describes the Application Architecture part of Phase C: Information Systems Architectures of the TOGAF Architecture Development Method (ADM).

Key Points Explained

Upon completion of this chapter you should be able to:

1. Understand the inputs to the phase, and explain Application Principles
2. Understand the steps, and be able to explain the considerations for selecting reference models, viewpoints, and tools
3. Understand the outputs, and be able to explain the following key elements:
   - Application Architecture components of the Architecture Definition Document
   - Application Architecture components of the Architecture Requirements Specification

---

7.2 Objectives

The objectives of the Application Architecture part of Phase C are to:

- Develop the Target Application Architecture that enables the Business Architecture and the Architecture Vision, while addressing the Request for Architecture Work and stakeholder concerns
- Identify candidate Architecture Roadmap components based upon gaps between the Baseline and Target Application Architectures

7.3 Inputs

(Syllabus Reference: Unit 11, Learning Outcome 1: You should understand the inputs to the phase.)

The inputs to this phase are:

- Request for Architecture Work
- Capability Assessment
- Communications Plan
- Organizational Model for Enterprise Architecture
- Tailored Architecture Framework
- Application principles, if existing
- Statement of Architecture Work
- Architecture Vision
- Architecture Repository
- Draft Architecture Definition Document:
  - Baseline Business Architecture (detailed)
  - Target Business Architecture (detailed)
  - Baseline Data Architecture (high-level or detailed)
  - Target Data Architecture (high-level or detailed)
  - Baseline Application Architecture (high-level)
  - Target Application Architecture (high-level)
  - Baseline Technology Architecture (high-level)
  - Target Technology Architecture (high-level)
- Draft Architecture Requirements Specification:
  - Gap Analysis results
  - Relevant technical requirements
- Business and Data Architecture components of an Architecture Roadmap, if available

7.3.1 Application Principles

(Syllabus Reference: Unit 11, Learning Outcome 1.1: You should be able to explain the following key element: Application Principles.)

Application principles form part of the overarching set of architecture principles, initially developed in the Preliminary Phase. Example application principles drawn from TOGAF 9 Part III, Chapter 23 (Architecture Principles) are summarized in Table 7.

Table 7:   Example Application Principles

Principle	Summary
Technology Independence	Applications are independent of specific technology choices and therefore can operate on a variety of technology platforms.
Ease-of-Use	Applications are easy to use. The underlying technology is transparent to users, so they can concentrate on tasks at hand.

7.4 Steps

(Syllabus Reference: Unit 11, Learning Outcome 2: You should understand the steps for this phase.)

Phase C: Application Architecture consists of the following steps:

1.   Select reference models, viewpoints, and tools
2.   Develop Baseline Application Architecture Description
3.   Develop Target Application Architecture Description
4.   Perform Gap Analysis
5.   Define candidate roadmap components
6.   Resolve impacts across the Architecture Landscape
7.   Conduct formal stakeholder review
8.   Finalize the Application Architecture
9.   Create Architecture Definition Document

The order of the steps should be adapted to the situation: in particular, you should determine whether it is appropriate to do the Baseline Application Architecture or the Target Application Architecture development first.

The steps are described in more detail in the following sections.

7.4.1 Select Reference Models, Viewpoints, and Tools

(Syllabus Reference: Unit 11, Learning Outcome 2.1: You should be able to explain the considerations for selecting reference models, viewpoints, and tools.)

Review and validate the set of application principles. Then, select relevant Application Architecture resources (reference models, patterns, etc.) from the Architecture Repository, on the basis of the business drivers, the stakeholders, and their concerns. Next, select relevant Application Architecture viewpoints (for example, stakeholders of the applications, viewpoints relevant to functional and individual users of applications, etc.), those that will enable the architect to demonstrate how the stakeholder concerns are being addressed in the Application Architecture. Then, identify appropriate tools and techniques to be used for the capture, modeling, and analysis of the Application Architecture, in association with the selected viewpoints.

7.4.1.1 *Determine Overall Modeling Process*

For each viewpoint, select the models needed to support the specific view required, using the selected tool or method. Examples of applications models include those from the TeleManagement Forum (TMF) and the Object Management Group (OMG). Confirm that all stakeholder concerns have been addressed. If they are not, create new models to address concerns not covered, or augment existing models (see above).

The recommended process for developing an Application Architecture is as follows:

- Understand the list of applications or application components that are required, based on the baseline Application Portfolio, what the requirements are, and the Business Architecture scope
- Simplify complicated applications by decomposing them into two or more applications
- Ensure that the set of application definitions is internally consistent, by removing duplicate functionality as far as possible, and combining similar applications into one
- Identify logical applications and the most appropriate physical applications
- Develop matrices across the architecture by relating applications to business services, business functions, data, processes, etc.
- Elaborate a set of Application Architecture views by examining how the applications will function, capturing integration, migration, development, and operational concerns

7.4.1.2 *Identify Required Catalogs, Matrices, and Diagrams*

TOGAF provides definitions of catalogs, matrices, and diagrams for use in development of an Application Architecture. TOGAF recommends that the catalogs, matrices, and diagrams shown in Table 8 be considered in Phase C: Application Architecture and provides guidance on their structure in TOGAF 9 Part IV, Chapter 34 (Content Metamodel).

Table 8:   Phase C: Application Architecture Catalogs, Matrices, and Diagrams

Catalogs	Matrices	Diagrams
Application Portfolio catalog Interface catalog	Application/ Organization matrix Role/Application matrix Application/Function matrix Application Interaction matrix	Application Communication diagram Application and User Location diagram Application Use-Case diagram Enterprise Manageability diagram Process/Application Realization diagram Software Engineering diagram Application Migration diagram Software Distribution diagram

7.4.1.3 *Identify Types of Requirement to be Collected*

Once the catalogs, matrices, and diagrams have been developed, modeling should be completed by formalizing the application-focused requirements for the Target Architecture. The architect should identify the types of requirements to be met by the architecture. These requirements may relate to the application domain, may provide requirements input into the Data and Technology Architectures, or may provide detailed guidance to be reflected during design and implementation.

7.4.2 Develop Baseline Application Architecture Description

Develop a Baseline Description of the existing Application Architecture to the extent necessary to support the Target Application Architecture. The scope and level of detail to be defined will depend on the extent to which existing applications are likely to be carried over into the Target Application Architecture, and on whether architecture descriptions exist. Where possible, identify the relevant Application Architecture building blocks, drawing on the Architecture Repository. If not already existing within the Architecture Repository, define each application in line with the Application Portfolio catalog. Where new architecture models need to be developed to satisfy stakeholder concerns, use the models identified within Step 1 as a guideline for creating new architecture content to describe the Baseline Architecture.

7.4.3   Develop Target Application Architecture Description

Develop a Target Description for the Application Architecture to the extent necessary to support the Architecture Vision, Target Business Architecture, and Target Data Architecture. The scope and level of detail to be defined will depend on the relevance of the application elements to attaining the Target Architecture Vision, and on whether architectural descriptions exist. Where possible, identify the relevant Application Architecture building blocks, drawing on the Architecture Repository. Where new architecture models need to be developed to satisfy stakeholder concerns, use the models identified within Step 1 as a guideline for creating new architecture content to describe the Target Architecture.

7.4.4   Perform Gap Analysis

First, check the architecture models for internal consistency and accuracy. Note changes to the viewpoint represented in the selected models from the Architecture Repository, and document the changes. Then, test the architecture models for completeness against requirements. Finally, identify gaps between the baseline and target using the Gap Analysis technique.

7.4.5   Define Candidate Roadmap Components

Following creation of a Baseline Architecture, Target Architecture, and Gap Analysis, an Application Roadmap is required to prioritize activities over the coming phases. This initial Application Architecture Roadmap will be used as raw material to support the more detailed definition of a consolidated, cross-discipline roadmap within Phase E: Opportunities & Solutions.

7.4.6   Resolve Impacts Across the Architecture Landscape

Once the Application Architecture is finalized, it is necessary to understand any wider impacts or implications. At this stage, other architecture artifacts in the Architecture Landscape should be examined to determine the following:

- Does this Application Architecture impact any pre-existing architectures?
- Have recent changes been made that impact the Application Architecture?
- Are there any opportunities to re-use work from this Application Architecture in other areas of the organization?

- Does this Application Architecture impact other projects (planned or in progress)?
- Will this Application Architecture be impacted by other projects (planned or in progress)?

7.4.7 Conduct Formal Stakeholder Review

Check the original motivation for the architecture project and the Statement of Architecture Work against the proposed Application Architecture. Conduct an impact analysis to identify any areas where the Business and Data Architectures (e.g., business practices) may need to change in light of changes in the Application Architecture (for example, changes to forms or procedures, applications, or database systems). If the impact is significant, this may warrant the Business and Data Architectures being revisited. Finally, identify any constraints on the Technology Architecture (especially the infrastructure) about to be designed.

7.4.8 Finalize the Application Architecture

Select standards for each of the building blocks, re-using as much as possible from the reference models selected from the Architecture Repository. Fully document each building block, and then conduct a final cross-check of overall architecture against business requirements. Document the rationale for building block decisions in the architecture document. Document the final requirements traceability report. Also document the final mapping of the architecture within the Architecture Repository. From the selected building blocks, identify those that might be re-used, and publish them in the Architecture Repository. Finalize all the work products.

7.4.9 Create Architecture Definition Document

Document the rationale for building block decisions in the Architecture Definition Document. Prepare the Application Architecture sections of the Architecture Definition Document (see Section 7.5.1). Send the document for review by relevant stakeholders, and incorporate feedback.

7.5 Outputs

(Syllabus Reference: Unit 11, Learning Outcome 3: You should understand the outputs of the phase.)

The outputs of this phase are:
- Statement of Architecture Work, updated if necessary
- Validated application principles, or new application principles
- Draft Architecture Definition Document, containing content updates (see Section 7.5.1).
- Draft Architecture Requirements Specification, including content updates (see Section 7.5.2)
- Application Architecture components of an Architecture Roadmap

The outputs may also include some or all of the catalogs, matrices, and diagrams listed in Table 8.

7.5.1 Components of the Architecture Definition Document
(Syllabus Reference: Unit 10, Learning Outcome 3.1: You should be able to explain the following key element: Application Architecture Components of the Architecture Definition Document.)

The topics that should be addressed in the Architecture Definition Document related to the Application Architecture are as follows:
- Baseline Application Architecture, if appropriate
- Target Application Architecture:
  - Process systems model
  - Place systems model
  - Time systems model
  - People systems model
- Application Architecture views corresponding to the selected viewpoints, addressing key stakeholder concerns

7.5.2 Components of the Architecture Requirements Specification
(Syllabus Reference: Unit 11, Learning Outcome 3.2: You should be able to explain the following key element: Application Architecture Components of the Architecture Requirements Specification.)

Application Architecture requirements populating the Architecture Requirements Specification in Phase C include:
- Gap Analysis results
- Applications interoperability requirements

- Relevant technical requirements that will apply to this evolution of the Architecture Development Cycle
- Constraints on the Technology Architecture about to be designed
- Updated business requirements, if appropriate
- Updated data requirements, if appropriate

7.6 Summary

This phase defines the *kinds* of applications necessary to process the data and support the business. The goal is to define the kinds of applications that are relevant and what those applications need to do. The applications are not described as computer systems but as logical groups of capabilities that manage data and support business functions. Thus, the applications and their capabilities should be defined without reference to particular technologies. This is because the applications should be stable, whereas the technology used to implement them may not be.

7.7 Exercises

Exercise 7-1

Identify five sources of information within your organization that could be used to draw up a Baseline Application Architecture Description.

Exercise 7-2

Which of the Phase C: Application Architecture catalogs, matrices, and diagrams would be most suitable for addressing the following concerns:
- Identifying which business functions use which applications within the enterprise
- Identifying all applications in the enterprise
- Identifying where the users of applications are located

Exercise 7-3

Which of the Phase C: Application Architecture catalogs, matrices, and diagrams would be most suitable for addressing the following stakeholders:
- External suppliers who need to exchange information

7.8 Recommended Reading

The following are recommended sources of further information for this chapter:

- TOGAF 9 Part II, Chapter 11 (Phase C: Information Systems Architectures – Application Architecture)
- TOGAF 9 Part IV, Chapter 36 (Architecture Deliverables)
- Sample Catalogs, Matrices, and Diagrams presentation: www.togaf.info/sg03

Phase D: Technology Architecture

8.1 Key Learning Points

This chapter describes Phase D: Technology Architecture of the TOGAF
Architecture Development Method (ADM).

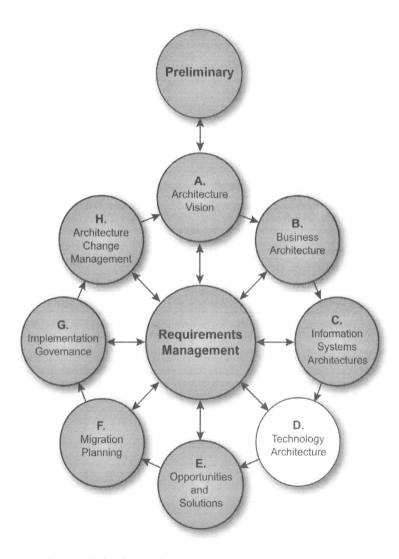

Figure 9:   Phase D: Technology Architectue

Key Points Explained

Upon completion of this chapter you should be able to:

1. Understand the inputs to the phase, and explain Technology Principles

2. Understand the steps, and be able to explain:

   - How the TRM can be used when developing a Technology Architecture

   - The role of Architecture Building Blocks (ABBs)

3. Understand the outputs and be able to explain the following key elements:

   - Technology Architecture components of the Architecture Definition Document

   - Technology Architecture components of the Architecture Requirements Specification

---

8.2 Objectives

The objectives of Phase D: Technology Architecture are to:

- Develop the Target Technology Architecture that enables the logical and physical application and data components and the Architecture Vision, addressing the Request for Architecture Work and stakeholder concerns

- Identify candidate Architecture Roadmap components based upon gaps between the Baseline and Target Technology Architectures

8.3 Inputs

(Syllabus Reference: Unit 14, Learning Outcome 1: You should understand the inputs to the phase.)

The inputs to this phase are:

- Request for Architecture Work
- Capability Assessment
- Communications Plan
- Organizational Model for Enterprise Architecture
- Tailored Architecture Framework
- Technology principles, if existing
- Statement of Architecture Work
- Architecture Vision
- Architecture Repository

- Draft Architecture Definition Document:
  - Baseline Business Architecture (detailed)
  - Target Business Architecture (detailed)
  - Baseline Data Architecture (detailed)
  - Target Data Architecture (detailed)
  - Baseline Application Architecture (detailed)
  - Target Application Architecture (detailed)
  - Baseline Technology Architecture (high-level)
  - Target Technology Architecture (high-level)
- Draft Architecture Requirements Specification:
  - Gap Analysis results
  - Relevant technical requirements
- Business, Data, and Application Architecture components of an Architecture Roadmap

8.3.1 Technology Principles

(Syllabus Reference: Unit 14, Learning Outcome 1.1: You should be able to explain the following key element: Technology Principles.)

Technology principles form part of the overarching set of architecture principles, initially developed in the Preliminary Phase. Example technology principles drawn from TOGAF 9 Part III, Chapter 23 (Architecture Principles) are summarized in Table 9.

Table 9:   Example Technology Principles

Principle	Summary
Requirements-based Change	Changes to applications and technology are made only in response to business needs.
Responsive Change Management	Changes to the enterprise information environment are implemented in a timely manner.
Control Technical Diversity	Technological diversity is controlled to minimize the non-trivial cost of maintaining expertise in and connectivity between multiple processing environments.
Interoperability	Software and hardware should conform to defined standards that promote interoperability for data, applications, and technology.

8.4 Steps

(Syllabus Reference: Unit 14, Learning Outcome 2: You should understand the steps in the phase.)

Phase D consists of the following steps:
1. Select reference models, viewpoints, and tools
2. Develop Baseline Technology Architecture Description
3. Develop Target Technology Architecture Description
4. Perform Gap Analysis
5. Define candidate roadmap components
6. Resolve impacts across the Architecture Landscape
7. Conduct formal stakeholder review
8. Finalize the Technology Architecture
9. Create Architecture Definition Document

The order of the steps should be adapted to the situation. In particular, you should determine whether it is appropriate to do the Baseline Technology Architecture or the Target Technology Architecture development first.

The steps are described in more detail in the following sections.

8.4.1 Select Reference Models, Viewpoints, and Tools

Review and validate the set of technology principles. Select relevant Technology Architecture resources (reference models, patterns, etc.) from the Architecture Repository on the basis of the business drivers, stakeholders, and their concerns. Select relevant Technology Architecture viewpoints that will enable the architect to demonstrate how the stakeholder concerns are being addressed in the Technology Architecture. Identify appropriate tools and techniques to be used for the capture, modeling, and analysis, in association with the selected viewpoints.

8.4.1.1 *Determine the Overall Modeling Process*

For each viewpoint, select the models needed to support the specific view required, using the selected tool or method. Ensure that all stakeholder concerns have been addressed. If they are not, create new models to address them, or augment existing models.

8.4.1.2 *Identify Required Catalogs, Matrices, and Diagrams*

Catalogs are inventories of the core assets of the business. They are hierarchical in nature and capture the decomposition of a metamodel entity and also decompositions across related model entities (e.g., platform service to logical technology component to physical technology component). The Technology Architecture should create technology catalogs as follows:

- Based on existing technology catalogs and the analysis of applications carried out in the Application Architecture phase, collect a list of products in use.
- If the requirements identified in the Application Architecture are not met by existing products, extend the product list by examining products that provide the required functionality and meet the required standards.
- Classify products against the TOGAF TRM if appropriate, extending the model as necessary to fit the classification of technology products in use.
- If technology standards are currently in place, apply these to the technology component catalog to gain a baseline view of compliance with technology standards.

Diagrams present the Technology Architecture from a set of different perspectives (viewpoints) according to the requirements of the stakeholders. This activity provides a link between platform requirements and hosting requirements, as a single application may need to be physically located in several environments to support local access, development lifecycles, and hosting requirements.

For major baseline applications or application platforms, produce a stack diagram showing how hardware, operating system, software infrastructure, and packaged applications combine. If appropriate, extend the Application Architecture diagrams of software distribution to show how applications map onto the technology platform. For each environment produce a logical diagram of hardware and software infrastructure showing the contents of the environment and logical communications between components. Where available, collect capacity information on the deployed infrastructure. For each environment, produce a physical diagram of communications infrastructure, such as routers, switches, firewalls, and network links. Where available, collect capacity information on the communications infrastructure.

TOGAF recommends that the catalogs, matrices, and diagrams shown in
Table 10 be considered in Phase D and provides guidance on their structure
in TOGAF 9 Part IV, Chapter 34 (Content Metamodel).

Table 10:   Phase D: Technology Architecture Catalogs, Matrices, and Diagrams

Catalogs	Matrices	Diagrams
Technology Standards catalog Technology Portfolio catalog	Application/Technology matrix	Environments and Locations diagram Platform Decomposition diagram Processing diagram Networked Computing/ Hardware diagram Communications Engineering diagram

8.4.1.3 Identify Types of Requirements to be Collected

Once the Technology Architecture catalogs, matrices, and diagrams have
been developed, modeling should be completed by formalizing the business
requirements for the Target Architecture. The architect should identify types
of requirements to be met by the architecture. These requirements may relate
to the technology domain, or may provide detailed guidance to be reflected
during design and implementation.

8.4.1.4 Select Services

The services portfolios are combinations of basic services from the service
categories in the TOGAF TRM that do not conflict. The combinations of
services are again tested to ensure support for the applications. This is a
prerequisite to the later step of fully defining the architecture.

For each building block, build up a service description portfolio as a set of
non-conflicting services. The set of services should be checked to ensure that
the functionality provided meets application requirements.

8.4.2 Develop Baseline Technology Architecture Description

Develop a Baseline Description of the existing Technology Architecture
to support the Target Technology Architecture. The scope and level of

detail to be defined will depend on the extent to which existing technology components are likely to be carried over into the Target Technology Architecture, and on whether architectural descriptions exist. Identify the relevant Technology Architecture building blocks, drawing on any artifacts held in the Architecture Repository. If nothing exists within the Architecture Repository, define each application in line with the Technology Portfolio catalog; see TOGAF 9 Part IV, Chapter 34 (Content Metamodel).

(Syllabus Reference: Unit 14, Learning Outcome 2.1: You should be able to explain how the TRM can be used when developing a Technology Architecture.)

Begin by converting the description of the existing environment into the terms of the organization's Foundation Architecture (e.g., the TOGAF Foundation Architecture's TRM). This will allow the team developing the architecture to gain experience with the model and to understand its component parts. The team may be able to take advantage of a previous architectural definition, but it is assumed that some adaptation may be required to match the architectural definition techniques described as part of this process. Another important task is to set down a list of key questions which can be used later in the development process to measure the effectiveness of the new architecture.

Where new architecture models need to be developed to satisfy stakeholder concerns, use the models identified within Step 1 as a guideline for creating new architecture content to describe the Baseline Architecture.

8.4.3 Develop Target Technology Architecture Description

Develop a Target Description for the Technology Architecture to the extent necessary to support the Architecture Vision, Target Business Architecture, and Target Information Systems Architecture. The scope and level of detail to be defined will depend on the relevance of the technology elements to the Target Architecture, and on whether architectural descriptions exist. As far as possible, identify the relevant Technology Architecture building blocks from the Architecture Repository.

(Syllabus Reference: Unit 14, Learning Outcome 2.2: You should be able to explain the role of ABBs when developing a Technology Architecture.)

A key process in the creation of a broad architectural model of the target system is the conceptualization of building blocks. Architecture Building Blocks (ABBs) describe the required functionality and how it may be implemented without the detail introduced by configuration or detailed design. The method of defining building blocks, along with some general guidelines for their use in creating an architectural model, is described in TOGAF 9 Part IV, Section 37.3 (Building Blocks and the ADM).

Where new architecture models need to be developed to satisfy stakeholder concerns, use the models identified within Step 1 as a guideline for creating new architecture content to describe the Target Architecture.

8.4.4   Perform Gap Analysis

Verify the architecture models for internal consistency and accuracy. Document any changes to the viewpoints represented in the selected models from the Architecture Repository. Test architecture models for completeness against requirements. Identify gaps between the baseline and target using Gap Analysis.

8.4.5   Define Candidate Roadmap Components

Following creation of a Baseline Architecture, Target Architecture, and Gap Analysis, a Technology Roadmap is required to prioritize activities over the coming phases. This initial Technology Architecture Roadmap will be used as raw material to support more detailed definition of a consolidated, cross-discipline roadmap within Phase E: Opportunities & Solutions.

8.4.6   Resolve Impacts Across the Architecture Landscape

Once the Technology Architecture is finalized, it is necessary to understand any wider impacts or implications. At this stage, other architecture artifacts in the Architecture Landscape should be examined to determine the following:

- Does this Technology Architecture impact any pre-existing architectures?
- Have recent changes been made that impact the Technology Architecture?
- Are there any opportunities to re-use work from this Technology Architecture in other areas of the organization?
- Does this Technology Architecture impact other projects (planned or those in progress)?
- Will this Technology Architecture be impacted by other projects (planned or those in progress)?

8.4.7 Conduct Formal Stakeholder Review

Check the original motivation for the architecture project and the Statement of Architecture Work against the proposed Technology Architecture, asking if it is fit for the purpose of supporting subsequent work in the other architecture domains. Refine the proposed Technology Architecture only if necessary.

8.4.8 Finalize the Technology Architecture

Select standards for each of the building blocks, re-using as much as possible from the reference models selected from the Architecture Repository. Fully document each building block, then conduct a final cross-check of overall architecture against business goals; document rationale for building block decisions in the architecture document. Document the final requirements traceability report. Document the final mapping of the architecture within the Architecture Repository. From the selected building blocks, identify those that might be re-used (working practices, roles, business relationships, job descriptions, etc.), and publish them in the Architecture Repository. Finalize all the work products.

8.4.9 Create Architecture Definition Document

Document the rationale for building block decisions in the Architecture Definition Document. Prepare the Technology Architecture sections of the Architecture Definition Document (see Section 8.5.1). Send the document for review by relevant stakeholders, and incorporate any feedback.

8.5 Outputs

(Syllabus Reference: Unit 14, Learning Outcome 3: You should understand the outputs of this phase.)

The outputs of this phase are:
- Statement of Architecture Work, updated if necessary
- Validated technology principles or new technology principles (if generated here)
- Draft Architecture Definition Document (see Section 4.5.1), containing content updates (see Section 8.5.1)
- Draft Architecture Requirements Specification (see Section 4.5.2) , including content updates (see Section 8.5.2)
- Technology Architecture components of an Architecture Roadmap

The outputs may also include some or all of the catalogs, matrices, and diagrams listed in Table 10.

8.5.1 Components of the Architecture Definition Document

(Syllabus Reference: Unit 14, Learning Outcome 3.1: You should be able to explain the following key element: Technology Architecture Components of the Architecture Definition Document.)

The topics that should be addressed in the Architecture Definition Document related to Technology Architecture are as follows:
- Baseline Technology Architecture, if appropriate
- Target Technology Architecture, including:
  - Technology components and their relationships to information systems
  - Technology platforms and their decomposition, showing the combinations of technology required to realize a particular technology "stack"
  - Environments and locations with a grouping of the required technology into computing environments (e.g., development, production)
  - Expected processing load and distribution of load across technology components
  - Physical (network) communications
  - Hardware and network specifications
- Views corresponding to the selected viewpoints addressing key stakeholder concerns

8.5.2 Components of the Architecture Requirements Specification

(Syllabus Reference: Unit 14, Learning Outcome 3.2: You should be able to explain the following key element: Technology Architecture Components of the Architecture Requirements Specification.)

Technology Architecture requirements added to the Architecture Requirements Specification in Phase D include:
- Gap Analysis results
- Updated technology requirements

8.6 Summary

This phase documents the Technology Architecture that will form the basis of subsequent implementation and migration work, in terms of hardware, software, and communications technology, their relationships to each other and the environment, and the principles governing its design and evolution.

8.7 Exercises

Exercise 8-1

Identify five sources of information within your organization that could be used to draw up a Baseline Technology Architecture Description.

Exercise 8-2

Which of the Phase D: Technology Architecture catalogs, matrices, and diagrams would be most suitable for addressing the following concerns:

- Identifying the types of all hardware platforms in the enterprise
- Identifying which business applications execute on which systems in the enterprise
- Identifying which locations host which applications

Exercise 8-3

Which of the Phase D: Technology Architecture catalogs, matrices, and diagrams would be most suitable for addressing the following stakeholders:

- Network managers
- Project Managers

8.8 Recommended Reading

The following are recommended sources of further information for this chapter:

- TOGAF 9 Part II, Chapter 12 (Phase D: Technology Architecture)
- TOGAF 9 Part IV, Chapter 36 (Architecture Deliverables)
- Sample Catalogs, Matrices, and Diagrams presentation: www.togaf.info/ sg03

Phase E: Opportunities & Solutions

9.1 Key Learning Points

This chapter describes Phase E: Opportunities & Solutions of the TOGAF
Architecture Development Method (ADM).

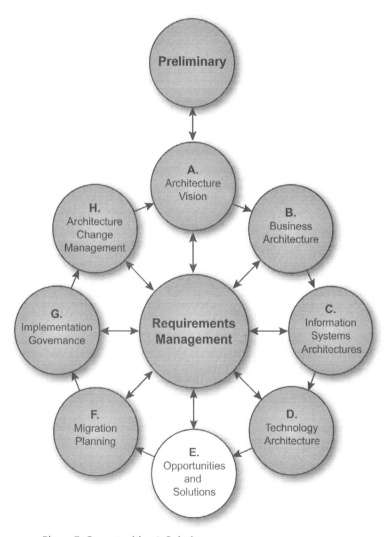

Figure 10:   Phase E: Opportunities & Solutions

> **Key Points Explained**
>
> Upon completion of this chapter you should be able to:
>
> 1. Describe the key stakeholders involved in this phase
> 2. Explain how migration planning techniques are used in this phase to review and consolidate the Gap Analysis results from earlier phases
> 3. Describe the steps to create the initial Implementation and Migration Strategy
> 4. Describe three basic approaches to implementation
> 5. Explain how to identify and group work packages
> 6. Explain how Transition Architectures are created and documented
>
> In addition you should be able to:
>
> - Describe how the Implementation Factor Assessment and Deduction matrix can be used to document factors impacting the Architecture Implementation and Migration Plan
> - Explain the purpose of the Consolidated Gaps, Solutions, and Dependencies matrix

9.2 Objectives

The objectives of Phase E: Opportunities and Solutions are to:

- Generate the initial complete version of the Architecture Roadmap, based upon the gap analysis and candidate Architecture Roadmap components from Phases B, C, and D
- Determine whether an incremental approach is required, and if so identify Transition Architectures that will deliver continuous business value

> **Stakeholders**
>
> *(Syllabus Reference: Unit 16, Learning Outcome 1: You should be able to describe the key stakeholders in this phase.)*
>
> Phase E is a collaborative effort with stakeholders required from both the business and IT sides. It should include both those that implement and those that operate the infrastructure. It should also include those responsible for strategic planning, especially for creating the Transition Architectures, if required.

9.3 Inputs

The inputs to this phase are:

- Product information
- Request for Architecture Work
- Capability Assessment
- Communications Plan
- Planning Methodologies
- Organizational Model for Enterprise Architecture
- Governance Models and Frameworks
- Tailored Architecture Framework
- Statement of Architecture Work
- Architecture Vision
- Architecture Repository
- Draft Architecture Definition Document
- Draft Architecture Requirements Specification
- Change Requests for existing programs and projects
- Candidate Architecture Roadmap components from Phases B, C, and D

9.4 Steps

Phase E consists of the following steps:

1. Determine/confirm key corporate change attributes
2. Determine business constraints for implementation
3. Review and consolidate Gap Analysis results from Phases B to D
4. Review consolidated requirements across related business functions
5. Consolidate and reconcile interoperability requirements
6. Refine and validate dependencies
7. Confirm readiness and risk for business transformation
8. Formulate Implementation and Migration Strategy
9. Identify and group major work packages
10. Identify Transition Architectures
11. Create the Architecture Roadmap & Implementation and Migration Plan

The steps are described in more detail in the following sections.

9.4.1 Determine/Confirm Key Corporate Change Attributes

This step determines how the enterprise architecture can be best implemented to take advantage of the organization's business culture. This should include the creation of an Implementation Factor Assessment and

Deduction matrix to serve as a repository for architecture implementation and migration decisions. The step also includes assessments of the transition capabilities of the organizations involved (including culture and abilities), and assessments of the enterprise (including culture and skill sets). The resulting factors from the assessments should be documented in the Implementation Factor Assessment and Deduction matrix. For organizations where enterprise architecture is well established, this step can be simple, but the matrix has to be established so that it can be used as an archive and record of decisions taken.

9.4.1.1　Implementation Factor Assessment and Deduction Matrix

(Syllabus Reference: Unit 15, Learning Outcome 1: You should be able to describe how the Implementation Factor Assessment and Deduction matrix can be used to document factors impacting the Architecture Implementation and Migration Plan.)

The Implementation Factor Assessment and Deduction matrix documents the factors that impact the Implementation and Migration Plan. The matrix should include a list of the factors, their descriptions with rationale, and the deductions (conclusions) that indicate the actions or constraints that have to be taken into consideration when formulating the plan. Production and use of this artifact can be considered as a Risk Management activity. An example matrix is shown in Table 11.

Table 11:　Example Implementation Factor Assessment and Deduction Matrix

Implementation Factor Assessment and Deduction Matrix		
Factor	**Description**	**Deduction**
<Name of the Factor>	<Description of the Factor>	<Impact on the Migration Plan>
Change in Technology	Replace the message centers with an email service, saving 700 personnel	Need for personnel training, re-assignment The switch to email has major personnel savings and should be given priority.
Consolidation of Services	...	...
Introduction of New Customer Service	...	...

9.4.2 Determine Business Constraints for Implementation

Identify any business drivers that would constrain the sequence of implementation. This should include a review of the business and strategic plans, at both a corporate and line-of-business level, and a review of the Enterprise Architecture Maturity Assessment.

9.4.3 Review and Consolidate Gap Analysis Results from Phases B to D

(Syllabus Reference: Unit 16, Learning Outcome 2: You should be able to explain how migration planning techniques are used in this phase to review and consolidate the Gap Analysis results from earlier phases.)

Consolidate and integrate the Gap Analysis results from the Business, Information Systems, and Technology Architectures (created in Phases B to D) and assess their implications with respect to potential solutions and inter-dependencies. This should be done by creating a Consolidated Gaps, Solutions, and Dependencies matrix, as shown in Section 9.4.3.1, which will enable the identification of Solution Building Blocks (SBBs) that could potentially address one or more gaps and their associated Architecture Building Blocks (ABBs).

Review the Phase B, C, and D Gap Analysis results and consolidate them in a single list. The gaps should be consolidated along with potential solutions to the gaps and dependencies. A recommended technique for determining the dependencies is to use sets of views such as the Business Interaction matrix, the Data Entity/Business Function matrix, and the Application/Function matrix to completely relate elements from different architectural domains.

Rationalize the Consolidated Gaps, Solutions, and Dependencies matrix. Once all of the gaps have been documented, re-organize the gap list and place similar items together. When grouping the gaps, refer to the Implementation Factor Assessment and Deduction matrix and review the implementation factors. Any additional factors should be added to the Implementation Factor Assessment and Deduction matrix.

9.4.3.1 *Consolidated Gaps, Solutions, and Dependencies Matrix*

(Syllabus Reference: Unit 15, Learning Outcome 2: You should be able to explain the purpose of the Consolidated Gaps, Solutions, and Dependencies matrix.)

The technique of creating a Consolidated Gaps, Solutions, and Dependencies matrix allows the architect to group the gaps identified in the domain architecture Gap Analysis results and assess potential solutions and dependencies to one or more gaps. An example is shown in Table 12. This matrix can be used as a planning tool when creating work packages. The identified dependencies drive the creation of projects and migration planning in Phases E and F.

Table 12:   Consolidated Gaps, Solutions, and Dependencies Matrix

Consolidated Gaps, Solutions, and Dependencies Matrix				
#	Architecture	Gap	Potential Solutions	Dependencies
1	Business	New Order Processing Process	Use COTS software tool process Implement custom solution	Drives Application #2
2	Application	New Order Processing Application	COTS software tool Acme Develop in-house	
3	Data	Consolidated Customer Information Base	Use COTS customer base Develop customer data mart	

9.4.4   Review Consolidated Requirements Across Related Business Functions

Assess the requirements, gaps, solutions, and factors to identify a minimal set of requirements whose integration into work packages would lead to a more efficient and effective implementation of the Target Architecture across the business functions that are participating in the architecture. This functional perspective leads to the satisfaction of multiple requirements through the provision of shared solutions and services. The implications of this consolidation of requirements with respect to architectural components can be significant with respect to the provision of resources. For example, several requirements raised by several lines of business can be resolved through the provision of a shared set of Business Services and Information System Services within a work package or project.

9.4.5 Consolidate and Reconcile Interoperability Requirements

This step consolidates the interoperability requirements identified in previous phases. The Architecture Vision and Target Architectures, as well as the Implementation Factor Assessment and Deduction matrix and Consolidated Gaps, Solutions, and Dependencies matrix, should be consolidated and reviewed to identify any constraints on interoperability required by the potential set of solutions. A key outcome is to minimize interoperability conflicts. Re-used Solution Building Blocks, Commercial Off-The-Shelf (COTS) products, and third-party service providers typically impose interoperability requirements that conflict. Any such conflicts must be addressed in the architecture.

Interoperability Requirements and Solutions

(Syllabus Reference: Unit 8, Learning Outcome 1: You should be able to explain how to reconcile Interoperability Requirements with potential solutions.)

The most significant issue to be addressed is business interoperability. Most SBBs or COTS will have their own embedded business processes. Changing the embedded business processes will often require so much work, that the advantages of re-using solutions will be lost with updates being costly and possibly requiring a complete rework. Furthermore, there may be a workflow aspect between multiple systems that has to be taken into account. The acquisition of COTS software has to be seen as a business decision that may require rework of the domain architectures. The enterprise architect will have to ensure that any change to the business interoperability requirements is signed off by the business architects and architecture sponsors in a revised Statement of Architecture Work.

9.4.6 Refine and Validate Dependencies

Refine the initial dependencies, ensuring that any constraints on the Implementation and Migration Plans are identified. There are several key dependencies that should be taken into account, such as dependencies on existing implementations of Business Services and Information Systems Services or changes to them. Dependencies should be used for determining the sequence of implementation and identifying the coordination required. A study of the dependencies should group activities together, creating a basis for projects to be established. Examine the relevant projects and see whether logical increments of deliverables can be identified. The dependencies will also help to identify when the identified increment can be delivered. Once finished, these dependencies should be documented as part of the Architecture Roadmap and any necessary Transition Architectures. Adding dependencies serves as the basis for most migration planning.

Capability-Based Planning and the ADM

Specific capabilities targeted for completion will be the focus of the Architecture Definition (Phases B, C, and D) and, based upon the identified work packages Phase E, projects will be conceived. The capability increments will be the drivers for the Transition Architectures (Phase E) that will structure the project increments. The actual delivery will be coordinated through the Implementation and Migration Plans (Phase F).

[Source: TOGAF 9, Part III, Chapter 32 (Capability-Based Planning)]

9.4.7 Confirm Readiness and Risk for Business Transformation

The architects should review the findings of the Business Transformation Readiness Assessment previously conducted in Phase A and determine their impact on the Architecture Roadmap and the Implementation and Migration Strategy. It is important to identify, classify, and mitigate risks associated with the transformation effort. Risks should be documented in the Consolidated Gaps, Solutions, and Dependencies matrix.

9.4.8 Formulate Implementation and Migration Strategy

(Syllabus Reference: Unit 16, Learning Outcome 3: You should be able to describe the steps to create the Implementation and Migration Strategy.)

(Syllabus Reference: Unit 16, Learning Outcome 4: You should be able to describe three basic approaches to implementation.)

Create an overall Implementation and Migration Strategy that will guide the implementation of the Target Architecture and structure any Transition Architectures. The first activity is to determine an overall strategic approach to implementing the solutions and/or exploiting opportunities. There are three basic approaches as follows:

- Greenfield: A completely new implementation.
- Revolutionary: A radical change (i.e., switch on, switch off).

- Evolutionary: A strategy of convergence, such as parallel running or a phased approach to introduce new capabilities.

Next, determine an approach for the overall strategic direction that will address and mitigate the risks identified in the Consolidated Gaps, Solutions, and Dependencies matrix. The most common implementation methodologies are:

- Quick win (snapshots)
- Achievable targets
- Value chain method (e.g., NASCIO[7] methodology)

These approaches and the identified dependencies should become the basis for the creation of the work packages. This activity terminates with agreement on the Implementation and Migration Strategy for the enterprise.

9.4.9   Identify and Group Major Work Packages

(Syllabus Reference: Unit 16, Learning Outcome 5: You should be able to explain how to identify and group work packages.)

Key stakeholders, planners, and the enterprise architect(s) should assess the missing business capabilities identified in the Architecture Vision and Target Architecture.

Using the Consolidated Gaps, Solutions, and Dependencies matrix together with the Implementation Factor Assessment and Deduction matrix, logically group the various activities into work packages (where a work package is an inter-dependent set of activities and deliverables that deliver a discrete enterprise outcome).

Fill in the "Solution" column in the Consolidated Gaps, Solutions, and Dependencies matrix that recommends the proposed solution mechanisms. Indicate for every gap/activity whether the solution should be oriented towards a new development or based upon an existing product and/or use a solution that can be purchased. An existing system may resolve the requirement with minor enhancements. For new development this is a good time to determine whether the work should be conducted in-house or through a contract.

---

7   NASCIO is the National Association of State Chief Information Officers; see www.nascio.org.

Classify every current system as:
- Mainstream: Part of the future information system.
- Contain: Expected to be replaced or modified in the planning horizon (next three years).
- Replace: To be replaced in the planning horizon.

Supporting top-level work packages should then in turn be decomposed into increments to deliver the capability increments, Analyze and refine these work packages, or increments, with respect to their business transformation issues and the strategic implementation approach. Finally, group the work packages into portfolios and then projects within the portfolios taking into consideration the dependencies and the strategic implementation approach.

9.4.10   Identify Transition Architectures

(Syllabus Reference: Unit 16, Learning Outcome 6: You should be able to explain how Transition Architectures are created and documented.)

Where the scope of change to implement the Target Architecture (see Section 10.5.2) requires an incremental approach, then one or more Transition Architectures may be necessary. These provide an ability to identify clear targets along the roadmap to realizing the Target Architecture. The Transition Architectures should provide measurable business value. The time-span between successive Transition Architectures does not have to be of uniform duration.

Development of Transition Architectures must be based upon the preferred implementation approach, the Consolidated Gaps, Solutions, and Dependencies matrix, the listing of projects and portfolios, as well as the enterprise's capacity for creating and absorbing change.

Determine where the difficult activities are, and unless there are compelling reasons, implement them after other activities that most easily deliver missing capability.

9.4.11   Create the Architecture Roadmap & Implementation and Migration Plan

Consolidate the work packages and Transition Architectures into the Architecture Roadmap, Version 0.1, which describes a timeline of the progression from the Baseline Architecture to the Target Architecture. The timeline informs the Implementation and Migration Plan. The Architecture Roadmap frames the migration planning in Phase F. Identified Transition Architectures and work packages should have a clear set of outcomes. The Architecture Roadmap must demonstrate how the selection and timeline of Transition Architectures and work packages realizes the Target Architecture.

The detail of the Architecture Roadmap, Version 0.1 should be expressed at a similar level of detail to the Architecture Definition Document developed in Phases B, C, and D. Where significant additional detail is required before implementation the architecture is likely transitioning to a different level. See TOGAF 9, Part III, Chapter 19 and 20 for techniques to manage iteration and different levels of detail.

The Implementation and Migration Plan must demonstrate the activity necessary to realize the Architecture Roadmap. The Implementation and Migration Plan forms the basis of the migration planning in Phase F. The detail of the Implementation and Migration Plan, Version 0.1 must be aligned to the detail of the Architecture Roadmap and be sufficient to identify the necessary projects and resource requirements to realize the roadmap.

When creating the Implementation and Migration Plan there are many approaches to consider, such as a data-driven sequence, where application systems that create data are implemented first, then applications that process the data. A clear understanding of the dependencies and lifecycle of in-place SBBs is required for an effective Implementation and Migration Plan.

Finally, update the Architecture Vision, Architecture Definition Document, and Architecture Requirements Specification with any additional relevant outcomes from this phase.

9.5 Outputs

The outputs of this phase are:
- Statement of Architecture Work, updated if necessary
- Architecture Vision, updated if necessary
- Draft Architecture Definition Document, updated if necessary, including:
  - Transition Architectures (see Section 10.5.2), if any

- Draft Architecture Requirements Specification, including:
  - Consolidated Gaps, Solutions, and Dependencies Assessment
- Capability Assessment (see Section 3.5.2), including:
  - Business Capability Assessment
  - IT Capability Assessment
- Architecture Roadmap, including:
  - Work package portfolio
  - Identification of Transition Architectures, if any
  - Implementation recommendations
- Implementation and Migration Plan (outline) (see Section 10.5.1)

The outputs may also include the following diagrams: a Project Context diagram and a Benefits diagram.

9.6 Summary

Phase E is the first phase which is directly concerned with implementation. It identifies the parameters of change, the work packages, and the necessary projects. The outputs include an outline Implementation and Migration Plan, the Architecture Roadmap, and Transition Architectures, if any.

9.7 Exercises

Exercise 9-1
Describe three or more migration options for phasing in a new business system while maintaining business continuity. You should describe the impact on services, users, and platforms in each option.

9.8 Recommended Reading

The following are recommended sources of further information for this chapter:

- TOGAF 9 Part II, Chapter 13 (Phase E: Opportunities & Solutions)
- TOGAF 9 Part III, Chapter 28 (Migration Planning Techniques)
- TOGAF 9 Part III, Chapter 29 (Interoperability Requirements)
- TOGAF 9 Part IV, Chapter 36 (Architecture Deliverables)

Chapter 10

Phase F: Migration Planning

10.1 Key Learning Points

This chapter describes Phase F: Migration Planning of the TOGAF
Architecture Development Method (ADM).

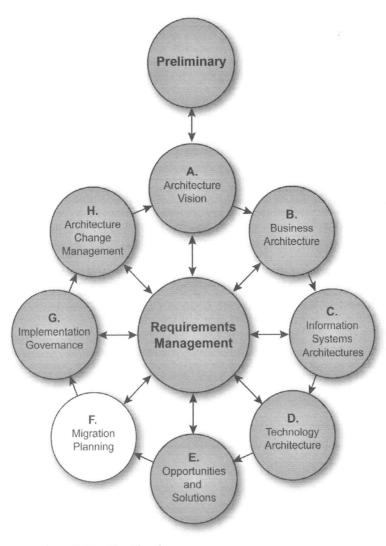

Figure 11: Phase F: Migration Planning

Key Points Explained

Upon completion of this chapter you should be able to:

1. Describe the management frameworks that have to be coordinated within this phase

2. Explain how business value is assigned to each work package

3. Describe the steps to prioritize the migration projects

4. Describe the steps to confirm the Architecture Roadmap

5. Explain key outputs of this phase, specifically:

   - Implementation and Migration Plan

   - Transition Architecture

   - Architecture Definition Document

In addition you should be able to:

- Explain how the Business Value Assessment technique can be used in architecture development

- Explain how the Transition Architecture State Evolution Table can be used in conjunction with the TRM

10.2 Objectives

The objectives of Phase F: Migration Planning are to:

- Finalize the Architecture Roadmap and the supporting Implementation and Migration Plan

- Ensure that the Implementation and Migration Plan is coordinated with the enterprise's approach to managing and implementing change in the enterprise's overall change portfolio

- Ensure that the business value and cost of work packages and Transition Architectures is understood by key stakeholders

10.3 Inputs

The inputs to this phase are:

- Request for Architecture Work

- Communications Plan

- Organizational Model for Enterprise Architecture

- Governance Models and Frameworks

- Tailored Architecture Framework

- Statement of Architecture Work

- Architecture Vision
- Architecture Repository
- Draft Architecture Definition Document, including:
  - Transition Architectures, if any
- Draft Architecture Requirements Specification
- Change Requests for existing programs and projects
- Architecture Roadmap, including:
  - Identification of work packages
  - Identification of Transition Architectures
  - Implementation Factor Assessment and Deduction Matrix
- Capability Assessment
- Implementation and Migration Plan (outline)

10.4 Steps

Phase F consists of the following steps:

1. Confirm management framework interactions for the Implementation and Migration Plan
2. Assign a business value to each work package
3. Estimate resource requirements, project timings, and availability/delivery vehicle
4. Prioritize the migration projects through the conduct of a cost/benefit assessment and risk validation
5. Confirm Architecture Roadmap and update Architecture Definition Document
6. Complete the Implementation and Migration Plan
7. Complete the architecture development cycle and document lessons learned

The steps are described in more detail in the following sections.

10.4.1 Confirm Management Framework Interactions for the Implementation and Migration Plan

(Syllabus Reference: Unit 17, Learning Outcome 1: You should be able to describe the management frameworks that have to be coordinated within this phase.)

This step is about coordinating the Implementation and Migration Plan with the management frameworks within the organization. There are typically four management frameworks that have to work closely together for the Implementation and Migration Plan to succeed:

- Business Planning that conceives, directs, and provides the resources for all of the activities required to achieve concrete business objectives/outcomes.
- Enterprise Architecture that structures and gives context to all enterprise activities delivering concrete business outcomes primarily but not exclusively in the IT domain.
- Portfolio/Project Management that co-ordinates, designs, and builds the business systems that deliver the concrete business outcomes.
- Operations Management that integrates, operates, and maintains the deliverables that deliver the concrete business outcomes.

The Implementation and Migration Plan will impact each one of these frameworks and consequently has to be reflected in them. In the course of this step, understand the frameworks within the organization and ensure that these plans are coordinated and inserted (in a summary format) within the plans of each one of these frameworks. The outcome of this step may well be that the Implementation and Migration Plan could be part of a different plan produced by another one of the frameworks with enterprise architecture participation.

10.4.2   Assign a Business Value to Each Work Package

(Syllabus Reference: Unit 17, Learning Outcome 2: You should be able to explain how business value is assigned to each work package.)

Establish and assign business values to all of the work packages. The intent is to first establish what constitutes business value within the organization, how value can be measured, and then apply this to each one of the projects and project increments.

If Capability-Based Planning has been used, then the business values associated with the capabilities and associated capability increments should be used to assign the business values for deliverables.

There are several issues to address in this activity:

- Performance Evaluation Criteria are used by portfolio and capability managers to approve and monitor the progress of the architecture transformation.
- Return-on-Investment Criteria have to be detailed and signed off by the various executive stakeholders.
- Business Value has to be defined as well as techniques, such as the value chain (e.g., NASCIO), which are to be used to illustrate the role in achieving tangible business outcomes. Business value will be used by portfolio and capability managers to allocate resources and, in cases where there are cutbacks, business value in conjunction with return-on-investment can be used to determine whether an endeavor proceeds, is delayed, or is canceled.
- Critical Success Factors (CSFs) should be established to define success for a project and/or project increment. These will provide managers and implementers with a gauge as to what constitutes a successful implementation.
- Measures of Effectiveness (MOE) are often performance criteria and many corporations include them in the CSFs. Where they are treated discretely, it should be clear as to how these criteria are to be grouped.
- Strategic Fit based upon the overall enterprise architecture (all tiers) will be the critical factor for allowing the approval of any new project or initiative and for determining the value of any deliverable.

Use the work packages as a basis of identifying projects that will be in the Implementation and Migration Plan. The identified projects will be fully developed in other steps in Phase F. The projects, and project increments, may require adjustment of the Architecture Roadmap and Architecture Definition Document.

Risks should then be assigned to the projects and project increments by aggregating risks identified in the Consolidated Gaps, Solutions, and Dependencies Matrix (from Phase E).

Estimate the business value for each project using the Business Value Assessment Technique.

10.4.2.1 *Business Value Assessment Technique*

(Syllabus Reference: Unit 15, Learning Outcome 5: You should be able to explain how the Business Value Assessment Technique can be used in architecture development.)

A technique to assess business value is to draw up a matrix based on a value index dimension and a risk index dimension. An example is shown in Figure 12. The value index should include criteria such as compliance to principles, financial contribution, strategic alignment, and competitive position. The risk index should include criteria such as size and complexity, technology, organizational capacity, and impact of a failure. Each criterion should be assigned an individual weight. The index and its criteria and weighting should be developed and approved by senior management. It is important to establish the decision-making criteria before the options are known.

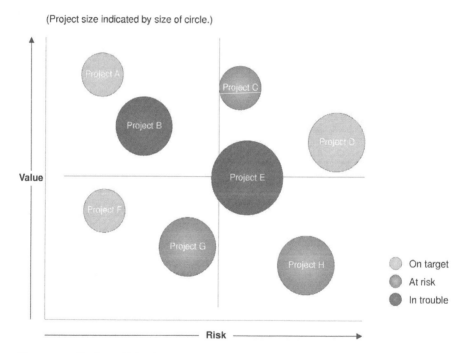

Figure 12:   Business Value Assessment Matrix

10.4.3 Estimate Resource Requirements, Project Timings, and Availability/ Delivery Vehicle

This step determines the required resources and times for each project and their increments and provides the initial cost estimates. The costs should be broken down into capital (to create the capability) and operations and maintenance (to run and sustain the capability). Opportunities should be identified where the costs associated with delivering new and/or better capability can be offset by decommissioning existing systems. Assign required resources to each activity and aggregate them at the project increment and project level.

10.4.4 Prioritize the Migration Projects through the Conduct of a Cost/Benefit Assessment and Risk Validation

(Syllabus Reference: Unit 17, Learning Outcome 3: You should be able to describe the steps to prioritize the migration projects.)

Prioritize the projects by ascertaining their business value against the cost of delivering them. The approach is to first determine, as clearly as possible, the net benefit of all of the SBBs delivered by the projects, and then verify that the risks have been effectively mitigated and factored in. Afterwards, the intent is to gain the requisite consensus to create a prioritized list of projects that will provide the basis for resource allocation.

It is important to discover all costs, and to ensure that decision-makers understand the net benefit over time.

Review the risks to ensure that the risks for the project deliverables have been mitigated as much as possible. The project list is then updated with risk-related comments.

Have the stakeholders agree upon a prioritization of the projects. Prioritization criteria will use elements identified in creation of the draft Architecture Roadmap in Phase E as well as those relating to individual stakeholders' agendas.

Formally review the risk assessment and revise it as necessary ensuring that there is a full understanding of the residual risk associated with the prioritization and the projected funding line.

10.4.5 Confirm Architecture Roadmap and Update Architecture Definition Document

(Syllabus Reference: Unit 17, Learning Outcome 4: You should be able to describe the steps to confirm the Architecture Roadmap.)

Update the Architecture Roadmap including any Transition Architectures. Review the work to date to assess what the time-spans between Transition Architectures should be, taking into consideration the increments in business value and capability and other factors, such as risk. Once the capability increments have been determined, consolidate the deliverables by project increment for each Transition Architecture. This will result in a revised Architecture Roadmap.

This is needed in order to co-ordinate the development of several concurrent instances of the various architectures. A Transition Architecture State Evolution Table (see Section 10.4.6.1) can be used to show the proposed state of the Domain Architectures at various levels of detail.

If the implementation approach has shifted as a result of confirming the implementation increments, update the Architecture Definition Document. This may include assigning project objectives and aligning projects and their deliverables with the Transition Architectures to create an Architecture Definition Increments Table.

10.4.5.1 *Architecture Definition Increments Table*

(Syllabus Reference: Unit 15, Learning Outcome 3: You should be able to describe the purpose of an Architecture Definition Increments Table.)

The technique of creating an Architecture Definition Increments Table allows the architect to plan a series of Transition Architectures outlining the status of the enterprise architecture at specified times. A table should be drawn up, as shown in Table 13, listing the projects and then assigning their incremental deliverables across the Transition Architectures.

Table 13:   Example Architecture Definition Increments Tab

Architecture Definition: Project Objectives by Increment				
	Stage 1: April 2009/2010	**Stage 2: April 2010/2011**	**Stage 3: April 2011/2012**	
Project	**Transition Architecture 1: Preparation**	**Transition Architecture 2: Initial Operational Capability**	**Transition Architecture 3: Benefits**	**Comments**
Enterprise e-Services Capability	Training and Business Process	e-Licensing Capability	e-Employment Benefits	
IT e-Forms	Design and Build			
IT e-Information Environment	Design and Build Information Environment	Client Common Data Web Content Design and Build	Enterprise Common Data Document Management Design and Build	
...	...	...	...	...

10.4.6   Generate the Implementation and Migration Plan

This step generates the completed Implementation and Migration Plan. Much of the detail for the plan has already been gathered and this step brings it all together using accepted planning and management techniques.

This should include integrating all of the projects, project increments, and activities as well as dependencies into a project plan. Any Transition Architectures will act as portfolio milestones.

All external dependencies should be captured and included, and the overall availability of resources assessed. The project plans may be included with the Implementation and Migration Plan.

10.4.6.1   *Transition Architecture State Evolution Table*

(Syllabus Reference: Unit 15, Learning Outcome 4: You should be able to explain how the Transition Architecture State Evolution Table can be used in conjunction with the TRM.)

The technique of creating the Transition Architecture State Evolution Table allows the architect to show the proposed state of the architectures at various levels using the Technical Reference Model (TRM). A table should be created listing the services from the TRM used in the enterprise, the Transition Architectures, and proposed transformations, as shown in Table 14.

All Solution Building Blocks (SBBs) should be described with respect to their delivery and impact on these services. They should also be marked to show the progression of the enterprise architecture. In the example, where target capability has been reached, this is shown as "new" or "retain"; where capability is transitioned to a new solution, this is marked as "transition"; and where a capability is to be replaced, this is marked as "replace".

Table 14:   Example Transition Architecture State Evolution Table

Architectural State Using the Technical Reference Model				
Sub-Domain	Service	Transition Architecture 1	Transition Architecture 2	Transition Architecture 3
Infrastructure Applications	Information Exchange Services	Solution System A (replace)	Solution System B-1 (transition)	Solution System B-2 (new)
	Data Management Services	Solution System D (retain)	Solution System D (retain)	Solution System D (retain)
...	...			

10.4.7 Complete the Architecture Development Cycle and Document Lessons Learned

This step transitions governance from the development of the architecture to the realization of the architecture. If the maturity of the Architecture Capability warrants, an Implementation Governance Model may be produced (see Section 1.1.1). Lessons learned should also be documented and captured by the appropriate governance process in Phase H as inputs to managing the Architecture Capability.

The detail of the Architecture Roadmap and the Implementation and Migration Plan should be expressed at a similar level of detail to the Architecture Definition Document developed in Phases B, C, and D. Where significant additional detail is required by the next phase the architecture is likely transitioning to a different level. Depending upon the level of the Target Architecture and Implementation and Migration Plan it may be necessary to iterate another ADM cycle at a lower level of detail.

10.5 Outputs

(Syllabus Reference: Unit 17, Learning Outcome 5: You should be able to describe the key outputs of this phase.)

The outputs of this phase are:
- Implementation and Migration Plan (detailed)
- Finalized Architecture Definition Document, including:
  - Finalized Transition Architectures, if any
- Finalized Architecture Requirements Specification
- Finalized Architecture Roadmap
- Re-Usable Architecture Building Blocks (ABBs)
- Requests for Architecture Work for a new iteration of the ADM cycle (if any)
- Implementation Governance Model
- Change Requests for the Architecture Capability arising from lessons learned

10.5.1 Implementation and Migration Plan

(Syllabus Reference: Unit 16, Learning Outcome 5.1: You should be able to describe the Implementation and Migration Plan.)

The Implementation and Migration Plan is developed in Phases E and F, and provides a schedule of the projects for implementation of the Target Architecture. The Implementation and Migration Plan includes executable projects grouped into managed portfolios and programs. The Implementation and Migration Strategy identifying the approach to change is a key element of the Implementation and Migration Plan.

Typical contents are as follows:
- Implementation and Migration Strategy:
  - Strategic implementation direction
  - Implementation sequencing approach

- Project and portfolio breakdown of implementation:
    - Allocation of work packages to project and portfolio
    - Capabilities delivered by projects
    - Milestones and timing
    - Work breakdown structure

It may contain:
- Project charters:
    - Included work packages
    - Business value
    - Risk, issues, assumptions, dependencies
    - Resource requirements and costs
    - Benefits of migration, determined (including mapping to business requirements)
    - Estimated costs of migration options

10.5.2 Architecture Definition Document, including Transition Architecture

(Syllabus Reference: Unit 16, Learning Outcome 5.2: You should be able to describe the Architecture Definition Document, including Transition Architectures (if any).)

The Architecture Definition Document is finalized in this phase. For a detailed description see Section 4.5.1.

Where the scope of change to implement the Target Architecture requires an incremental approach, one or more Transition Architectures are defined within the Architecture Definition Document output from Phase E. A Transition Architecture shows the enterprise at an architecturally significant state between the Baseline and Target Architectures. Transition Architectures are used to describe transitional Target Architectures necessary for effective realization of the Target Architecture. These provide an ability to identify clear targets along the roadmap to realizing the Target Architecture.

The following contents are typical within a Transition Architecture:
- Transition Architecture:
    - Definition of transition states
    - Business Architecture for each transition state
    - Data Architecture for each transition state

- Application Architecture for each transition state
- Technology Architecture for each transition state

10.5.3 Implementation Governance Model

Once an architecture has been defined, it is necessary to plan how the Transition Architecture that implements the architecture will be governed through implementation. Within organizations that have established architecture functions, there is likely to be a governance framework already in place, but specific processes, organizations, roles, responsibilities, and measures may need to be defined on a project-by-project basis.

The Implementation Governance Model produced as an output of Phase F ensures that a project transitioning into implementation also smoothly transitions into appropriate Architecture Governance (for Phase G).

Typical contents of an Implementation Governance Model are:
- Governance processes
- Governance organization structure
- Governance roles and responsibilities
- Governance checkpoints and success/failure criteria

10.6 Summary

Phase F addresses migration planning; that is, how to move from the Baseline to the Target Architectures. It includes creating the finalized Architecture Definition Document, Architecture Roadmap, and the detailed Implementation and Migration Plan. After completion of this phase the preparation for implementation has been completed.

10.7 Exercises

Exercise 10-1

A project has completed Phase E with delivery of the outline Implementation and Migration Plan. Your role is to lead the Migration Planning phase. Describe your approach to creating the detailed Implementation and Migration Plan, including who you would involve, the steps, and what you would deliver.

10.8 Recommended Reading

The following are recommended sources of further information for this chapter:

- TOGAF 9 Part II, Chapter 14 (Phase F: Migration Planning)
- TOGAF 9 Part III, Chapter 28 (Migration Planning Techniques)
- TOGAF 9 Part IV, Chapter 36 (Architecture Deliverables)

Phase G: Implementation Governance

11.1 Key Learning Points

This chapter describes Phase G: Implementation Governance of the TOGAF
Architecture Development Method (ADM).

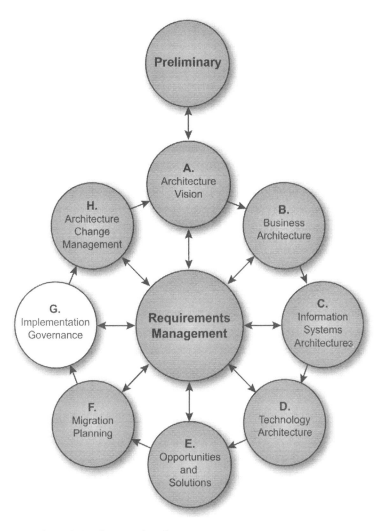

Figure 13:   Phase G: Implementation Governance

Key Points Explained

Upon completion of this chapter you should be able to:

1. Understand the inputs to the phase

2. Understand the steps, and be able to describe the following:

   • Explain how to tailor and conduct an Architecture Compliance Review

3. Understand the outputs, and be able to explain the following key elements:

   • The contents of Architecture Contracts

   • Their relationship to Architecture Governance

4. Demonstrate the role that risk monitoring plays in this phase

11.2 Objectives

The objectives of Phase G: Implementation Governance are to:

• Ensure conformance with the Target Architecture by implementation projects

• Perform appropriate Architecture Governance functions for the solution and any implementation-driven architecture Change Requests

Architecture Governance

The Architecture Contract produced in this phase features prominently in the area of Architecture Governance (see Chapter 22). It is often used as the means to driving change. In order to ensure that the Architecture Contract is effective and efficient, the following aspects of the governance framework should be introduced in this phase:

• Simple process

• People-centered authority

• Strong communication

• Timely responses and effective escalation process

• Supporting organization structures

11.3 Inputs

(Syllabus Reference: Unit 18, Learning Outcome 1: You should understand the inputs to the phase.)

The inputs to this phase are:
- Request for Architecture Work
- Capability Assessment
- Organizational Model for Enterprise Architecture
- Tailored Architecture Framework
- Statement of Architecture Work
- Architecture Vision
- Architecture Repository
- Architecture Definition Document
- Architecture Requirements Specification
- Architecture Roadmap
- Implementation Governance Model
- Architecture Contract
- Request for Architecture Work identified in Phases E and F
- Implementation and Migration Plan

11.4 Steps

(Syllabus Reference: Unit 18, Learning Outcome 2: You should understand the steps for this phase.)

Phase G consists of the following steps:
- Confirm scope and priorities for deployment with development management
- Identify deployment resources and skills
- Guide development of solutions deployment
- Perform enterprise Architecture Compliance Reviews
- Implement business and IT operations
- Perform post-implementation review and close the implementation

The steps are described in more detail in the following sections.

11.4.1 Confirm Scope and Priorities for Deployment with Development Management

This step takes the migration planning outputs and produces recommendations for deployment. This includes identifying priorities for the development teams, identifying issues for the deployment together with recommendations, and identifying building blocks for replacement and update. A Gap Analysis should be performed between the enterprise architecture and the solutions framework to identify specific Solution Building Blocks (SBBs). The solutions architects should consider whether some SBBs can be used across more than one project.

11.4.2 Identify Deployment Resources and Skills

The deployment resources will need to be educated in the overall enterprise architecture deliverables and expectations for the specific development and implementation projects. Considerations addressed in this step should include the identification of the system development methods required for the solutions development, ensuring that they include feedback on the designs to the architecture team.

11.4.3 Guide Development of Solutions Deployment

Project recommendations are created for each separate implementation and deployment project by documenting the scope of the individual project, the strategic requirements (from the architectural perspective), any change requests (such as support for a standard interface), rules for conformance, and timeline requirements from the roadmap.

The Architecture Contract (see Section 11.5.1) is documented and signatures are obtained from all developing organizations and the sponsoring organization. The Enterprise Continuum and Architecture Repository should then be populated with the solutions. The Architecture Contract is then used to guide the development of the business and IT operating models for the identified services. This guidance is based upon the business and IT operational requirements derived from the enterprise architecture by undertaking a Gap Analysis between the Solution Architecture and current operations in order to identify missing elements. This can then be used to develop an Implementation Plan.

11.4.4 Perform Enterprise Architecture Compliance Reviews

(Syllabus Reference: Unit 18, Learning Outcome 2.1: You should be able to explain how to tailor and conduct an Architecture Compliance Review.)

Prerequisite Knowledge: Architecture Compliance Review Process Steps
TOGAF defines a 12-step process for conducting Compliance Reviews. This is omitted here as it is included in the TOGAF 9 Foundation Study Guide. [See Section 9.7.4 of the TOGAF 9 Foundation Study Guide]

Once an architecture has been defined, it is necessary to govern that architecture through implementation to ensure that the original Architecture Vision is realized and that any implementation lessons are fed back into the architecture process. Periodic compliance reviews of implementation projects in Phase G provide a mechanism to review project progress and ensure that the design and implementation are proceeding according to the strategic and architectural objectives.

11.4.4.1   *Timing of Compliance Reviews*

Compliance reviews should be held at appropriate project milestones or checkpoints in a project's lifecycle. Specific checkpoints should be included:

* Development of the architecture itself (ADM compliance)
* Implementation of the architecture(s) (architecture compliance)

Architecture project timings for assessments should include project initiation, initial design, major design changes, and any *ad hoc* assessments needed.

An Architecture Compliance Review is typically targeted at a point in time when the business requirements and the enterprise architecture are reasonably firm, and the project architecture is taking shape well before its completion. The aim is to hold the review as soon as practical, at a stage when there is still time to correct any major errors or shortcomings.

11.4.4.2   *Review Scenarios*

In all cases, the Architecture Compliance Review process needs the backing of senior management, and should be mandated as part of corporate Architecture Governance policies. Normally the enterprise CIO or enterprise Architecture Board will mandate architecture reviews for all major projects, including subsequent annual reviews. TOGAF provides the following guidance for possible review scenarios:

* For smaller-scale projects, the review process could simply take the form of a series of questions that the project architects or project leaders pose to themselves, using the checklists provided to create a project report for management.
* Where the project under review has not involved a practicing or full-time architect to date (for example, in an application-level project), the purpose of the review is typically to bring in architectural expertise. In

such a case, the enterprise architecture function would be organizing, leading, and conducting the review, with the involvement of business domain experts. In such a scenario, the review is not a substitute for the involvement of architects in a project, but it can be a supplement or a guide to their involvement.

- In most scenarios, particularly in larger-scale projects, the architecture function will have been deeply involved in, and perhaps leading, the development project under review. In such a scenario, the review will be coordinated by the lead enterprise architect, who will assemble a team of business and technical domain experts for the review, and compile the answers to the questions posed during the review into some form of report. The questions will typically be posed by the business and technical domain experts. Alternatively, the review might be led by a representative of an Architecture Board or some similar body with enterprise-wide responsibilities.

11.4.4.3   Risk Monitoring

(Syllabus Reference: Unit 18, Learning Outcome 5: You should be able to demonstrate the role that risk monitoring plays in Phase G.)

Risk is pervasive in any enterprise architecture activity and is present in all phases within the ADM. Risks will have initially been identified in Phase A as part of the Business Transformation Readiness Assessment. The risk identification and mitigation assessment worksheets created at that stage will have become governance artifacts, and part of the compliance review process should include risk monitoring to ensure that any residual risks accepted are being mitigated to an acceptable level. For critical risks that are not being mitigated, a change request should be generated that might require another full or partial ADM cycle.

11.4.5   Implement Business and IT Operations

Carry out the deployment projects including IT services delivery implementation, business services delivery implementation, skills development and training implementation, and communications documentation publication. Publish new Baseline Architectures to the Architecture Repository and update other impacted repositories, such as operational configuration management stores.

11.4.6 Perform Post-Implementation Review and Close the Implementation

This step consists of conducting post-implementation reviews, publishing reviews, and closing implementation projects. Closure of Phase G occurs once the solutions are fully deployed.

11.5 Outputs

(Syllabus Reference: Unit 18, Learning Outcome 3: You should understand the outputs of this phase.)

The outputs of this phase are:

- Architecture Contract (signed) (see Section 11.5.1)
- Compliance Assessments
- Change Requests
- Impact Analysis – Implementation Recommendations
- Architecture-compliant solutions deployed, including:
    - The architecture-compliant implemented system
    - Populated Architecture Repository
    - Architecture compliance recommendations and dispensations
    - Recommendations on service delivery requirements
    - Recommendations on performance metrics
    - Service Level Agreements (SLAs)
    - Architecture Vision, updated post-implementation
    - Architecture Definition Document, updated post-implementation
    - Transition Architecture, updated post-implementation
    - Business and IT operating models for the implemented solution

11.5.1 Architecture Contracts

(Syllabus Reference: Unit 18, Learning Outcome 3.2: You should be able to explain the relationship of Architecture Contracts to Architecture Governance.)

The Architecture Contracts produced in Phase G are the joint agreements between development partners and sponsors on the deliverables, quality, and fitness-for-purpose of an architecture. Successful implementation of these agreements will be delivered through effective architecture. By implementing a governed approach to the management of contracts, the following can be ensured:

- A system of continuous monitoring to check integrity, changes, decision-making, and audit of all architecture-related activities within the organization
- Adherence to the principles, standards, and requirements of the existing or developing architectures
- Identification of risks in all aspects of the development and implementation of the architecture(s) covering the internal development against accepted standards, policies, technologies, and products as well as the operational aspects of the architectures such that the organization can continue its business within a resilient environment
- A set of processes and practices that ensure accountability, responsibility, and discipline with regard to the development and usage of all architectural artifacts
- A formal understanding of the governance organization responsible for the contract, their level of authority, and scope of the architecture under the governance of this body

TOGAF identifies two example contracts: the Architecture Design and Development Contract and the Business Users' Architecture Contract.

(Syllabus Reference: Unit 18, Learning Outcome 3.1: You should be able to explain the contents of Architecture Contracts.)

Typical contents of an Architecture Design and Development Contract are:
- Introduction and background
- The nature of the agreement
- Scope of the architecture
- Architecture and strategic principles and requirements
- Conformance requirements
- Architecture development and management process and roles
- Target Architecture measures
- Defined phases of deliverables
- Prioritized joint work plan
- Time window(s)
- Architecture delivery and business metrics

Typical contents of a Business Users' Architecture Contract are:
- Introduction and background
- The nature of the agreement
- Scope
- Strategic requirements
- Conformance requirements
- Architecture adopters
- Time window
- Architecture business metrics
- Service architecture (includes SLA)
    - This contract is also used to manage changes to the enterprise architecture in Phase H.

11.5.2 Compliance Assessments

Typical contents of a Compliance Assessment are:
- Overview of project progress and status
- Overview of project architecture/design
- Completed architecture checklists:
    - Hardware and operating system checklist
    - Software services and middleware checklist
    - Applications checklists
    - Information management checklists
    - Security checklists
    - System management checklists
    - System engineering checklists
    - Methods and tools checklists

11.6 Summary

Phase G: Implementation Governance defines architecture constraints on the implementation projects and obtains signatures on an Architecture Contract. The contract, along with all the documentation, is then delivered to the implementation team. This phase includes governing the architecture through implementation by conducting compliance reviews, and by risk monitoring as well as post-implementation reviews.

11.7 Exercises

Exercise 11-1

The CIO has asked you to organize a compliance review for an enterprise architecture project that is migrating the organization's customer information systems to a new platform (both hardware and software platform). She is concerned that the systems meet all applicable regulations for managing personal information. Summarize five key questions for the compliance checklist.

11.8 Recommended Reading

The following are recommended sources of further information for this chapter:

- TOGAF 9 Part II, Chapter 15 (Phase G: Implementation Governance)
- TOGAF 9 Part IV, Chapter 36 (Architecture Deliverables)
- TOGAF 9 Part VII, Chapter 49 (Architecture Contracts)
- TOGAF 9 Part VII, Chapter 50 (Architecture Governance)

Phase H: Architecture Change Management

12.1 Key Learning Points

This chapter describes Phase H: Architecture Change Management of the TOGAF Architecture Development Method (ADM).

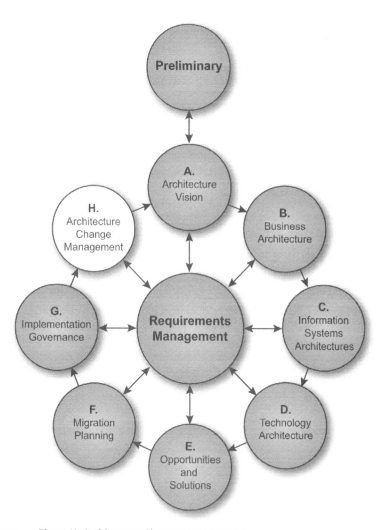

Figure 14: Phase H: Architecture Change Management

Key Points Explained

Upon completion of this chapter you should be able to:

1. Understand the inputs to the phase, and be able to explain the following:

   - Change Requests

2. Understand the steps, and be able to describe the following:

   - Architecture Board meetings

3. Understand the outputs, and be able to explain when the following can occur:

   - Updated Architecture Contracts

   - A new Request for Architecture Work

12.2 Objectives

The objectives of Phase H: Architecture Change Management are to:

- Ensure that the architecture lifecycle is maintained
- Ensure that the Architecture Governance Framework is executed
- Ensure that the enterprise Architecture Capability meets current requirements

12.3 Inputs

(Syllabus Reference: Unit 19, Learning Outcome 1: You should understand the inputs to the phase.)

The inputs to this phase are:

- Request for Architecture Work identified in Phases E and F
- Organizational Model for Enterprise Architecture
- Tailored Architecture Framework
- Statement of Architecture Work
- Architecture Vision
- Architecture Repository
- Architecture Definition Document
- Architecture Requirements Specification
- Architecture Roadmap
- Change Requests due to technology changes
- Change Requests due to business changes
- Change Requests from lessons learned
- Implementation Governance Model
- Architecture Contract (signed)

- Compliance Assessments
- Implementation and Migration Plan

12.3.1 Change Requests

(Syllabus Reference: Unit 19, Learning Outcome 1.1: You should be able to explain Change Requests.)

Requests for Architecture Change are considered in this phase. During implementation of an architecture, as more facts become known, it is possible that the original architecture definition and requirements are not suitable or are not sufficient to complete the implementation of a solution. In these circumstances, it is necessary for implementation projects to either deviate from the suggested architectural approach or to request scope extensions. Additionally, external factors, such as market factors, changes in business strategy, and new technology opportunities, may open up opportunities to extend and refine the architecture. In these circumstances, a Change Request can be submitted in order to initiate a further cycle of architecture work.

Typical contents of a Change Request are:
- Description of the proposed change
- Rationale for the proposed change
- Impact assessment of the proposed change, including:
  - Reference to specific requirements
  - Stakeholder priority of the requirements to date
  - Phases to be revisited
  - Phase to lead on requirements prioritization
  - Results of phase investigations and revised priorities
  - Recommendations on management of requirements
- Repository reference number

12.4 Steps

(Syllabus Reference: Unit 19, Learning Outcome 2: You understand the steps in this phase.)

Phase H consists of the following steps:
1. Establish value realization process
2. Deploy monitoring tools

3. Manage risks
4. Provide analysis for architecture change management
5. Develop change requirements to meet performance targets
6. Manage governance process
7. Activate the process to implement change

The steps are described in more detail in the following sections.

12.4.1 Establish Value Realization Process

This step should establish a process to ensure that business projects realize value from the enterprise architecture. The value can be measured in terms of quantifiable measures (reduced costs, reduced time-to-market length) and indirect measures (such as new skills and capabilities).

12.4.2 Deploy Monitoring Tools

Here we deploy and apply tools to enable the following:

- Monitor technology changes which could impact the Baseline Architecture
- Monitor business changes which could impact the Baseline Architecture
- Track business value (e.g., investment appraisal method to determine value metrics for the business objectives)
- Monitor enterprise architecture capability maturity
- Track and assess asset management programs
- Track the QoS performances and usage
- Determine and track business continuity requirements

12.4.3 Manage Risks

In this step the enterprise architecture risks should be assessed and recommendations made for risk mitigation.

12.4.4 Provide Analysis for Architecture Change Management

Provide analysis for architecture change management:

- Analyze performance
- Conduct enterprise architecture performance reviews with service management
- Assess Change Requests and reporting to ensure that the expected value realization and Service Level Agreement (SLA) expectations of the customers are met

- Undertake a Gap Analysis of the performance of the enterprise architecture
- Ensure change management requests adhere to the enterprise Architecture Governance and framework

12.4.5 Develop Change Requirements to Meet Performance Targets

Make recommendations concerning change requirements to meet performance targets and development of position to act.

12.4.6 Manage Governance Process

(Syllabus Reference: Unit 19, Learning Outcome 2.1: You are able to describe Architecture Board meetings.)

Manage the governance process and framework for the architecture. This includes scheduling and holding meetings of the Architecture Board. The purpose of these meetings is to decide how to handle change requests (technology and business) as well as dispensation requests. See also Section 22.4 and Section 22.5.

12.4.7 Activate the Process to Implement Change

Activate the architecture process to implement change by producing a new Request for Architecture Work and request for investment. Ensure any changes implemented in this phase are captured and documented in the Architecture Repository.

12.5 Outputs

(Syllabus Reference: Unit 19, Learning Outcome 3: You understand the outputs of this phase.)

The outputs of this phase are:
- Architecture updates (for maintenance changes)
- Changes to Architecture Framework and principles (for maintenance changes)
- New Request for Architecture Work, to initiate another cycle of the ADM (for major changes)
- Statement of Architecture Work, updated if necessary
- Architecture Contract, updated if necessary
- Compliance Assessments, updated if necessary

(Syllabus Reference: Unit 19, Learning Outcome 3.1: You should be able to explain when Architecture Contracts might be updated.)

The impact of a Change Request may require Architecture Contracts to be updated to reflect the changes agreed.

(Syllabus Reference: Unit 19, Learning Outcome 3.2: You should be able to explain when a new Request for Architecture Work might occur.)

A new Request for Architecture Work should be produced for change requests that require a major change. These are called "Re-architecting Changes" and require putting the whole architecture through the ADM cycle.

12.6 Summary

Phase H ensures that changes to the architecture are managed in a cohesive and controlled manner in line with the Architecture Governance processes. It also establishes and supports the enterprise architecture to provide flexibility to evolve the architecture rapidly in response to changes in the technology or business environment.

12.7 Exercises

Exercise 12-1

There are three main categories of architecture change:
1. Simplification: This can be handled via change management techniques.
2. Incremental: This may be handled via change management techniques, or it may require partial re-architecting.
3. Re-architecting: This requires putting the whole architecture through the Architecture Development Cycle again.

Explain why each of these changes might occur.

Exercise 12-2

Describe the change impact of the following scenarios:
1. The required change is part of the business strategy and is substantial.
2. A new technology or standard emerges.

3. The change is at an infrastructure level; for example, ten systems are reduced to one system.
4. The Foundation Architecture needs to be re-aligned with the business strategy.
5. Substantial change is required to components and guidelines for use in deployment of the architecture.

12.8 Recommended Reading

The following are recommended sources of further information for this chapter:

- TOGAF 9 Part II, Chapter 16 (Phase H: Change Management)
- TOGAF 9 Part IV, Chapter 36 (Architecture Deliverables)
- TOGAF 9 Part VII, Chapter 47 (Architecture Board)
- TOGAF 9 Part VII, Chapter 50 (Architecture Governance)

ADM Architecture Requirements Management

13.1 Key Learning Points

This chapter describes ADM Architecture Requirements Management. The process of managing architecture requirements applies to all phases of the ADM cycle, as shown in Figure 15.

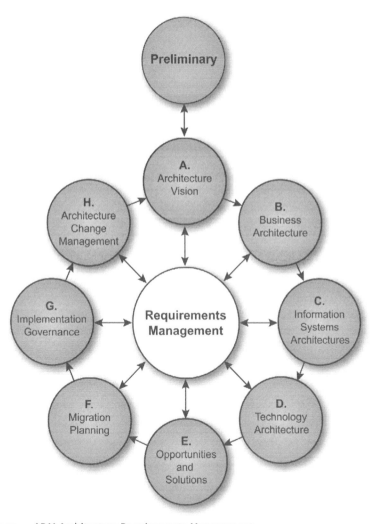

Figure 15: ADM Architecture Requirements Management

> **Key Points Explained**
>
> Upon completion of this chapter you should be able to:
>
> 1. Understand the inputs to the Requirements Management process
> 2. Understand the steps and their correspondence to phases
> 3. Explain how the Requirements Management steps correspond to ADM phases
> 4. Explain the purpose of the outputs of Requirements Management

13.2 Objectives

The objectives of the Requirements Management phase are to:

- Ensure that the Requirements Management process is sustained and operates for all relevant ADM phases
- Manage architecture requirements identified during any execution of the ADM cycle or a phase
- Ensure that relevant architecture requirements are available for use by each phase as the phase is executed

13.3 Inputs

(Syllabus Reference: Unit 20, Learning Outcome 1: You should understand the inputs to the Requirements Management process.)

The inputs to the Requirements Management process are the requirements-related outputs from each ADM phase. The first high-level requirements are produced as part of the Architecture Vision. Each architecture domain then generates detailed requirements. Deliverables in later ADM phases contain mappings to new types of requirements (e.g., conformance requirements).

13.4 Steps

(Syllabus Reference: Unit 20, Learning Outcome 2: You should understand the steps and their correspondence to ADM phases.)

(Syllabus Reference: Unit 20, Learning Outcome 3: You should be able to explain how the Requirements Management steps correspond to ADM phases.)

Table 15 lists the correspondence between Requirements Management process steps and ADM phase steps.

Table 15:   Correspondence between Requirements Managements and the ADM Phases

Step	Requirements Management Steps	ADM Phase Steps
1		Identify/document requirements – use Business Scenarios or an analogous technique
2	Baseline requirements: 1. Determine priorities arising from current phase of ADM 2. Confirm stakeholder buy-in to resultant priorities 3. Record requirements priorities and place in Requirements Repository	—
3	Monitor baseline requirements	
4		Identify changed requirement: 1. Remove or re-assess priorities 2. Add requirements and re-assess priorities 3. Modify existing requirements
5	Identify changed requirements and record priorities: 1. Identify changed requirements. Ensure the requirements are prioritized by the architect(s) responsible for the current phases and by the relevant stakeholders 2. Record new priorities 3. Ensure that any conflicts are identified and managed throughout the phases 4. Generate Requirements Impact Statement for steering the architecture team **Notes:** 1. Changed requirements can come in through any route. To ensure that the requirements are properly assessed and prioritized, this process needs to direct the ADM phases and record the decisions related to the requirements. 2. The Requirements Management phase needs to determine stakeholder satisfaction with the decisions. Where there is dissatisfaction, the phase remains accountable to ensure the resolution of the issues and determine the next steps.	

Step	Requirements Management Steps	ADM Phase Steps
6		1. Assess impact of changed requirements on current (active) phase 2. Assess impact of changed requirements on previous phases 3. Determine whether to implement change, or defer to a later ADM cycle; if the decision is to implement, assess the timescale for change management implementation 4. Issue Requirements Impact Statement, Version n+1
7		Implement requirements arising from Phase H The architecture can be changed through its lifecycle by the Architecture Change Management phase (Phase H). The Requirements Management process ensures that new or changing requirements that are derived from Phase H are managed accordingly.
8	Update the Requirements Repository with information relating to the changes requested, including stakeholder views affected.	
9		Implement the change in the current phase
10		Assess and revise Gap Analysis for past phases The Gap Analysis in the ADM Phases B through D identifies the gaps between Baseline and Target Architectures; certain types of gap can give rise to gap requirements. The ADM describes two kinds of gap: 1. Something that is present in the baseline, but not in the target (i.e., eliminated – by accident or design) 2. Something not in the baseline, but present in the target (i.e., new) A "gap requirement" is anything that has been eliminated by accident, and therefore requires a change to the Target Architecture. If the Gap Analysis generates gap requirements, then this step will ensure that they are addressed, documented, and recorded in the Requirements Repository, and that the Target Architecture is revised accordingly.

13.5 Outputs

(Syllabus Reference: Unit 20, Learning Outcome 4: You should be able to explain the purpose of the outputs of Requirements Management.)

The outputs of the Requirements Management process are:
- Updated Architecture Requirements Specification (see Section 4.5.2)
- Requirements Impact Assessment

The Requirements Repository will be updated as part of the Requirements Management phase and should contain all requirements information.

13.5.1 Requirements Impact Assessment

Throughout the ADM, new information is collected relating to an architecture. As this information is gathered, new facts may come to light that invalidate existing aspects of the architecture; for example, new requirements arising or existing requirements changing. A Requirements Impact Assessment assesses the current architecture requirements and specification to identify changes that should be made and the implications of those changes. It documents an assessment of the changes and the recommendations for change to the architecture. The statement goes through various iterations until the final version, which includes the full implications of the requirements (e.g., costs, timescales, business metrics) on the architecture development. The recommended contents are as follows:
- Reference to specific requirements
- Stakeholder priority of the requirements to date
- Phases to be revisited
- Phase to lead on requirements prioritization
- Results of phase investigations and revised priorities
- Recommendations on management of requirements
- Repository reference number

These are often produced as a response to a Change Request.

13.6 Summary

Requirements Management is an ongoing activity of the ADM. The Requirements Repository contains the current requirements for the Target Architecture. When new requirements arise, or existing ones are changed, a

Requirements Impact Statement is generated, which identifies the phases of the ADM that need to be revisited to address the changes.

13.7 Exercises

Exercise 13-1

You have been asked to recommend candidate tools for Requirements Management. Identify three or more suitable tools, together with a rationale for why they would suitable for use. (Hint: The Volere website has a useful list of tools.[8])

13.8 Recommended Reading

The following are recommended sources of further information for this chapter:

- TOGAF 9 Part II, Chapter 17 (ADM Architecture Requirements Management)
- TOGAF 9 Part IV, Chapter 36 (Architecture Deliverables)

---

8   Refer to www.volere.co.uk/tools.htm.

PART 2

Guidelines for Adapting the ADM

In this Part, we examine three guidelines for adapting the Architecture Development Method:

- Chapter 14 describes how to apply iteration to the ADM, and how to apply the ADM at different enterprise levels.
- Chapter 15 describes security considerations during the application of the ADM.
- Chapter 16 describes SOA as an architectural style.

Iteration and Levels

14.1 Key Learning Points

This chapter describes the guidelines for adapting the ADM using iteration and different levels of architecture engagement. This chapter will help you to apply these guidelines during application of the ADM.

Key Points Explained

Upon completion of this chapter you should be able to:

1. Describe the concept of iteration and how it applies to TOGAF
2. Describe the factors influencing the use of iteration
3. Describe some suggested iteration cycles
4. Describe how the ADM supports different types of engagements within the organization
5. Explain how to apply iteration cycles to the ADM phases
6. Explain how the concepts of levels and the Enterprise Continuum are used to organize the Architecture Landscape
7. Identify the different levels of architecture that exist in an organization

---

14.2 The Concept of Iteration

(Syllabus Reference: Unit 23, Learning Outcome 1: You should be able to describe the concept of iteration and how it applies to TOGAF.)

The ADM supports a number of concepts that can be characterized as iteration. First, iteration describes the process of both describing a comprehensive Architecture Landscape through multiple ADM cycles based upon individual initiatives bound to the scope of the Request for Architecture Work. Second, iteration describes the integrated process of developing an architecture where the activities described in different ADM phases interact to produce an integrated architecture. In order to concisely describe the activity and outputs, this latter iteration is described in sequential terms. Third, iteration describes the process of managing change to the organization's Architecture Capability. These are described further below.

14.2.1   Iteration to Develop a Comprehensive Architecture Landscape

Projects will exercise through the entire ADM cycle, commencing with Phase A. Each cycle of the ADM will be bound by a Request for Architecture Work. The architecture output will populate the Architecture Landscape, either extending the landscape described, or changing the landscape where required.

Separate projects may operate their own ADM cycles concurrently, with relationships between the different projects.

One project may trigger the initiation of another project. Typically, this is used when higher-level architecture initiatives identify opportunities or solutions that require more detailed architecture, or when a project identifies landscape impacts outside the scope of its Request for Architecture Work.

14.2.2   Iteration within an ADM Cycle (Architecture Development Iteration)

Projects may operate multiple ADM phases concurrently. Typically, this is used to manage the inter-relationship between Business Architecture, Information Systems Architecture, and Technology Architecture.

Projects may cycle between ADM phases, in planned cycles covering multiple phases. Typically, this is used to converge on a detailed Target Architecture when higher-level architecture does not exist to provide context and constraint.

Projects may return to previous phases in order to circle back and update work products with new information. Typically, this is used to converge on an executable Architecture Roadmap or Implementation and Migration Plan, when the implementation details and scope of change trigger a change or re-prioritization of stakeholder requirements.

14.2.3   Iteration to Manage the Architecture Capability (Architecture Capability Iterations)

Projects may require a new iteration of the Preliminary Phase to (re-) establish aspects of the Architecture Capability identified in Phase A to address a Request for Architecture Work.

Projects may require a new iteration of the Preliminary Phase to adjust the organization's Architecture Capability as a result of identifying new or changed requirements for Architecture Capability as a result of a change request in Phase H.

14.3 Factors Influencing the Use of Iteration

(Syllabus Reference: Unit 23, Learning Outcome 2: You should be able to describe the factors influencing the use of iteration.)

Factors influencing the use of iteration include:

- **The formality and nature of established process checkpoints within the organization.** Does the organization mandate that certain groups of activities are carried out between checkpoints? Does the organization mandate that certain activities must be finalized before other activities can be carried out?
- **The level of stakeholder involvement expected within the process.** Are stakeholders expecting to be closely involved within the development of a solution, or are they expecting to see a complete set of deliverables for review and approval?
- **The number of teams involved and the relationships between different teams.** Is the entire architecture being developed by a specific team, or is there a hierarchy of teams with governance relationships between them?
- **The maturity of the solution area and the expected amount of re-work and refinement required to arrive at an acceptable solution.** Can the solution be achieved in a single pass, or does it require extensive proof-of-concept and prototyping work to evolve a suitable outcome?
- **Attitude to risk.** Does the organizational culture react negatively to partially complete work products being circulated? Does the organizational culture require solutions to be proved in a trial environment before they can be implemented for mainstream application?
- **The class of engagement.** What is the context for development of the enterprise architecture?

14.4 Iteration Cycles

(Syllabus Reference: Unit 23, Learning Outcome 3: You should be able to describe some suggested iteration cycles.)

The suggested iteration cycles for the TOGAF ADM are shown in Figure 16 and can be used to effectively group related architectural activities to achieve a specific purpose.

Architecture Capability iterations support the creation and evolution of the required Architecture Capability. This includes the initial mobilization of architecture activity for a given purpose or architecture engagement type by establishing or adjusting the architecture approach, principles, scope, vision, and governance.

Architecture Development iterations allow for the creation of architecture content by cycling through, or integrating, Business, Information Systems, and Technology Architecture phases. These iterations ensure that the architecture is considered as a whole. In this type of iteration stakeholder reviews are typically broader. As the iterations converge on a target, extensions into the Opportunities and Solutions and Migration Planning phases ensure that the viability of the architecture's implementation is considered as the architecture is finalized.

Transition Planning iterations support the creation of formal change roadmaps for a defined architecture.

Architecture Governance iterations support governance of change activity progressing towards a defined Target Architecture.

Figure 16: Iteration Cycles

Styles of Architecture Definition

TOGAF suggests two process styles when defining architectures:

Baseline First

An assessment of the current state (baseline) is used to identify problem areas and opportunities for improvement. This is a suitable approach when the baseline is complex, not clearly understood or agreed upon.

Target First

The target solution is elaborated in detail and then mapped back to the baseline. This is a suitable approach if the target state is agreed at a high level and where the enterprise wishes to effectively transition to the target model.

14.5 Classes of Architecture Engagement

(Syllabus Reference: Unit 23, Learning Outcome 4: You should be able to describe how the ADM supports different types of engagement within an organization.)

An architecture function or services organization may be called on to assist in the development of an enterprise in a number of different contexts, as architectures range from summary to detail, broad to narrow coverage, and current state to future state. In these contexts the concept of iteration should be used in developing the architecture.

TOGAF defines three typical areas of engagement for architects which are classified as *Identification, Definition,* or *Implementation* of the required change. Each of the classifications has its own scenarios or engagement types; for example, supporting a business strategy, architecture portfolio management of the Architecture Landscape, foundational change initiative, etc. These are shown in Figure 17 and described in the following sections.

14.5.1 Identification of Required Change

Outside the context of any change initiative, enterprise architecture can be used as a technique to provide visibility of the IT capability to support strategic decision-making and alignment of execution.

14.5.2 Definition of Change

Where a need to change has been identified in an enterprise, enterprise architecture can be used as a technique to define the nature and extent of change in a structured fashion. Within large-scale change initiatives, architectures can be developed to provide detailed architecture initiatives that are bounded by the scope of a program or portfolio.

14.5.3 Implementation of Change

Architecture at all levels of the enterprise can be used as a technique to provide design governance to change initiatives by providing overall visibility, and structural constraints, and defining criteria by which to evaluate technical decisions.

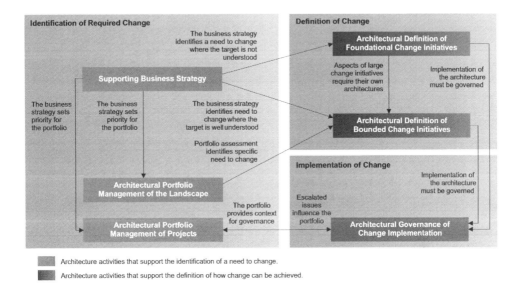

Figure 17:   Classes of Enterprise Architecture Engagement

Within the three areas of engagement, TOGAF defines a number of classes of engagement, which are summarized in Figure 17 Table 16.

Table 16:   Areas and Classes of Enterprise Architecture Engagement

Area of Engagement	Class of Engagement/ Iteration Focus	Description
Identification of Required Change	Supporting Business Strategy Architecture Capability and Architecture Development (Baseline First) Iterations	This type of engagement is suitable for merger and acquisitions. As the business strategies, objectives, goals, and drivers change, it is necessary for IT to change in order to maintain alignment. The creation of new business strategies can be supported by the enterprise architecture by: • Providing visibility of change opportunities • Providing elaboration on the practical impacts of a particular strategic choice • Providing tests on the feasibility or viability of a particular strategic direction In this engagement type, as business strategies change or new business strategies are created that might impact the whole enterprise, then the focus is to look at the baseline first, with broad shallow consideration given to the Architecture Landscape in order to address a specific strategic question. It should define terms for more detailed efforts to realize the strategy.

Area of Engagement	Class of Engagement/ Iteration Focus	Description
	Architectural Portfolio Management of the Landscape Architecture Capability and Architecture Development (Baseline First) Iterations	This type of engagement is typical for service providers and management to manage a complex IT landscape. It is common practice across large organizations for a Service Management organization to provide operational reporting and management of the IT portfolio. Enterprise Architecture can add a further dimension to Service Management reporting by supporting a linkage between operational performance and the strategic need for IT. Using the traceability between IT and business inherent in enterprise architecture, it is possible to evaluate the IT portfolio against operational performance data and business needs (e.g., cost, functionality, availability, responsiveness) to determine areas where misalignment is occurring and change needs to take place. In this type of engagement the focus is to look at the baseline first and to focus on the physical assessment of the current applications and technology infrastructure to identify opportunities for improvement.
	Architectural Portfolio Management of Projects Transition Planning and Architecture Governance Iterations	It is common practice across large organizations for a Program Management organization to provide operational reporting and management of the change portfolio. Enterprise Architecture can add a further dimension to project portfolio management reporting by supporting a link between project scope, architectural impact, and business value. Architectural factors can be added to other quantitative project factors to support strategic decision-making on project priority and funding levels. This type of engagement is focused on projects and their dependencies, aligning the project sequence to optimize the architecture.
Definition of Change	Architectural Definition of Foundational Change Initiatives Architecture Capability, Architecture Development (Baseline First), and Transition Planning Iterations	Foundational change initiatives are change efforts that have a known objective, but are not strictly scoped or bounded by a shared vision or requirements. The initial priority is to understand the nature of the problem and to bring structure to the definition of the problem. Once the problem is more effectively understood, it is possible to define appropriate solutions and to align stakeholders around a common vision and purpose. The focus should be to look at the baseline first and to identify what needs to change to transition to the target.

Area of Engagement	Class of Engagement/ Iteration Focus	Description
	Architectural Definition of Bounded Change Initiatives Architecture Development (Target First) and Transition Planning Iterations	Bounded change initiatives are change efforts that typically arise as the outcome of a prior architectural strategy, evaluation, or vision. Here, the desired outcome is already understood and agreed. The focus of the architecture is to effectively elaborate a future state solution that addresses the identified issues, drivers, and constraints. The focus should be to look at the target first and then to do transition planning. Focus on elaborating the target to meet a previously defined and agreed vision, scope, or set of constraints. Use the target as a basis for analysis to avoid perpetuation of current, sub-optimal architectures.
Implementation of Change	Architectural Governance of Change Implementation Architecture Governance Iteration	Once an architectural solution model has been defined, it provides a basis for solution architecture, design, and implementation. In order to ensure that the objectives and value of the defined enterprise architecture are appropriately realized, it is necessary for continuing enterprise Architecture Governance of the implementation process to support design review, architecture refinement, and issue escalation. Use the Architecture Vision, constraints, principles, requirements, Target Architecture definition, and transition roadmap to ensure that projects realize their intended benefit, are aligned with each other, and are aligned with wider business need.

14.6 Mapping TOGAF Phases to Iteration Cycles

(Syllabus Reference: Unit 23, Learning Outcome 5: You should be able to explain how to apply iteration cycles to the ADM phases.)

14.6.1 Iteration between ADM Cycles

In this approach each iteration completes an ADM cycle at a single level of architecture description with Phase F (Migration Planning) being used to initiate new more detailed architecture development projects. This type of iteration highlights the need for a higher-level architecture to guide and constrain more detailed architecture(s) and is a method to develop the complete Architecture Landscape for a project in multiple iterations. This approach is shown in Figure 18.

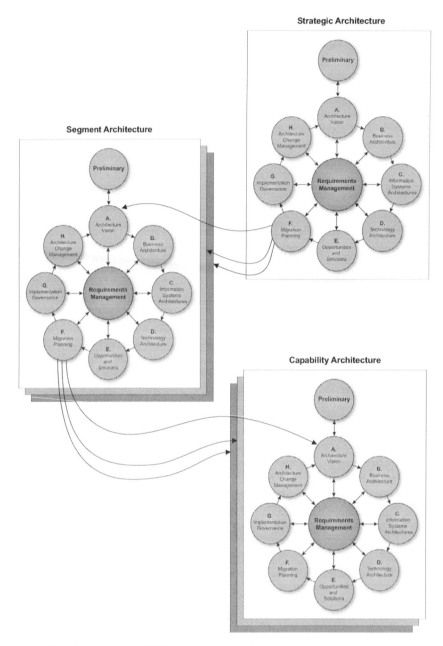

Figure 18:   A Hierarchy of ADM Processes Example

14.6.2 Iteration within an ADM Cycle

TOGAF includes suggested iteration cycles for both baseline first and target first architecture definitions. The example for target first is shown in Figure 19.

TOGAF Phase		Architecture Development			Transition Planning		Architecture Governance	
		Iteration 1	Iteration 2	Iteration n	Iteration 1	Iteration n	Iteration 1	Iteration n
Preliminary		Informal	Informal	Informal				Light
Architecture Vision		Informal	Informal	Informal	Informal	Informal		Light
Business Architecture	Baseline	Informal	Core	Core	Informal	Informal		Light
	Target	Core	Light	Core	Informal	Informal		Light
Application Architecture	Baseline	Informal	Core	Core	Informal	Informal		Light
	Target	Core	Light	Core	Informal	Informal		Light
Data Architecture	Baseline	Informal	Core	Core	Informal	Informal		Light
	Target	Core	Light	Core	Informal	Informal		Light
Technology Architecture	Baseline	Informal	Core	Core	Informal	Informal		Light
	Target	Core	Light	Core	Informal	Informal		Light
Opportunities and Solutions		Light	Light	Light	Core	Core	Informal	Informal
Migration Planning		Light	Light	Light	Core	Core	Informal	Informal
Implementation Governance					Informal	Informal	Core	Core
Change Management		Informal	Informal	Informal	Informal	Informal	Core	Core

▓ Core: primary focus activity for the iteration
▒ Light: secondary focus activity for the iteration
☐ Informal: potential activity for the iteration, not formally mentioned in the method

Figure 19:   Activity by Iteration for Target First Architecture Definition

The suggested iteration cycles mapped to the TOGAF phases are described in the following sections.

14.6.2.1 Architecture Development Iteration (Baseline First)

Iteration 1 – Define the Baseline Architecture

This iteration comprises a pass through the Business Architecture, Information Systems Architecture, and Technology Architecture phases of the ADM, focusing on definition of the Baseline Architecture. Opportunities, solutions, and migration plans are also considered to identify the focus for change and test feasibility.

Iteration 2 – Define the Target Architecture and Gaps

This iteration comprises a pass through the Business Architecture, Information Systems Architecture, and Technology Architecture phases of the ADM, focusing on definition of the Target Architecture and analyzing gaps against the Baseline Architecture. Opportunities, solutions, and migration plans are also considered to test viability.

Iteration *n* – Refine the Baseline Architecture, Target Architecture, and Gaps

Subsequent iterations attempt to correct and refine the Baseline and Target Architectures to achieve an outcome that is beneficial, feasible, and viable.

14.6.2.2 *Architecture Development Iteration (Target First)*

Iteration 1 – Define the Target Architecture

This iteration comprises a pass through the Business Architecture, Information Systems Architecture, and Technology Architecture phases of the ADM, focusing on definition of the Target Architecture. Opportunities, solutions, and migration plans are also considered to identify the focus for change and test feasibility.

Iteration 2 – Define the Baseline Architecture and Gaps

This iteration comprises a pass through the Business Architecture, Information Systems Architecture, and Technology Architecture phases of the ADM, focusing on definition of the Baseline Architecture and analyzing gaps against the Target Architecture. Opportunities, solutions, and migration plans are also considered to test viability.

Iteration *n* – Refine the Baseline Architecture, Target Architecture, and Gaps

Subsequent iterations attempt to correct and refine the Baseline and Target Architectures to achieve an outcome that is beneficial, feasible, and viable.

14.6.2.3 *Transition Planning Iteration*

Iteration 1 – Define and Agree a Set of Improvement Opportunities

The initial iteration of transition planning seeks to gain buy-in to a portfolio of solution opportunities in the Opportunities & Solutions phase of the ADM. This iteration also delivers a provisional Implementation and Migration Plan.

Iteration n – Refine the Improvement Opportunities

Subsequent iterations of transition planning seek to agree on the Transition Architecture, and refine the Implementation and Migration Plan by feeding back issues into the Opportunities & Solutions phase.

14.6.2.4 Architecture Governance Iteration

Iteration 1 – Mobilize Architecture Governance and Change Management Processes

The initial Architecture Governance iteration establishes a process for the governance of change and also puts in place the appropriate people, processes, and technology to support managed access to and changes of the defined architecture.

Iteration n – Carry out Architecture Governance and Change Control

Subsequent iterations of the Architecture Governance cycle focus on reviews of change initiatives to resolve issues and ensure compliance. Results of a change request may trigger another phase to be revisited; for example, feeding back a new requirement to the Preliminary Phase to improve the Architecture Capability, or a new requirement for the architecture into the Architecture Development phases.

14.7 Applying the ADM across the Architecture Landscape

(Syllabus Reference: Unit 23, Learning Outcome 6: You should be able to explain how the concepts of levels and the Enterprise Continuum are used to organize the Architecture Landscape.)

In a typical enterprise, multiple architectures will exist in the Architecture Landscape at any point in time. Some architectures will address very specific needs; others will be more general. Some will address detail; some will provide a big picture. To address this complexity TOGAF uses the concepts of levels and the Enterprise Continuum, to provide a conceptual framework for organizing the Architecture Landscape.

14.7.1 The Architecture Landscape

(Syllabus Reference: Unit 23, Learning Outcome 7: You should be able to identify the different levels of architecture that exist in an organization.)

Levels provide a framework for dividing the Architecture Landscape into three levels of granularity as shown in Figure 20, and described below.

Figure 20:   Summary Classification Model for Architecture Landscapes

1. Strategic Architecture provides an organizing framework for operational and change activity and allows for direction setting at an executive level.
2. Segment Architecture provides an organizing framework for operational and change activity and allows for direction setting and the development of effective architecture roadmaps at a program or portfolio level.
3. Capability Architecture provides an organizing framework for change activity and the development of effective architecture roadmaps realizing capability increments.

14.7.2   The Architecture Continuum

The Architecture Continuum provides a method of dividing each level of
the Architecture Landscape by abstraction. It offers a consistent way to
define and understand the generic rules, representations, and relationships
in an architecture, including traceability and derivation relationships. The
Architecture Continuum shows the relationships from foundation elements
to organization-specific architecture, as shown in Figure 21.

Figure 21:   Summary of the Architecture Continuum

The classification methods of the Architecture Continuum can be used
to partition and organize the Architecture Landscape into a set of related
architectures with:

- Manageable complexity for each individual architecture or solution
- Defined groupings
- Defined hierarchies and navigation structures
- Appropriate processes, roles, and responsibilities attached to each
  grouping

14.7.3   Organizing the Architecture Landscape

The following characteristics can be used to organize the Architecture
Landscape:

- Breadth: The breadth (subject matter) area is generally the primary
  organizing characteristic for describing an Architecture Landscape.
  Architectures are functionally decomposed into a hierarchy of specific
  subject areas or segments.
- Depth: With broader subject areas, less detail is needed to ensure that
  the architecture has a manageable size and complexity. More specific
  subject matter areas will generally permit (and require) more detailed
  architectures.
- Time: For a specific breadth and depth an enterprise can create a Baseline
  Architecture and a set of Target Architectures that stretch into the future.

Broader and less detailed architectures will generally be valid for longer periods of time and can provide a vision for the enterprise that stretches further into the future.

- Recency: Finally, each architecture view will progress through a development cycle where it increases in accuracy until finally approved. After approval, an architecture will begin to decrease in accuracy if not actively maintained. In some cases recency may be used as an organizing factor for historic architectures.

Using the criteria above, architectures can be grouped into Strategic, Segment, and Capability Architecture levels, as described in Figure 20.

14.8 Summary

TOGAF provides guidelines for adapting the ADM for iteration. This includes proposed iteration cycles to suit different classes of architecture engagement. Guidance is also provided on how to use levels for architecture development across the Architecture Landscape.

14.9 Exercises

Exercise 14-1

When applying iteration to the ADM it is sometimes best to produce the Baseline Architecture first. Give two examples of when a Baseline First approach to architecture development would be most appropriate.

Exercise 14-2

When applying iteration to the ADM it is sometimes best to produce the Target Architecture first. Give two examples of when a Target First approach to architecture development would be most appropriate.

Exercise 14-3

For the following example, identify a suitable class of architecture engagement, and describe the context and the approach you would take for the engagement:

- The CIO requests your advice on the following issues:
    - How to control the increasing IT operational costs
    - How to accurately forecast IT spend
    - How to remove the duplication of systems

Exercise 14-4

For the following example, identify a suitable class of architecture engagement, and describe the context and the approach you would take for the engagement:

- The CEO announces that the organization is merging with its number three competitor, and requests your advice on:
    - How to keep up with the major rivals in the industry
    - How to achieve the merger successfully in the shortest time

14.10 **Recommended Reading**

The following are recommended sources of further information for this chapter:

- TOGAF 9 Part III, Chapter 19 (Applying Iteration to the ADM)
- TOGAF 9 Part III, Chapter 20 (Applying the ADM across the Architecture Landscape)

Chapter 15

Security

15.1 Key Learning Points

This chapter describes the guidelines for adapting the ADM for security. This chapter will help you understand the security considerations that need to be addressed during application of the ADM.

Key Points Explained

Upon completion of this chapter you should be able to:

1. Describe the responsibility that Enterprise Architects have towards Security Architecture
2. Describe the recommended security adaptations to the ADM

15.2 Introduction

TOGAF 9 introduces guidance on security architecture and the ADM in order to help practitioners avoid missing critical security concerns. This guidance is intended to inform the enterprise architect of what the security architect will need to carry out during the security architecture work.

15.2.1 Characteristics of Security Architectures

A security architecture generally has the following characteristics:

- It has its own methods.
- It composes its own discrete views and viewpoints.
- It addresses non-normative flows.
- It introduces its own unique normative flows.
- It introduces unique, single-purpose components in the design.
- It calls for a unique set of skills from the enterprise architect.

15.2.2 Security Responsibilities of the Enterprise Architect

(Syllabus Reference: Unit 24, Learning Outcome 1: You should be able to describe the responsibility that Enterprise Architects have towards Security Architecture.)

Enterprise architects have a responsibility to ensure that stakeholder concerns related to security are addressed in the enterprise architecture. All groups of stakeholders in the enterprise will have security concerns. These concerns might not be obvious as security-related concerns unless there is special awareness on the part of the enterprise architect. To assist the enterprise architect, TOGAF recommends bringing a security architect into a project as early as possible.

Figure 22:   Stakeholder Concerns Related to Security

The typical set of stakeholder concerns related to security is shown in Figure 22. The specific concerns are briefly described as follows:

- Authentication: The substantiation of the identity of a person or entity related to the enterprise or system in some way.
- Authorization: The definition and enforcement of permitted capabilities for a person or entity whose identity has been established.

- Audit: The ability to provide forensic data attesting that the systems have been used in accordance with stated security policies.
- Assurance: The ability to test and prove that the enterprise architecture has the security attributes required to uphold the stated security policies.
- Availability: The ability of the enterprise to function without service interruption or depletion despite abnormal or malicious events.
- Asset Protection: The protection of information assets from loss or unintended disclosure, and resources from unauthorized and unintended use.
- Administration: The ability to add and change security policies, add or change how policies are implemented in the enterprise, and add or change the persons or entities related to the systems.
- Risk Management: The organization's attitude and tolerance for risk.

Typical security artifacts that should be produced as part of addressing these concerns are as follows:
- Business rules regarding handling of data and information assets
- Written and published security policy
- Codified data/information asset ownership and custody
- Risk analysis documentation
- Data classification policy documentation

15.3 Adapting the ADM for Security

(Syllabus Reference: Unit 24, Learning Outcome 2: You should be able to describe the recommended security adaptations to the ADM.)

Table 17 provides summary security guidance for adapting each phase of the ADM.

Table 17:   Security Adaptations for the ADM

Phase	Guidance
ADM Requirements Management	Security Policy and Security Standards should become part of the Requirements Management process. Monitor for new security requirements. Typical sources include: 1. A new statutory or regulatory mandate 2. A new threat realized or experienced 3. A new architecture initiative discovers new stakeholders with new requirements For 1 and 2, these new requirements would be drivers for input to the change management process in Phase H. A new architecture initiative might be launched to examine the existing infrastructure and applications to determine the extent of changes required to meet the new demands. For 3, a new security requirement will enter the Requirements Management process.
Preliminary Phase	Scope the enterprise organizations impacted by the security architecture. Define and document applicable regulatory and security policy requirements (and communicate them regularly to employees). Define the required security capability as part of the Architecture Capability. Implement security architecture tools.
Phase A: Architecture Vision	In similar fashion to obtaining management recognition and endorsement for the overall architecture project, obtain the endorsement for the security-related aspects of the architecture development effort. Define the security-related management sign-off milestones. Determine the applicable disaster recovery or business continuity requirements. Identify and document the anticipated physical/business and regulatory environments in which the systems will be deployed. Determine the criticality of the system: safety-critical, mission-critical, non-critical.
Phase B: Business Architecture	Determine the legitimate actors who will interact with the system (Business Scenarios can be used). Produce a baseline of the current security-specific business processes. Determine whom/how much it is acceptable to inconvenience with security measures. Identify and document the interconnecting systems beyond project control and determine trust levels. Determine the assets at risk if something goes wrong (sometimes assets are not tangible; e.g., customer goodwill or a credit rating). Determine the cost of asset loss/impact in failure cases. Identify and document the ownership of assets.

Phase	Guidance
	Determine and document appropriate security forensic processes (which are used to enforce security policies).
	Identify the criticality of the availability and correct operation of the overall service.
	Determine and document how much security (cost) is justified by the threats and value of the assets (by a risk analysis).
	Reassess and confirm Architecture Vision decisions.
	Assess alignment or conflict of identified security policies with business goals.
	Determine what can go wrong by performing a threat analysis.
Phase C: Information Systems Architectures	Assess and baseline current security-specific architecture elements, including a full inventory of architecture elements that implement security services.
	Identify safe default actions and failure states, which need to take into account the current state, business environment, applicable policies, and regulatory obligations.
	Identify and evaluate applicable guidelines and standards.
	In light of the previous risk assessment, revisit assumptions regarding interconnecting systems beyond project control.
	Determine and document the sensitivity or classification level of information stored/created/used (include any legislative burdens on the system and/or data).
	Identify and document custody of assets.
	Identify the criticality of the availability and correct operation of each function.
	Determine whether the system under design is accommodated by existing business disaster/continuity plans. If not, determine the gap and the costs.
	Identify what aspects of the system must be configurable to reflect changes in policy/business environment/access control.
	Identify the lifespan of information used, as defined by business needs and regulatory requirements.
	Determine approaches to address identified risks.
	Identify actions/events that warrant logging for later review or triggering forensic processes.
	Identify and document requirements for rigor in proving accuracy of logged events (e.g., non-repudiation to ensure logged data has not been tampered with).
	Identify potential/likely avenues of attack.
	Determine what can go wrong.

Phase	Guidance
Phase D: Technology Architecture	Assess and baseline current security-specific technologies. Revisit assumptions regarding interconnecting systems beyond project control. Identify and evaluate applicable recognized guidelines and standards. Identify methods to regulate consumption of resources. Engineer a method by which the effectiveness of security measures will be measured and communicated on an ongoing basis. Identify the trust (clearance) levels for the system. Identify the minimal privileges required for any entity to achieve a technical or business objective. Identify mitigating security measures, where justified by risk assessment. Determine what can go wrong.
Phase E: Opportunities & Solutions	Identify existing security services available for re-use from the Baseline Architecture and the Architecture Repository. Implement and deploy mitigation measures addressing identified risks. Evaluate tested and re-usable security software and resources. Identify new code/resources/assets appropriate for re-use. Determine what can go wrong.
Phase F: Migration Planning	Assess the impact of new security measures upon other new components or existing systems. Implement assurance methods by which the effectiveness of security measures will be measured and communicated on an ongoing basis. Identify correct secure installation parameters, initial conditions, and configurations. Implement disaster recovery and business continuity plans. Determine what can go wrong.
Phase G: Implementation Governance	Establish design and code reviews. Implement methods and procedures to review evidence that reflects operational stability and adherence to security policies. Implement training to ensure correct deployment, configuration, and operations. Determine what has gone wrong by implementing a feedback loop to verify execution of the plan and implement corrections if necessary.
Phase H: Architecture Change Management	Changes in security requirements are often more disruptive than a simplification or incremental change. Changes in security policy can be driven by statute, regulation, or something that has gone wrong. Changes in security standards are usually less disruptive since the trade-off for their adoption is based on the value of the change. However, standards changes can also be mandated. Determine what has gone wrong. Good security forensic practices in conjunction with a written published security policy make determination of this possible. Incorporate security-relevant changes to the environment into the requirements for future enhancement.

15.4 Security Input/Output Summary

TOGAF Part III, Chapter 21 (Security Architecture and the ADM) recommends additional inputs and outputs for the ADM as shown in Table 18.

Table 18: Security Inputs and Outputs

Phase	Inputs	Outputs
Preliminary Phase	Written security policy Relevant statutes List of applicable jurisdictions	List of applicable regulations List of applicable security policies Security team roster List of security assumptions and boundary conditions
Phase A: Architecture Vision	List of applicable security policies List of applicable jurisdictions Complete disaster recovery and business continuity plans	Physical security environment statement Business security environment statement Regulatory environment statement Security policy cover letter signed by CEO or delegate List of architecture development checkpoints for security sign-off List of applicable disaster recovery and business continuity plans Systems criticality statement
Phase B: Business Architecture	Initial business and regulatory security environment statements List of applicable disaster recovery and business continuity plans List of applicable security policies and regulations	List of forensic processes List of new disaster recovery and business continuity requirements Validated business and regulatory environment statements List of validated security policies and regulations List of target security processes List of baseline security processes List of security actors List of interconnecting systems Statement of security tolerance for each class of security actor Asset list with values and owners List of trust paths Availability impact statement(s) Threat analysis matrix

Phase	Inputs	Outputs
Phase C: Information Systems Architectures	Threat analysis matrix Risk analysis Documented forensic processes Validated business policies and regulations List of interconnecting systems New disaster recovery and business continuity requirements	Event log-level matrix and requirements Risk management strategy Data lifecycle definitions List of configurable system elements Baseline list of security-related elements of the system New or augmented security-related elements of the system Security use-case models: • Normative models • Non-normative models List of applicable security standards: • Protocols • Object libraries • Others ... Validated interconnected system list Information classification report List of asset custodians Function criticality statement Revised disaster recovery and business continuity plans Refined threat analysis matrix
Phase D: Technology Architecture	List of security-related elements of the system List of interconnected systems List of applicable security standards List of security actors Risk management strategy Validated security policies Validated regulatory requirements Validated business policies related to trust requirements	Baseline list of security technologies Validated interconnected systems list Selected security standards list Resource conservation plan Security metrics and monitoring plan User authorization policies Risk management plan User trust (clearance) requirements

15.5 Summary

TOGAF introduces guidance on security and the ADM to help practitioners avoid missing a critical security concern. The guidance is not intended to be a security architecture development methodology. It is intended to inform the enterprise architect of the security architecture task and role.

15.6 Exercises

Exercise 15-1

A new regulation regarding security compliance of e-commerce systems is being introduced. Describe the high-level approach you would take to manage its introduction using the TOGAF ADM.

15.7 Recommended Reading

The following are recommended sources of further information for this chapter:

- TOGAF 9 Part III, Chapter 21 (Security Architecture and the ADM)

Chapter 16

SOA

16.1 Key Learning Points

This chapter will help you understand SOA as a style of architecture, and how enterprise architecture can be used to support SOA.

Key Points Explained

Upon completion of this chapter you should be able to:

1. Describe SOA as an architectural style
2. Explain how enterprise architecture supports SOA
3. Describe the recommended SOA adaptations to the ADM

16.2 SOA as an Architectural Style

(Syllabus Reference: Unit 25, Learning Outcome 1: You should be able to describe SOA as an architectural style.)

TOGAF 9 defines SOA as "an architectural style that supports service-orientation", where the term architectural style is defined as "the combination of distinctive features in which architecture is performed or expressed" and the term service-orientation is defined as "a way of thinking in terms of services and service-based development and the outcomes of services".

The use of SOA as an architectural style is intended to simplify the business, including interoperation of parts of the business. By structuring capability as meaningful, granular services as opposed to opaque, silo'ed business units, it becomes possible to quickly identify functional capabilities of an organization and to avoid duplicating similar capabilities across different areas of the organization. By standardizing the behavior and interoperation of services, it is possible to limit the impacts of change and also to understand in advance the likely chain of impacts. From a software development perspective, it also allows for applications to be structured so as to facilitate flexibility and agility.

16.3 Enterprise Architecture and SOA

(Syllabus Reference: Unit 25, Learning Outcome 2: You should be able to explain how enterprise architecture supports SOA.)

Enterprise architecture can be used to support SOA by providing frameworks, tools, and techniques to address the development and maintenance of SOAs. Some of the key benefits that enterprise architecture provides include:

- Consistent abstractions of high-level strategies and deliverables to support planning and analysis
- The ability to link different perspectives to a single business problem providing a consistent model to address various domains and tests for completeness
- Identification of clear roadmaps to achieve future state
- Traceability that links IT and other assets to the business they support
- Support for impact assessment, risk/value analysis, and portfolio management
- Identified and documented principles, constraints, frameworks, patterns, and standards
- Governance frameworks and process that ensure the appropriate authority for decision-making

Enterprise architecture becomes a foundation for service-orienting an organization, because it links stakeholders together, ensuring that the needs of each stakeholder community are met and that each stakeholder community is aware of appropriate context. This linkage is the enabler for interoperability and re-use.

Through its linking of the business context to IT, enterprise architecture identifies and provides justification for the cost of change programs in relation to the business value to be derived from the effort. Enterprise architecture provides the context and analysis capabilities to:

- Show how SOA solutions can be effectively architected to support business capabilities
- Show which services should be built and which should be re-used
- Show how services should be designed

Without enterprise architecture, the negative effects can include one or more of the following:

- Limited agility
- Difficulty identifying and orchestrating SOA services
- Service sprawl
- Exponentially growing governance challenges
- Limited SOA service interoperability
- Limited SOA service re-use
- Multiple silo'ed SOAs
- Difficulty evolving and changing SOA implementations

16.4 Adapting the ADM for SOA

This section describes, for each phase of the TOGAF ADM, what should be considered when looking to apply the principle of service-orientation, and how this affects the phase.

16.4.1 Preliminary Phase

The Preliminary Phase is where the Architecture Capability is adapted to support SOA. The key outputs of this phase are the principles, organizational structure, governance, and initial content of the Architecture Repository.

The starting point for SOA development with TOGAF is that the enterprise adopts service-orientation as an architecture principle (from TOGAF 9, Chapter 23). An enterprise wishing to use TOGAF for SOA should include this principle, either as it stands or in modified form, in its set of architecture principles.

Successful SOA depends in part on the readiness of the enterprise to become service-oriented. The organization can conduct an SOA maturity assessment during the Preliminary Phase, using The Open Group Service Integration Maturity Model (OSIMM) as part of the review of the organizational context for conducting enterprise architecture.

A review should occur of the existing governance procedures, confirming that they are appropriate for SOA. If they are not, then recommendations should be made for change to make them appropriate. The Open Group has a standardized governance framework that focuses on SOA and may be used to enhance existing governance frameworks (see The Open Group SOA Governance Framework Technical Standard).

It is recommended that the team established to implement SOA be established as a Center of Excellence (CoE).

There are a number of SOA resources that should be considered when initially populating the Architecture Repository as described in The Open Group SOA Reference Architecture. These include:

- The Building Blocks of SOA, which describes a set of Architecture Building Blocks (ABBs) that represent the key elements of SOA
- A High-Level Perspective of the SOA Reference Architecture, which gives an overview of the nine layers of the reference architecture, with examples and rationale describing the main responsibilities of the layers and their primary building blocks
- Detailed Building Blocks of the SOA Reference Architecture, which presents detailed models that show how some of the features of SOA can be implemented using the reference architecture
- Infrastructure for SOA, which describes ABBs that correspond to infrastructure products that are available today to support service-oriented applications
- Industry SOA standards, such as the TeleManagement Forum Integration Framework

16.4.2   Phase A Vision

The high-level description produced in Phase A will reflect the service-oriented nature of the architecture that is envisaged. One obvious difference between an SOA architecture description and a description of an architecture of another style is the language. The SOA description uses different language, with words such as "policy", "composition", and "task", and it has different models, such as matrices showing use of services by business processes and use of applications by services. The Open Group SOA Ontology provides a taxonomy and ontology for SOA.

In an SOA project it is important to ensure that stakeholders understand the implications of SOA and are prepared for the organizational impacts of SOA services. This impact is applicable whether SOA services are made available as wrapped legacy applications, using exposed services on purchased products, bespoke services, Cloud Computing Software as a Service (SaaS), etc.

TOGAF provides guidance on the Content Metamodel entities that are key to SOA, and also describes extensions necessary to support SOA.

16.4.3 Phase B: Business Architecture

The starting point for the artifacts that are developed in this phase is the set of key business requirements identified in Phase A. The following artifacts shown in Table 19 should be considered for SOA because they contribute to the definition of SOA building blocks in Phase C and Phase D.

Table 19:   Summary of SOA-Specific Phase B Artifacts

Artifact	Purpose
Business Service Interaction Diagram	This shows all the business services in scope and their relations and the information flowing between the business services. It will indicate what business services are commonly re-used by other business services indicating opportunities for possible re-use of supporting IS services. This is also used to define business processes and the relationships between those business processes since each process is composed by a subset of this model.
Business Process Diagram	This is a set of diagrams that show the business processes and their decomposition, their interactions, and the information with which they are concerned.
Business Vocabulary Catalog	This is a list of the key terms used in describing the business processes and information. It is important that the Business Architecture phase establishes the information context for the software services, as described in the Information Architecture for SOA section of The Open Group SOA Source Book, and a catalog of business terms is an important part of this context. The business vocabulary can be derived while developing the business service model.
Business Services Catalog	This is a list of the enterprise's business services and their non-functional requirements. It is used to analyze the non-functional requirements
Business Service/Location Catalog	To understand where the Business Services need to be executed.
Event/Process Catalog	To understand which process is run in relation to an event.
Contract/Service Quality Catalog	To understand the non-functional properties of a contract.
Business Service Interaction Matrix	To show relations between Business Services.
Business Service/Information Matrix (CRUD)	To show how information elements are used by Business Services and to find faults in that model.
Information Component Model	To define the logical structure of the information in the organization. It can be used as an input to the exchange model defining the input and outputs from SOA services.

16.4.4   Phase C: Information Systems Architectures

SOA makes little difference to the Data Architecture sub-phase, but it has a major impact on the Applications Architecture. As well as affecting the artifacts that are developed, the views that are produced, the concerns that are discussed, and the requirements that are identified, SOA affects the way that the architect does the gap analysis between Baseline and Target Architectures in Phase C.

With SOA, the traditional software applications are replaced by sets of loosely-coupled services. Existing applications should still be described, as should any new applications of a traditional kind that are required, and these applications should be included in the applications portfolio. In addition, areas of application functionality that are covered by services should be identified. These will (probably as part of the implementation) be decomposed into services, which will be included in the services portfolio.

In each of Phases B, C, and D a gap analysis should be performed between the Baseline and Target Architectures to determine what needs to be done to move from the baseline to the target. For Phases B and D, and the Data Architecture sub-phase of Phase C, this is not much affected by SOA. For the Applications Architecture sub-phase of Phase C, however, SOA makes a difference to the way that the gap analysis is performed.

The ABBs defined in Phase C will include traditional applications and groups of services covering areas of application functionality. Both kinds of building block should be included in the gap analysis. However, it may be the intent that a group of services be implemented as a "wrapper" over existing applications. This situation, which is special for SOA, should be indicated in the gap analysis, as well as situations where old applications are to be removed or replaced, or new applications are to be added.

But SOA is not only about services, it is also the solutions created by using combinations of services. These solutions are usually structured using the Business Processes and Business Services defined in Phase B.

Table 20:   Summary of SOA-Specific Phase C Artifacts

Artifact	Purpose
IS Service Interaction Diagram	This shows requirements for potential SOA services (IS Services) and the interactions between them, and their use of information. It is used to show the full set of requirements for the solution and the relationships between the requirements.
Business Process/IS Service Matrix	This shows the relation between each Business Process and the IS Services supporting the process. It is used to show the full set of requirements for SOA services for a given Business Process.
IS Service Contract Catalog	This lists all IS Services, their Contracts, and the related Service Qualities to enable analysis of the non-functional requirements (e.g., security, performance, loading, availability, policies, etc.) for potential SOA Services. This catalog is an important input to the Service Portfolio Management process in SOA governance.
IS Service/Application (existing) Catalog	This catalog connects IS Services (potential SOA Services), Contracts, and Service Qualities with existing applications (as-is Physical Application Components). It is used to specify wrapping scenarios on existing applications and to analyze non-functional requirements.
IS Service/Data Entity Matrix	This matrix shows what data is handled by potential SOA Services (IS Services). It is used to identify potential data handling SOA Services.
Logical SOA Component Matrix	This matrix shows the relationship between the logical SOA Components (Logical Application Components) and the potential SOA Services (IS Services). It is used to structure Logical Components from the requirements.
Logical SOA Solution Diagram	This diagram shows the relations between the logical SOA components (Logical Application Components) and other logical solutions (Logical Application Components). It is used to show and analyze the functional and non-functional requirements of the interfaces between solutions.
Service Distribution Matrix	This matrix shows the services distributed on physical locations to fulfill legal or other requirements. The purpose is to show and analyze whether there are any location requirements on services. This can be done on either IS Services or Logical Application Components.

16.4.5   Phase D: Technology Architecture

For SOA, the Technology Architecture defines the software and hardware infrastructure needed to support the portfolio of services. A starting point for the Technology Architecture is The Open Group SOA Reference Architecture which contains most platform services possible for an SOA infrastructure. Each organization will need to customize the SOA Reference Architecture to their needs.

The Open Group has produced additional information concerning adapting an organization's infrastructure for service-orientation, including The Open Group Service-Oriented Infrastructure (SOI) Reference Model.

Using the artifacts (listed below), and SOI Reference Model, the architect should develop views that demonstrate to the stakeholders how their SOA-specific concerns relating to the Technology Architecture are addressed.

In doing this, the architect adds further requirements to those identified in Phases A, B, and C, and addresses the requirements that can be satisfied by the Technology Architecture. All architecture requirements should have been addressed by the end of this phase. If there are still outstanding architecture requirements, then it is necessary to go back to Phase B or Phase C to address them. Implementation requirements will be addressed by the projects that are identified in Phase E.

Table 21:   Summary of SOA-Specific Phase D Artifacts

Artifact	Purpose
Logical Technology Architecture Diagram	This diagram is used to show and analyze the instance of The Open Group SOA Reference Architecture. It will contain all ABBs and capabilities deemed necessary for the SOA Solution.
Logical Application and Technology Matrix	This matrix is used to show and analyze the relations between the Logical Application Components and the Logical Technology Components to ensure the architect understands what technology will be used for the Logical Application Components. It will also be used to derive and validate the non-functional requirements for the technology components.

16.4.6   Phase E: Opportunities and Solutions

The identification of SOA solutions is a key task for SOA. The questions of what SOA solutions the enterprise will have, and how they will be managed, should be considered in this phase.

Solution delivery options are normally considered as part of this phase. A delivery option that should be considered particularly for SOA is the use of services provided by external companies, as opposed to the development of services in-house or the acquisition of software products that perform the services.

Table 22: Summary of SOA-Specific Phase E Artifacts

Artifact	Purpose
Physical SOA Solution Matrix	This matrix shows the relationship between the physical SOA solutions (Physical Application Components) and the Logical SOA Components. It is used to define the physical structure of the SOA solution.
Physical SOA Solution Diagram	This diagram shows the relations between the physical SOA solution (Physical Application Components) and other solutions (Physical Application Components). It is used to show and analyze the functional and non-functional requirements of the interfaces between solutions.
Physical Service Solution Matrix	This matrix shows which existing services are re-used, which services could be provided by external services (SaaS), and which services need to be developed as wrappings of new/existing applications and which need to be developed. It is an input to the SOA Governance Service Portfolio Management process.
Application Guidelines	This document provides guidelines on how to develop SOA solutions and services. Suggestions of possible guidelines can be found in Appendix A of The Open Group SOA Governance Framework.
Physical Technology Architecture Diagram	This diagram is used to show and analyze the physical technical solution for the SOA infrastructure.
Physical Application and Technology Matrix	This matrix is used to show and analyze the physical infrastructure used to run the physical application and to ensure that the non-functional requirements are derived properly and understood.
Technology Portfolio Catalog	This is a list of products and kinds of product that will be used in the implementation, including SOA run-time infrastructure, SOA development environment, service component technology, and service interface (portal, channel, etc.) technology. It will also include non-functional requirements.
Technology Guidelines	This document provides guidelines on how to use SOA infrastructure. Suggestions of possible guidelines can be found in Appendix A of The Open Group SOA Governance Framework.

The implementation projects that are identified, and the implementation and migration strategy, will depend on the decisions taken on the level of detail of implementation specification when the architect team scoped the architecture development in Phase A.

16.4.7 Phase F: Migration Planning

The Implementation Governance Model is reviewed in Phase F in order to ensure that it is in place before the next phase – Implementation Governance – commences. SOA requires particular governance rules and procedures. The governance and support strategy is reviewed in the Preliminary Phase. If it needs to be updated for SOA, then this should be done before implementation starts.

16.4.8 Phase G: Implementation Governance

The activities performed in the Implementation Governance phase will depend in part on the decisions taken on the level of detail of implementation specification when the architect team scoped the architecture development in Phase A. During the Implementation Governance phase, the monitoring part of the SOA Governance Vitality Method (from The Open Group SOA Governance Framework Technical Standard) should be put in operation to ensure that the SOA governance activities are performed at the correct level.

16.4.9 Phase H: Architecture Change Management

It is at this point that the architect should determine whether it is necessary to revisit the Preliminary Phase to adjust the Architecture Capability. Where SOA has not previously been used within an enterprise, Phase H of an architecture development is an opportunity to assess the contribution that SOA could make, and to consider adopting the principle of service-orientation.

16.5 Summary

The use of SOA as an architectural style is intended to simplify the business, including interoperation of parts of the business. Enterprise architecture can be used to support SOA by providing a set of tools and techniques to address many of the non-technical challenges associated with SOA adoption. TOGAF provides guidance and a set of resources for adapting the ADM for SOA development.

16.6 **Recommended Reading**

The following are recommended sources of further information for this chapter:

- TOGAF 9 Part III, Chapter 22 (Using TOGAF to Define & Govern SOAs)
- The SOA Source Book
- The Open Group Service Integration Maturity Model (OSIMM)
- The Open Group SOA Governance Framework

PART 3

The Architecture Content Framework

In this Part, we introduce the Architecture Content Framework and high-level concepts of the TOGAF Content Metamodel. The Content Framework describes the relationships between all the concepts in an enterprise architecture.

Architecture Content Framework

17.1 Key Learning Points

This chapter will help you understand the TOGAF Architecture Content Framework and the high-level concepts of the TOGAF Content Metamodel.

Key Points Explained

Upon completion of this chapter you should be able to:

1. Explain the purpose of the Architecture Content Framework
2. Describe the relationship between the Architecture Content Framework and the TOGAF ADM
3. Describe the main components of the TOGAF Content Metamodel
4. Describe the core metamodel concepts
5. Explain the purpose of dividing the metamodel into core and extensions
6. Describe the key concepts related to the core metamodel entities

---

17.2 Introduction

(Syllabus Reference: Unit 5, Learning Outcome 1: You should be able to explain the purpose of the Architecture Content Framework.)

The Architecture Content Framework provides a detailed model of architectural work products, including deliverables, artifacts within deliverables, and the Architecture Building Blocks (ABBs) that deliverables represent. It helps to improve the consistency of the TOGAF outputs by presenting outputs in a consistent and structured way, and also helps to reference and classify them.

The benefits of using the Architecture Content Framework include that it provides a comprehensive checklist of architecture outputs, it promotes better integration of work products, and provides a detailed open standard for how architectures should be described.

Using TOGAF with Other Content Frameworks

The Architecture Content Framework provided in TOGAF 9 allows TOGAF to be used as a stand-alone framework for architecture within an enterprise. However, other content frameworks exist and it is expected that some enterprises may opt to use an external framework in conjunction with the ADM instead. In these cases, the TOGAF Architecture Content Framework provides a useful reference and starting point for TOGAF content to be mapped to the metamodels of other frameworks.

17.3 The Content Framework and the TOGAF ADM

(Syllabus Reference: Unit 5, Learning Outcome 3: You should be able to describe the relationship between the Architecture Content Framework and the TOGAF ADM.)

The ADM addresses a business need through a process of vision, definition, planning, and governance. At each stage the ADM takes information as inputs and creates outputs. The content framework provides a structure for the ADM that defines inputs and outputs in detail and puts each deliverable into the context of the architecture. So the content framework is a companion to the ADM. The ADM describes what needs to be done to create an architecture and the content framework describes what it should look like in the end.

17.4 Why do we Need a Metamodel?

The use of models helps to simplify complex subjects, such as an enterprise, to make them simpler to understand. A content metamodel is used to formalize the definition of an enterprise architecture, structuring architectural information in an ordered way so that it can be processed to meet the stakeholder needs, which aids communication and understanding.

The majority of architecture stakeholders do not actually need to know what the architecture metamodel is and are only concerned with specific issues, such as the functionality that the application supports, or the processes which will be impacted by the project. In order to meet the needs of these stakeholders, the TOGAF concepts of building blocks, catalogs, matrices, and diagrams are used. A content metamodel can also formalize the relationship between objects, allowing for traceability. Most importantly it can be used as a data schema mapping for enterprise architecture tools.

What is a Metamodel?
A model that describes how and with what the architecture will be described in a structured way.
[Source: TOGAF 9.1 Part I, Chapter 3 (Definitions)]

17.5 Components of the Content Metamodel

(Syllabus Reference: Unit 5, Learning Outcome 2: You should be able to describe the main components of the Content Metamodel.)

The Architecture Content Framework is based on a standard content metamodel that defines all the types of building blocks in an architecture, showing how these building blocks can be described and how they relate to one another. For example, when creating an architecture, an architect will identify applications, data entities held within applications, and technologies that implement those applications. These applications will in turn support particular groups of business users or actors, and will be used to fulfill business services. The content metamodel identifies all of these concerns (i.e., application, data entity, technology, actor, and business service), shows the relationships that are possible between them (e.g., actors consume business services), and identifies artifacts that can be used to represent them.

Figure 23 shows the highest level abstraction of the TOGAF Content Metamodel, which closely corresponds to the ADM.

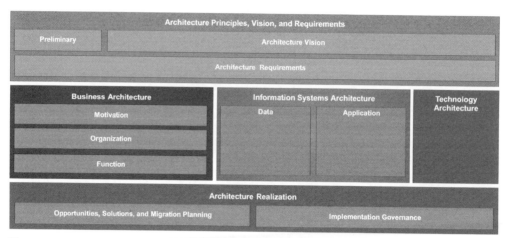

Figure 23:   Content Metamodel Simplified

The metamodel can be thought of as having three layers as follows:

Layer 1: Architecture Principles, Vision, and Requirements

The artifacts in this layer are intended to capture the surrounding context of formal architecture models, including general architecture principles, strategic context that forms input for architecture modeling, and requirements generated from the architecture. The architecture context is typically collected in the Preliminary and Architecture Vision phases.

Layer 2: The Architecture Domains

Business Architecture artifacts capture architectural models of business operation, looking specifically at factors that motivate the enterprise, how the enterprise is organizationally structured, and also what functional capabilities the enterprise has.

Information Systems Architecture artifacts capture architecture models of IT systems, looking at applications and data in line with the TOGAF ADM phases.

Technology Architecture artifacts capture procured technology assets that are used to implement and realize information system solutions.

Layer 3: Architecture Realization

The artifacts in this layer capture change roadmaps showing the transition between architecture states and binding statements that are used to steer and govern an implementation of the architecture.

Figure 24 shows a more detailed representation of the content metamodel. Further detailed diagrams including the detailed relationships are provided in TOGAF 9 Part IV: Architecture Content Framework.

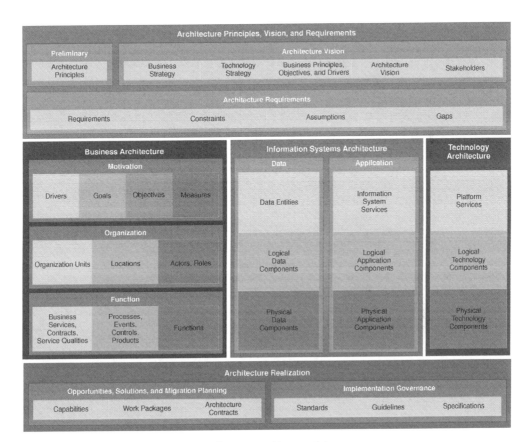

Figure 24:   Detailed Representation of the Content Metamodel

17.6 Core Metamodel Concepts

(Syllabus Reference: Unit 7, Learning Outcome 1: You should be able to describe the Core Metamodel Concepts.)

A TOGAF architecture is based on defining ABBs within architecture catalogs, specifying the relationships between those building blocks in architecture matrices, and presenting communication diagrams that show in a precise way what the architecture is. The core concepts that make up the content metamodel are described in the following subsections.

17.6.1 Core and Extension Content

(Syllabus Reference: Unit 7, Learning Outcome 2: You should be able to describe the purpose of dividing the metamodel into core and extensions.)

In order for TOGAF to be usable in many different scenarios and situations, it is necessary to provide both a fully featured enterprise architecture metamodel for content and also the ability to avoid carrying out unnecessary activities. The metamodel supports this through partitioning into Core and Extension content, as shown in Figure 25, with the Core Content designed not to be altered.

Figure 25:   Core Content Metamodel and its Extensions

The Core Content Metamodel provides a minimum set of architectural content to support traceability across artifacts. Additional metamodel concepts to support more specific or more in-depth modeling are contained within a set of extensions that logically group together extension catalogs, matrices, and diagrams.

All extension modules are optional and should be selected during the Preliminary Phase of the architecture development to meet the needs of the organization. Additionally, the extension groupings described by the content metamodel are only a suggestion and further tailoring may be carried out to suit specific needs at the discretion of the architects.

This Core Content and Extension concept is intended as a move towards supporting formal method extension approaches within TOGAF, such as the method plug-in concept found within the Software Process Engineering Metamodel (SPEM) developed by the Object Management Group (OMG).

17.6.2 Core Metamodel Entities

(Syllabus Reference: Unit 7, Learning Outcome 3: You should be able to describe the key concepts related to the core metamodel entities.)

The content metamodel uses the core terms listed in Table 23 to describe metamodel entities.

Table 23:   Core Metamodel Entit

Entity	Description
Actor	A person, organization, or system that is outside the consideration of the architecture model, but interacts with it.
Application Component	An encapsulation of application functionality that is aligned to implementation structuring.
Business Service	Supports business capabilities through an explicitly defined interface and is explicitly governed by an organization.
Data Entity	An encapsulation of data that is recognized by a business domain expert as a discrete concept. Data entities can be tied to applications, repositories, and services and may be structured according to implementation considerations.
Function	Delivers business capabilities closely aligned to an organization, but not explicitly governed by the organization.
Information System Service	The automated elements of a business service. An information system service may deliver or support part or all of one or more business services.
Organization Unit	A self-contained unit of resources with goals, objectives, and measures. Organization units may include external parties and business partner organizations.
Platform Service	A technical capability required to provide enabling infrastructure that supports the delivery of applications.
Role	An actor assumes a role to perform a task.
Technology Component	An encapsulation of technology infrastructure that represents a class of technology product or specific technology product.

The relationships between these core metamodel entities are summarized as follows:

- **Process should normally be used to describe flow**. A process is a flow of interactions between functions and services and cannot be physically deployed. All processes should describe the flow of execution for a function and therefore the deployment of a process is through the function it supports; i.e., an application implements a function that has a process.

- **Function describes units of business capability at all levels of granularity**. The term function is used to describe a unit of business capability at all levels of granularity, encapsulating terms such as value chain, process area, capability, business function, etc. Any bounded unit of business function should be described as a function.

- **Business services support organizational objectives and are defined at a level of granularity consistent with the level of governance needed**. A business service operates as a boundary for one or more functions. The granularity of business services is dependent on the focus and emphasis of the business (as reflected by its drivers, goals, and objectives). A service in Service Oriented Architecture (SOA) terminology (i.e., a deployable unit of application functionality) is actually much closer to an application service, application component, or technology component, which may implement or support a business service.

- **Business services are deployed onto application components**. Business services may be realized by business activity that does not relate to IT, or may be supported by IT. Business services that are supported by IT are deployed onto application components. Application components can be hierarchically decomposed and may support one or more business services. It is possible for a business service to be supported by multiple application components, but this is problematic from a governance standpoint and is symptomatic of business services that are too coarse-grained, or application components that are too fine-grained.

- **Application components are deployed onto technology components**. An application component is implemented by a suite of technology components. For example, an application, such as "HR System", would typically be implemented on several technology components, including hardware, application server software, and application services.

17.6.3 Building Blocks, Catalogs, Matrices, and Diagrams

In order to meet the needs of most stakeholders who do not need to know what the TOGAF Content Metamodel is, the TOGAF concepts of building blocks, catalogs, matrices, and diagrams are used.

Building blocks are entities of a particular type within the metamodel (for example, a business service called "Purchase Order"). Building blocks carry metadata according to the metamodel, which supports query and analysis. For example, business services have a metadata attribute for *owner*, which allows a stakeholder to query all business services owned by a particular organization. Building blocks may also include dependent or contained entities as appropriate to the context of the architecture (e.g., a business service called "Purchase Order" may implicitly include a number of processes, data entities, application components, etc.).

Catalogs are lists of building blocks of a specific type, or of related types, that are used for governance or reference purposes (e.g., an organization chart, showing locations and actors). As with building blocks, catalogs carry metadata according to the metamodel, which supports query and analysis. Matrices are grids that show relationships between two or more model entities. Matrices are used to represent relationships that are list-based rather than graphical (e.g., a CRUD matrix showing which applications Create, Read, Update, and Delete a particular type of data is difficult to represent visually).

Diagrams are renderings of architectural content in a graphical format. Diagrams can be used as a technique for graphically populating architecture content or for checking the completeness of information that has been collected. TOGAF defines a set of architecture diagrams to be created (e.g., organization chart). Each of these diagrams may be created several times for an architecture with different styles or content coverage to suit stakeholder concerns.

Building blocks, catalogs, matrices, and diagrams are all concepts that are well supported by leading enterprise architecture tools. In environments where tools are used to model the architecture, such tools typically support mechanisms to search, filter, and query the Architecture Repository. The interactions are summarized in Figure 26.

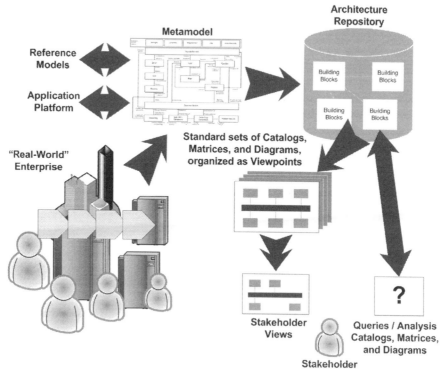

Figure 26:   Interactions between Metamodel, Building Blocks, Matrices, Diagrams, and Stakeholders

17.7 **Summary**

The Architecture Content Framework presents outputs in a consistent and structured way. It has three categories of work products: deliverables, artifacts, and building blocks. There is a mapping from the Architecture Content Framework to the TOGAF ADM phases.

The TOGAF Content Metamodel is used to structure architectural information in a particular way. A metamodel is a precise definition of the constructs and rules needed for creating models. The TOGAF Metamodel has both a core and a set of extension modules.

17.8 Exercises

Exercise 17-1

You are establishing a Content Metamodel for your organization based on the TOGAF Content Framework. Which extensions would be most appropriate for the following scenarios:

- The organization has to comply with several statutory regulations on how it handles customer data.
- The organization is taking its first steps to develop an enterprise architecture.
- The organization is merging with a competitor and needs to consolidate its service offerings.

17.9 Recommended Reading

The following are recommended sources of further information for this chapter:

- TOGAF 9 Part IV, Chapter 33 (Introduction)
- TOGAF 9 Part IV, Chapter 34 (Content Metamodel)
- TOGAF 9 Architecture Content Metamodel Overview presentation: www.togaf.info/sg04

PART 4

The Enterprise Continuum

In this Part, we examine the Enterprise Continuum in more depth:

- Chapter 18 describes Architecture Partitioning.
- Chapter 19 describes the Architecture Repository, which is a model for a physical instance of the Enterprise Continuum.

Recommended reading before commencing this part of the Study Guide includes:

- TOGAF 9 Foundation Study Guide, Chapter 6, The Enterprise Continuum and Tools

Chapter 18

Architecture Partitioning

18.1 Key Learning Points

The purpose of this chapter is to help you understand how architecture partitioning can be used to simplify the development and maintenance of an enterprise architecture.

> **Key Points Explained**
>
> Upon completion of this chapter you should be able to:
>
> 1. Describe the purpose of Architecture Partitioning
> 2. Describe the classification criteria for solutions and architectures when considering partitioning
> 3. Describe how Architecture Partitioning can be employed in the Preliminary Phase of the ADM

18.2 Introduction

(Syllabus Reference: Unit 21, Learning Outcome 1: You should be able to describe the purpose of Architecture Partitioning.)

The main purpose of Architecture Partitioning is to manage complexity by simplifying the development and management of the enterprise architecture. Architectures are partitioned in order to:

- **Manage Complexity**: Addressing all problems within a single architecture can be too complicated.
- **Manage Conflicts**: Different organizational unit architectures conflict with one another.
- **Manage Parallel Developments**: Different teams need to work on different elements of architecture at the same time and partitions allow for specific groups of architects to own and develop specific segments of the architecture.

- **Manage Re-use**: Effective architecture re-use requires modular architecture segments that can be taken and incorporated into broader architectures and solutions.

18.3 Applying Classification to Partitioned Architectures

(Syllabus Reference: Unit 21, Learning Outcome 2: You should be able to describe the classification criteria for solutions and architectures when considering partitioning.)

The following classification criteria can be used to support solution partitioning:

- **Subject Matter (Breadth)**: Solutions are naturally organized into groups to support operational management and control. Examples of solution partitions according to subject matter would include applications, departments, divisions, products, services, service centers, sites, etc. Solution decomposition by subject matter is typically the fundamental technique for structuring both solutions and the architectures that represent them.
- **Time**: Solution lifecycles are typically organized around a timeline, which allows the impact of solution development, introduction, operation, and retirement to be managed against other business activity occurring in similar time periods.
- **Maturity/Volatility**: The maturity and volatility of a solution will typically impact the speed of execution required for the solution lifecycle. Additionally, volatility and maturity will shape investment priorities. Solutions existing in highly volatile environments may be better suited to rapid, agile development techniques.

The following classification criteria can be used to support partitioning of architectures:

- **Depth**: The level of detail within an architecture has a strong correlation to the stakeholder groups that will be interested in the architecture. Typically less detailed architectures will be of interest to executive stakeholders. As architectures increase in detail, their relevance to implementation and operational personnel will also increase.

The following characteristics are generally not used to partition an Architecture Landscape:

- Architectures used to describe the Architecture Landscape are generally not abstract.
- Solution volatility generally prevents architectures from being defined that are far in the future. Volatility also reduces the accuracy of historic architectures over time, as the organization changes and adapts to new circumstances.

Using the classification criteria above, architectures can be grouped into partitions.

18.4 Applying Partitioning to the ADM

(Syllabus Reference: Unit 21, Learning Outcome 7: You should be able to describe how Architecture Partitioning can be employed in the Preliminary Phase of the ADM.)

The key objective of the Preliminary Phase is to establish the Architecture Capability for the enterprise. In practical terms this activity will require the establishment of a number of architecture partitions, with defined boundaries and ownership.

Generally speaking, each team carrying out architecture activity within the enterprise will own one or more architecture partitions and will execute the ADM to define, govern, and realize their architectures. If more than one team is expected to work on a single architecture, this can become problematic, as the precise responsibilities of each team are difficult to establish. For this reason, it is preferable to apply partitioning to the architecture until each architecture has one owning team.

Steps within the Preliminary Phase to support architecture partitioning are as follows:
- Determine the organization structure for architecture within the enterprise and identify the teams. For each team, establish appropriate boundaries including:
  - Subject matter areas
  - Level of detail
  - Time periods
  - Stakeholders

- Determine the responsibilities for each architecture team. This step
  applies partitioning logic to the enterprise architecture in order to firstly
  identify the scope of each team and secondly to partition the architecture
  under the remit of a single team. Once complete, this step should
  have partitioned the entire scope of the enterprise and should have
  assigned responsibility for each partitioned architecture to a single team.
  Partitioning should create a definition of each architecture that includes:
  - Subject matter areas
  - Level of detail
  - Time period
  - Stakeholders
- Determine the relationships between architectures by considering where
  the architectures overlap and the compliance requirements between
  architectures. This step allows governance relationships to be formalized
  and also shows where artifacts from an architecture are expected to be
  re-used within other architectures.

Once the Preliminary Phase is complete, the teams conducting the
architecture should be defined. Each team should have a defined scope and
the relationships between teams and architecture should be understood. An
example of an allocation of teams to architecture is shown in Figure 27.

Figure 27:   Allocation of Teams to Architecture Scope

18.5 Summary

TOGAF provides guidance on classifying and partitioning architectures. The use of partitioning can be beneficial to manage complexity, allow for parallel developments, and facilitate re-use.

18.6 Recommended Reading

The following are recommended sources of further information for this chapter:

- TOGAF 9 Part IV, Chapter 33 (Introduction)
- TOGAF 9 Part IV, Chapter 34 (Content Metamodel)

Architecture Repository

19.1 Key Learning Points

The purpose of this chapter is to help you understand the Architecture Repository, its constituent parts, and its relationship to other parts of TOGAF.

> **Key Points Explained**
>
> Upon completion of this chapter you should be able to:
>
> 1. Explain the relationship between the Architecture Repository and the Enterprise Repository
> 2. Describe the purpose of the repository areas that hold the outputs of projects, specifically:
>   - Architecture Landscape
>   - Reference Library
>   - Standards Information Base
>   - Governance Log

19.2 Introduction

(Syllabus Reference: Unit 22, Learning Outcome 1: You should be able to explain the relationship between the Architecture Repository and the Enterprise Repository.)

Operating a mature architecture capability within a large enterprise creates a huge volume of architectural output. Effective management and leverage of these architectural products requires a formal taxonomy for different types of architectural assets, alongside dedicated processes and tools for architectural content storage.

This section of TOGAF provides a structural framework for an Architecture Repository that allows an enterprise to distinguish between different types of architectural assets that exist at different levels of abstraction in the organization.

This Architecture Repository is one part of the wider Enterprise Repository. While the Architecture Repository holds information concerning the enterprise architecture and associated artifacts there are a number of enterprise repositories that support the architecture. These include the Requirements Repository for requirements and the Solutions Repository for Solution Building Blocks (SBBs) as shown in Figure 28. The Architecture Repository also provides the capability to link architectural assets to components of the Detailed Design, Deployment, and Service Management Repositories.

19.3 The Repository in Detail

(Syllabus Reference: Unit 22, Learning Outcome 2: You should be able to describe the purpose of the repository areas that hold outputs of projects.)

The Architecture Repository is a logical information store for outputs of executing the ADM and is shown in Figure 28.

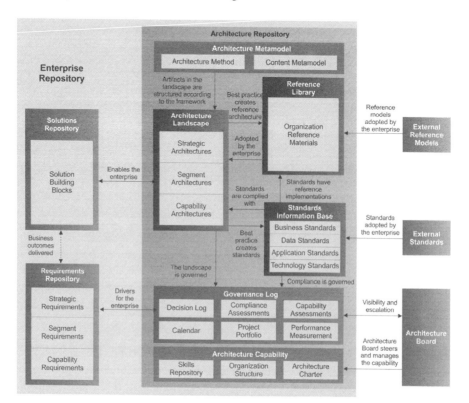

Figure 28:   The Architecture Repository

19.3.1 Architecture Metamodel

The Architecture Metamodel describes the Architecture Framework in use within the enterprise.

19.3.2 Architecture Landscape

(Syllabus Reference: Unit 22, Learning Outcome 2.1: You should be able to describe the purpose of the Architecture Landscape.)

The Architecture Landscape shows the state of the operating enterprise at particular points in time. Due to the sheer volume and the diverse stakeholder needs throughout an entire enterprise, the Architecture Landscape is divided into three levels of granularity:

1. **Strategic Architectures** show a long-term summary view of the entire enterprise. Strategic Architectures provide an organizing framework for operational and change activity and allow for direction setting at an executive level.
2. **Segment Architectures** provide more detailed operating models for areas within an enterprise. Segment Architectures can be used at the program or portfolio level to organize and operationally align more detailed change activity.
3. **Capability Architectures** show in a more detailed fashion how the enterprise can support a particular unit of capability. Capability Architectures are used to provide an overview of current capability, target capability, and capability increments and allow for individual work packages and projects to be grouped within managed portfolios and programs.

19.3.3 Reference Library

(Syllabus Reference: Unit 22, Learning Outcome 2.2: You should be able to describe the purpose of the Reference Library.)

The Reference Library contains re-usable architecture work products. The Reference Library provides a repository area to hold reference materials that should be used to develop architectures. Reference materials held may be obtained from a variety of sources, including standards bodies, product and service vendors, industry communities or forums, standard templates, and enterprise best practice. The Reference Library should contain reference architectures, reference models, a viewpoint library, and templates.

In order to segregate different classes of architecture reference materials, the Reference Library can use the Architecture Continuum as a method for classification.

19.3.4 Standards Information Base

(Syllabus Reference: Unit 22, Learning Outcome 2.3: You should be able to describe the purpose of the Standards Information Base.)

The Standards Information Base defines the compliance criteria for work governed by architecture. It is a repository area to hold the set of specifications to which architectures must conform.

Establishment of a Standards Information Base provides an unambiguous basis for architectural governance since the standards are easily accessible to projects and therefore the obligations of the project can be understood and planned for. Also standards are stated in a clear and unambiguous manner, so that compliance can be objectively assessed.

19.3.5 Governance Log

(Syllabus Reference: Unit 22, Learning Outcome 2.4: You should be able to describe the purpose of the Governance Log.)

The Governance Log is a repository area for holding shared information relating to the ongoing governance of projects, capturing results of governance activity such as compliance assessments. Maintaining a shared repository of governance information is important because decisions made during projects (such as standards deviations or the rationale for a particular architectural approach) need to be accessed on an ongoing basis. For example, if a system is to be replaced, having sight of the key architectural decisions that shaped the initial implementation is highly valuable, as it will highlight constraints that may otherwise be obscured. Also, many stakeholders are interested in the outcome of project governance (e.g., other projects, customers of the project, the Architecture Board, etc.).

19.3.6 Architecture Capability

The Architecture Capability describes the organization, roles, skills, and responsibilities of the enterprise architecture practice.

19.4 Relationship to Other Parts of TOGAF

The ADM has reminders regarding when to use assets from the Architecture Repository. The Architecture Repository is a model for an implementation of the Enterprise Continuum.

19.5 Summary

TOGAF provides a structural framework for a repository that is one part of a wider Enterprise IT Repository. The Architecture Repository is a logical information store for the outputs which result from executing the ADM and for inputs to it. It is a model for a physical instance of the Enterprise Continuum.

19.6 Recommended Reading

The following are recommended sources of further information for this chapter:

- TOGAF 9 Part V, Chapter 41 (Architecture Repository)

PART 5

TOGAF Reference Models

In this Part, we describe the two reference models provided with TOGAF:
the Technical Reference Model and the Integrated Information Infrastructure
Reference Model.

Recommended reading before commencing this part of the Study Guide
includes:

- TOGAF 9 Foundation Study Guide, Chapter 13, TOGAF Reference
  Models

The Technical Reference Model (TRM)

20.1 Key Learning Points

This chapter describes the TOGAF Technical Reference Model (TRM) in detail.

Key Points Explained

Upon completion of this chapter you should be able to:

1. Explain the TRM graphic, including the following key elements:
   - Application Software Categories
   - Application Platform Interface
   - Application Platform
   - Communications Infrastructure Interface
   - Qualities
2. Briefly describe the structure of the TRM
3. Briefly explain the main architecture objectives of using the TRM
4. Explain what the Platform Services Taxonomy is
5. Explain what the Service Quality Taxonomy is
6. Explain how to customize the TRM to meet an organization's specific needs

---

20.2 Structure of the TRM

(Syllabus Reference: Unit 12, Learning Outcome 2: You should be able to briefly describe the structure of the TRM.)

The TRM has two main components:

1. A *taxonomy* that defines terminology, and provides a coherent description of the components and conceptual structure of an information system
2. A model, with an associated *TRM graphic*, that provides a visual representation of the taxonomy, as an aid to understanding

Figure 29 shows the high-level model of the TRM. The three main parts of the TRM (Application Software, Application Platform, and Communications Infrastructure) are connected by two interfaces (Application Platform Interface and Communications Infrastructure Interface).

Figure 29:   Technical Reference Model – High-Level Model View

(Syllabus Reference: Unit 12, Learning Outcome 3: You should be able to briefly explain the main architectural objectives of using the TRM.)

The use of the TRM emphasizes two major common architecture objectives:

1. **Application Portability**, via the Application Platform Interface, identifying the set of services that are to be made available in a standard way to applications via the platform
2. **Interoperability**, via the Communications Infrastructure Interface, identifying the set of Communications Infrastructure services that are to be built on in a standard way

20.3 The TRM in Detail

(Syllabus Reference: Unit 12, Learning Outcome 1: You should be able to explain the TRM graphic.)

Figure 30 shows the detail of the TRM. This highlights the platform service categories together with the external environment entities, such as Applications and Communications Infrastructure.

Figure 30:   Detailed Technical Reference Model (Showing Service Categories)

The following sections look at various elements from the TRM.

20.3.1 Application Software

(Syllabus Reference: Unit 12, Learning Outcome 1.1: You should be able to explain Application Software Categories within the TRM.)

The TRM recognizes two categories of Application Software:
1. **Business Applications**, which implement business processes for an enterprise or vertical industry. These are specific to the enterprise or vertical industry. The internal structure of business applications relates closely to the specific Application Software configuration selected by an organization. Examples of business applications include patient record management services used in the medical industry, inventory management services used in the retail industry, geological data modeling services used in the petroleum industry, etc.

2. **Infrastructure Applications**, which provide general-purpose business functionality, based on infrastructure services. This is usually widespread commercial off-the-shelf (COTS) software, where it is uneconomic to consider custom implementation. Examples of applications in this category include electronic payment and funds transfer services, electronic mail client services, calendaring and scheduling services, spreadsheet, presentation and document editing software, etc.

20.3.2 Application Platform Interface

(Syllabus Reference: Unit 12, Learning Outcome 1.2: You should be able to explain the Application Software Interface within the TRM.)

The Application Platform Interface specifies a complete interface between the Application Software and the underlying Application Platform across which all services are provided. A rigorous definition of the interface results in application portability, provided that both platform and application conform to it. For this to work, the API definition must include the syntax and semantics of not just the programmatic interface, but also all necessary protocol and data structure definitions.

20.3.3 Application Platform

(Syllabus Reference: Unit 12, Learning Outcome 1.3: You should be able to explain the Application Platform within the TRM.)

The Application Platform is a single conceptual entity that includes Operating System Services, Network Services, and a generic set of platform services. This is the set of all possible services. A specific Target Architecture will contain only those services needed to support the required function. A typical architecture will also contain several Application Platforms; for example, a desktop client, file server, print server, internet server, database server, etc, each of which comprises a specific set of services to support the defined functionality.

20.3.4 Interfaces between Services

In addition to supporting Application Software through the Application Platform Interface (API), services in the Application Platform may support each other, either by openly specified interfaces or by private, unexposed interfaces. A key goal of architecture development is for service modules to be capable of replacement by other modules providing the same service functionality via the same service API.

20.3.5 Communications Infrastructure

The Communications Infrastructure provides the basic services to interconnect systems and provide the basic mechanisms for opaque transfer of data. It contains the hardware and software elements which make up the networking and physical communications links used by a system, and all the other systems connected to the network. It deals with the complex world of networks and the physical Communications Infrastructure, including switches, service providers, and the physical transmission media.

20.3.6 Communications Infrastructure Interface

(Syllabus Reference: Unit 12, Learning Outcome 1.4: You should be able to explain the Communications Infrastructure Interface within the TRM.)

The Communications Infrastructure Interface is the interface between the Application Platform and the Communications Infrastructure.

20.3.7 Qualities

(Syllabus Reference: Unit 12, Learning Outcome 1.5: You should be able to explain Qualities within the TRM.)

Besides the set of components making up the TRM, there is also a set of attributes that are termed "qualities" that apply across all components. Examples of qualities, which typically must apply through all elements of an architecture, include manageability and security. Qualities are specified in detail during the development of a Target Architecture. Some qualities are easier than others to describe in terms of standards. For instance, support for a set of locales can be defined to be part of the specification for the international operation quality. Other qualities can better be specified in terms of measures rather than standards (e.g., performance).

20.4 Taxonomy of Application Platform Services

(Syllabus Reference: Unit 12, Learning Outcome 4: You should be able to explain what the Platform Services Taxonomy is.)

The taxonomy of Platform Services provides a coherent description of an information system and is widely accepted as a useful, consistent structured definition of the Application Platform entity. It consists of a number of components termed "service categories", with further services defined within each category (see Table 24).

The taxonomy of the TOGAF TRM can be used in structuring a Standards Information Base, and is used in the database of standards maintained by The Open Group.[9]

Table 24:   TRM Service Categories

Service Category	Description
Data Interchange Services	Data Interchange Services provide specialized support for the interchange of information between applications and the external environment. These services are designed to handle data interchange between applications on the same platform and applications on different (heterogeneous) platforms.
Data Management Services	Data Management Services provide for the management of data independently of the processes that create or use it, allow data to be maintained indefinitely, and shared among many processes.
Graphics and Imaging Services	Graphics and Imaging Services provide functions required for creating, storing, retrieving, and manipulating images.
International Operation Services	International Operation Services provide a set of services and interfaces that allow a user to define, select, and change between different culturally-related application environments supported by the particular implementation.
Location and Directory Services	Location and Directory Services provide specialized support for locating required resources and for mediation between service consumers and service providers.

---

9   Refer to www.opengroup.org/sib.

Service Category	Description
Network Services	Network Services are provided to support distributed applications requiring data access and applications interoperability in heterogeneous or homogeneous networked environments.
Object-Oriented Provision of Services	This section shows how services are provided in an object-oriented manner. "Object Services" does not appear as a category in the TRM since all the individual object services are incorporated as appropriate in the other service categories.
Operating System Services	Operating System Services are responsible for the management of platform resources, including the processor, memory, files, and input and output. They generally shield applications from the implementation details of the machine.
Security Services	Security Services are necessary to protect sensitive information in the information system. The appropriate level of protection is determined based upon the value of the information to the business end users and the perception of threats to it.
Software Engineering Services	Software Engineering Services provide the tools for professional system developers appropriate to the development and maintenance of applications.
System and Network Management Services	System and Network Management Services provide for managing a wide variety of diverse resources of information systems.
Transaction Processing Services	Transaction Processing Services provide support for the online processing of information in discrete units called transactions, with assurance of the state of the information at the end of the transaction.
User Interface Services	User Interface Services define how users may interact with an application.

A detailed description of the Service Categories and services within each is given in TOGAF 9 Part VI, Chapter 43 (Foundation Architecture: Technical Reference Model).

20.5 Taxonomy of Application Platform Service Qualities

((Syllabus Reference: Unit 12, Learning Outcome 5: You should be able to explain what the Service Quality Taxonomy is.)

A service quality describes behaviour such as adaptability or manageability. Service qualities have a pervasive effect on the operation of most or all of the functional service categories.

> **Qualities**
>
> Qualities are referred to as "non-functional requirements" elsewhere.
> During the process of architecture development, the architect must be aware of the required or desired qualities and the extent of their influence on the choice of software building blocks used in implementing the architecture. The best way of making sure that qualities are not forgotten is to create a quality matrix, describing the relationships between each functional service and the qualities that influence it.

The service qualities presently identified in the TRM taxonomy are:

- **Availability** (the degree to which something is available for use), including:
  - **Manageability**, the ability to gather information about the state of something and to control it
  - **Serviceability**, the ability to identify problems and take corrective action, such as to repair or upgrade a component in a running system
  - **Performance**, the ability of a component to perform its tasks in an appropriate time
  - **Reliability**, resistance to failure
  - **Recoverability**, the ability to restore a system to a working state after an interruption
  - **Locatability**, the ability of a system to be found when needed
- **Assurance**, including:
  - **Security**, the protection of information from unauthorized access
  - **Integrity**, the assurance that data has not been corrupted
  - **Credibility**, the level of trust in the integrity of the system and its data

- **Usability** (ease-of-operation by users), including:
  - International Operation, including multi-lingual and multi-cultural abilities
- **Adaptability**, including:
  - **Interoperability**, whether within or outside the organization (for instance, interoperability of calendaring or scheduling functions may be key to the usefulness of a system)
  - **Scalability**, the ability of a component to grow or shrink its performance or capacity appropriately to the demands of the environment in which it operates
  - **Portability**, of data, people, applications, and components
  - **Extensibility**, the ability to accept new functionality
  - The ability to offer access to services in new paradigms such as object-orientation, or web-services

20.6 Using the TRM

(Syllabus Reference: Unit 12, Learning Outcome 6: You should be able to explain how to customize the TRM to meet an organization's specific needs.)

When building an architecture, users of TOGAF should assess their requirements and select the services, interfaces, and standards that satisfy their business needs. The objective of the TRM is to facilitate definition of the standardized Application Platform and its associated interfaces. Other entities are only addressed in the TRM insofar as they influence the Application Platform. The aim of this approach is to ensure that the higher-level building blocks which make up business solutions have a complete, robust platform on which to run.

It is important to recognize that the Application Platform in the TOGAF TRM is a single, generic, conceptual entity. From the viewpoint of the TOGAF TRM, the Application Platform contains all possible services. It is important to recognize that many of the real-world IT systems that are procured and used today come fully equipped with many advanced services. Service bundles are represented in a Technology Architecture in the form of building blocks. The architect must analyze the services needed in order to implement an IT infrastructure that meets the enterprise's business requirements in the optimal manner, and define the set of Solution Building Blocks using real-world platforms to implement that architecture.

Other architecture models may be preferable for some enterprises. For example, an enterprise may prefer to represent the TOGAF taxonomy using a different form of graphic, which better captures legacy concepts and proves easier for internal communication. There is no problem with using other architecture taxonomies and/or graphics with TOGAF. The core of TOGAF is its ADM: the TRM is a tool used in applying the ADM in the development of specific architectures.

20.7 Summary

The TOGAF Technical Reference Model (TRM) provides a model and core taxonomy of generic platform services. It can be used to build any system architecture. The taxonomy of platform services defines terminology and provides a coherent description of an information system. It is a widely accepted, useful, consistent structural definition of the Application Platform entity, although it should be noted that it is not intended to be an exclusive or an optimal definition. The taxonomy of Application Platform Service Qualities provides a number of "qualities", also termed non-functional requirements, which an architect must be aware of when implementing the architecture. The TOGAF ADM is not dependent on the TRM and can be used without reference to it.

20.8 Exercises

Exercise 20-1

Describe how you would adapt the TRM for your organization.

20.9 Recommended Reading

The following are recommended sources of further information for this chapter:
- TOGAF 9 Part VI, Chapter 43 (Foundation Architecture: Technical Reference Model)

Integrated Information Infrastructure Reference Model (III-RM)

21.1 Key Learning Points

This chapter takes a detailed look at the Integration Information Infrastructure Reference Model (III-RM). This chapter builds on the information contained in the TOGAF 9 Foundation Study Guide.

Key Points Explained

Upon completion of this chapter you should be able to:

1. Describe the business and technical drivers for Boundaryless Information Flow

2. Explain how the III-RM fulfills the solution space for Boundaryless Information Flow

3. Briefly describe the high-level structure of the III-RM

4. Explain the III-RM graphic, including the following components:

   - Business Applications
   - Infrastructure Applications
   - Application Platform
   - Interfaces
   - Qualities

21.2 Drivers for Boundaryless Information Flow

(Syllabus Reference: Unit 13, Learning Outcome 1: You should be able to describe the business and technical drivers for Boundaryless Information Flow.)

The key driver for Boundaryless Information Flow is the problem of supplying information to the right people at the right time, in a secure reliable manner. Readers are referred to Section 13.4 of the TOGAF 9 Foundation Study Guide for more information.

21.3 How the III-RM Fulfills the Solution Space

(Syllabus Reference: Unit 13, Learning Outcome 2: You should be able to explain how the III-RM fulfills the solution space for Boundaryless Information Flow.)

The III-RM addresses the solution space for Boundaryless Information Flow by providing a reference model for an implementation addressing this problem space.

21.4 The High-Level Structure of the III-RM

(Syllabus Reference: Unit 13, Learning Outcome 3: You should be able briefly describe the high-level structure of the III-RM.)

The model includes the key components for developing, managing, and operating an integrated information infrastructure. It also models a set of applications that sit on top of an application platform.

The III-RM is a subset of the TOGAF TRM which uses a slightly different orientation from the one usually presented. This relationship is depicted in Figure 31. The left side is the familiar view of the TOGAF TRM; it is a side view, where we look at the model as if looking at a house from the side, revealing the contents of the "floors". The top-down view on the right-hand side depicts what one might see if looking at a house from the "roof" down.

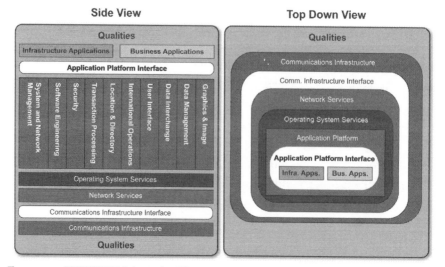

Figure 31:   TOGAF TRM Orientation Views

The subset of the TRM that comprises the III-RM is contained within the "Application Platform" box in the center. This shows that the resulting focus is on the Application Software, Application Platform, and Qualities subset of the TOGAF TRM.

The resulting model is shown in Figure 32

Figure 32:   III-RM – High Level

The III-RM is fundamentally an Application Architecture reference model; that is, a model of the application components and application services software essential for an integrated information infrastructure. There are more business applications and infrastructure applications than these in the environment, but these are the subsets relevant to the Boundaryless Information Flow problem space. Also, the model assumes the underlying existence of a computing and network platform, and does not depict them explicitly.

21.5 Components of the III-RM

(Syllabus Reference: Unit 13, Learning Outcome 4: You should be able to explain the III-RM graphic.)

The detailed III-RM graphic is shown in Figure 33.

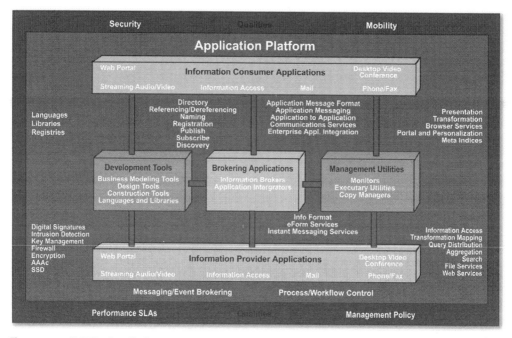

Figure 33:   III-RM – Detailed

There are human and computing actors in the business environment that need information, called information consumers. There are human and computing actors that have information, called information providers. Information consumers need technology services to help them request information. Information providers need services to help them liberate the information in their control.

There are numerous types of information consumer and information providers, as in the stock market where brokers help information consumers get the information they need. Thus, we have Brokering services in the reference model.

In the business environment there are development organizations and management organizations. These organizations are supported by tools and utilities to develop and manage the information services.

In the business environment people and information are spread out and mobile. So there is a need for a directory. This is provided to the tools, utilities, and services through the directory services in the reference model.

Finally, the business environment must be secure, mobile, manageable, and must meet business needs. This is depicted by the qualities that the reference model must support.

(Syllabus Reference: Unit 13, Learning Outcome 4.1: You should be able to explain the following component of the III-RM graphic: Business Applications.)

There are three types of Business Applications in the model:
1. **Brokering Applications**, which manage the requests from any number of clients to and across any number of Information Provider Applications
2. **Information Provider Applications**, which provide responses to client requests and rudimentary access to data managed by a particular server
3. **Information Consumer Applications**, which deliver content to the user of the system, and provide services to request access to information in the system on the user's behalf

The overall set of Information Provider, Information Consumer, and Brokerage Applications collectively creates an environment that provides a rich set of end-user services for transparently accessing heterogeneous systems, databases, and file systems.

(Syllabus Reference: Unit 13, Learning Outcome 4.2: You should be able to explain the following component of the III-RM graphic: Infrastructure Applications.)

There are two types of Infrastructure Application in the model:
1. **Development Tools**, which provide all the necessary modeling, design, and construction capabilities to develop and deploy applications that require access to the integrated information infrastructure, in a manner consistent with the standards of the environment

2. **Management Utilities**, which provide all the necessary utilities to understand, operate, tune, and manage the run-time system in order to meet the demands of an ever-changing business, in a manner consistent with the standards of the environment

(Syllabus Reference: Unit 13, Learning Outcome 4.3: You should be able to explain the following component of the III-RM graphic: Application Platform.)

The Application Platform provides supporting services to all the above applications – in areas such as location, directory, workflow, data management, data interchange, etc. – and thereby provides the ability to locate, access, and move information within the environment. This set of services constitutes a subset of the total set of services of the TRM Application Platform.

The services of the Application Platform component can be used to support conventional applications as well as Brokerage, Information Consumer, and Information Provider applications. When used as part of an overall Application Architecture in this way, such an approach enables maximum leverage of a single operational environment that is designed to ensure effective and consistent transfer of data between processes, and to support fast and efficient development, deployment, and management of applications.

(Syllabus Reference: Unit 13, Learning Outcome 4.4: You should be able to explain the following component of the III-RM graphic: Interfaces.)

The Interfaces used between the components include formats and protocols, application programming interfaces, switches, data values, etc.

(Syllabus Reference: Unit 13, Learning Outcome 4.5: You should be able to explain the following component of the III-RM graphic: Qualities.)

The Application Software and Application Platform must adhere to the policies and requirements depicted by the Qualities. The Qualities component of the model is supported by services required to maintain the quality of the system as specified in Service Level Agreements (SLAs).

21.6 Summary

The III-RM is an Application Architecture reference model; that is, a model of the application components and application services. The III-RM provides help in addressing one of the key challenges facing the enterprise architect today: the need to design an integrated information infrastructure to enable Boundaryless Information Flow.

21.7 Recommended Reading

The following are recommended sources of further information for this chapter:

- TOGAF 9 Part VI, Chapter 44 (Integrated Information Infrastructure Reference Model)

PART 6

Architecture Capability

In this Part, we look at three aspects of Architecture Capability:

- Chapter 22 describes the relationship between Architecture Governance and the ADM. It also describes how to establish and operate an Architecture Board.
- Chapter 23 describes Architecture Maturity Models.
- Chapter 24 describes the Architecture Skills Framework.

Recommended reading before commencing this part of the Study Guide includes:

- TOGAF 9 Foundation Study Guide, Chapter 9, Architecture Governance

Chapter 22
Architecture Governance

22.1 Key Learning Points

The purpose of this chapter is to help you understand how to apply Architecture Governance in development of an enterprise architecture. This chapter builds on the Architecture Governance chapter contained in the TOGAF 9 Foundation Study Guide.

Key Points Explained

Upon completion of this chapter you should be able to:

1. Explain how Architecture Governance fits within the ADM cycle
2. Discuss the key success factors for putting Architecture Governance into practice
3. Discuss the factors that should be considered when setting up an Architecture Board
4. Explain how to operate an Architecture Board

22.2 Architecture Governance and the ADM

(Syllabus Reference: Unit 2, Learning Outcome 1: You should be able to explain how Architecture Governance fits within the ADM cycle.)

TOGAF defines Architecture Governance as follows:
"The practice and orientation by which enterprise architectures and other architectures are managed and controlled at an enterprise-wide level. It is concerned with change processes (design governance) and operation of product systems (operational governance)."

[Source: TOGAF 9 Part I, Chapter 3 (Definitions)]

In the Preliminary Phase, decisions are made on how to govern the Architecture Framework, and how to integrate it with the existing governance and support models for the organization. Decisions are also taken as to the type of governance repository characteristics required.

In Phase F, the Implementation Governance Model produced ensures that a project transitioning into implementation smoothly transitions into the appropriate Architecture Governance for Phase G.

Phase G includes production of the Architecture Contract which features prominently in Architecture Governance as a means to ensure compliance and drive change. Periodic compliance reviews of projects are held to review progress and ensure that the design and implementation are in-line with the strategic and architectural objectives. Risk monitoring should also occur in this phase.

Phase H manages the governance process and framework for the architecture. This includes scheduling and holding meetings of the Architecture Board. The purpose of these meetings is to decide how to handle requests for change to the architecture. These can arise either from issues found in the original architecture definition and requirements, or from external factors such as business strategy changes and new technology opportunities. The Architecture Board should also ensure that the ADM is being applied correctly to ensure that all considerations are made and all required deliverables are produced.

22.3 Key Success Factors

(Syllabus Reference: Unit 2, Learning Outcome 2: You should be able to discuss the key success factors for putting Architecture Governance into practice.)

It is important to consider the following to ensure a successful approach to Architecture Governance, and effective management of the Architecture Contract:

- Establishment and operation of best practices for submission, adoption, re-use, reporting, and retirement of architecture policies, procedures, roles, skills, organizational structures, and support services
- Establishment of correct organizational responsibilities and structures to support Architecture Governance processes and reporting requirements
- Integration of tools and processes to facilitate take-up of processes (both procedural and cultural)
- Management of criteria for control of Architecture Governance processes, dispensations, compliance assessments, Service Level Agreements (SLAs), and Operational Level Agreements (OLAs)

- Meeting internal and external requirements for effectiveness, efficiency, confidentiality, integrity, availability, compliance, and reliability of Architecture Governance-related information, services, and processes

22.4 Setting up the Architecture Board

(*Syllabus Reference: Unit 2, Learning Outcome 3: You should be able to discuss the factors that should be considered when setting up an Architecture Board.*)

Factors to consider include identification of the executive sponsor, the size of the board, the structure of the board, and its relationship to other organizational groups and responsibilities.

In many companies, the executive sponsor of the initial architecture effort is the CIO (or other senior executive). However, to gain broad corporate support, a sponsoring body can have more influence. This sponsoring body is called an Architecture Board. The Architecture Board is the sponsor of the architecture within the enterprise, but the Architecture Board itself needs an executive sponsor from the highest level of the corporation. This commitment must span the planning process and continue into the maintenance phase of the architecture project. In many companies that fail in an architecture planning effort, there is a notable lack of executive participation and encouragement for the project.

The recommended size for an Architecture Board is four or five permanent members and the recommended upper limit is ten. A technique to manage the size of the board is to rotate the membership. This may be required due to some Architecture Board members finding that time constraints prevent long-term active participation. However, some continuity must exist on the Architecture Board, to prevent the corporate architecture from fluctuating from one set of ideas to another. One technique for ensuring rotation with continuity is to have set terms for the members, and to have the terms expire at different times.

The TOGAF Architecture Governance Framework provides a generic organizational framework that positions the Architecture Board in the context of the broader governance structures of the enterprise. This structure identifies the major organizational groups and responsibilities, as well as the relationship between each group. This is a best practice structure, and may be subject to change depending on the organization's form and existing structures.

The structure of the Architecture Board should reflect the form of the organization. The Architecture Governance structure required may well go beyond the generic structures outlined in the TOGAF Architecture Governance Framework. The organization may need to define a combination of the IT governance process and the existing organizational structures and capabilities, which typically may include a global governance board, local governance board, design authorities, and working parties.

22.5 Operating an Architecture Board

(Syllabus Reference: Unit 2, Learning Outcome 4: You should be able to explain how to operate an Architecture Board.)

TOGAF provides guidance on the operation of the Architecture Board, particularly from the governance perspective. This focuses primarily on how to prepare and conduct meetings and is summarized below.

22.5.1 General

Architecture Board meetings should be conducted with clearly identified agendas with explicit objectives, content coverage, and defined actions. These meetings will provide key direction in:

- Supporting the production of quality governance material and activities
- Providing a mechanism for formal acceptance through consensus and authorized publication
- Providing a fundamental control mechanism for ensuring the effective implementation of the architectures
- Establishing and maintaining the link between the implementation of the architectures and the stated strategy and objectives of the organization (business and IT)
- Identifying divergence from the contract and planning activities to realign with the contract through dispensations or policy updates

22.5.2 Preparation

Prior to a meeting, each participant should receive an agenda and any supporting documentation (e.g., dispensation requests, performance management reports, etc.). Each participant is expected to be familiar with the contents of each. Where actions have been allocated to an individual, it is that person's responsibility to report on progress against these. Each participant must confirm their availability and attendance at the Architecture Board meeting.

22.5.3 Agenda

TOGAF provides an outline set of contents for an Architecture Board meeting agenda. Each agenda item is described in terms of its content only.

Minutes of Previous Meeting

Minutes contain the details of the previous Architecture Board meeting as per standard organizational protocol.

Requests for Change

Items under this heading are normally change requests for amendments to architectures, principles, etc., but may also include business control with regard to Architecture Contracts; e.g., ensure that voice traffic to premium numbers, such as weather reports, are barred and data traffic to certain web sites is controlled.

Any request for change is made within agreed authority levels and parameters defined by the Architecture Contract.

Dispensations

A dispensation is used as the mechanism to request a change to the existing architectures, contracts, principles, etc. outside of normal operating parameters; e.g., exclude provision of service to a subsidiary, request for unusual service levels for specific business reasons, deploy non-standard technology or products to support specific business initiatives.

Dispensations are granted for a given time period and set of identified services and operational criteria that must be enforced during the lifespan of the dispensation. Dispensations are not granted indefinitely, but are used as a mechanism to ensure that service levels and operational levels, etc. are met while providing a level flexibility in their implementation and timing. The time-bound nature of dispensations ensures that they are a trigger to the Architecture Compliance activity.

Compliance Assessments

Compliance is assessed against Service Level Agreements (SLAs), Operational
Level Agreements (OLAs), cost targets, and required architecture refreshes.
These assessments will be reviewed and either accepted or rejected depending
on the criteria defined within the Architecture Governance Framework. The
Architecture Compliance assessment report will include details as described.

Dispute Resolution

Disputes that have not been resolved through the Architecture Compliance
and dispensation processes are identified here for further action and
are documented through the Architecture Compliance assessments and
dispensation documentation.

Architecture Strategy and Direction Documentation

This describes the architecture strategies, direction, and priorities and will
only be formulated by the global Architecture Board. It should take the form
of standard architecture documentation.

Actions Assigned

This is a report on the actions assigned at previous Architecture Board
meetings. An action tracker is used to document and keep the status of all
actions assigned during the Architecture Board meetings and should consist
of at least the following information:

- Reference
- Priority
- Action description
- Action owner
- Action details
- Date raised
- Due date
- Status
- Type
- Resolution date

Contract Documentation Management

This is a formal acceptance of updates and changes to architecture
documentation for onward publication.

Any Other Business (AOB)

Description of issues not directly covered under any of the above. These may not be described in the agenda but should be raised at the beginning of the meeting. Any supporting documentation must be managed as per all Architecture Governance documentation.

Schedule of Meetings

All meeting dates should be detailed and published.

22.6 Summary

Architecture Governance is the practice and orientation by which enterprise architectures and other architectures are managed and controlled at an enterprise-wide level. TOGAF provides guidance on aspects of Architecture Governance in the Architecture Capability Framework.

22.7 Exercises

Exercise 22-1

You have been asked to establish an Architecture Board for your organization. Draw up a list of the candidates with explanation of why they should be included, and set the agenda for the first meeting.

22.8 Recommended Reading

The following are recommended sources of further information for this chapter:

- TOGAF 9 Part VII, Chapter 47 (Architecture Board)
- TOGAF 9 Part VII, Chapter 50 (Architecture Governance)
- TOGAF 9 Foundation Study Guide, Chapter 9, Architecture Governance

Architecture Maturity Models

23.1 Key Learning Points

This chapter introduces Architecture Maturity Models. The purpose of this chapter is to help you understand their role in enabling an enterprise to determine the state of the enterprise architecture and to evaluate risks and options during the development of the enterprise architecture.

Key Points Explained

Upon completion of this chapter you should be able to:

1. Explain the role of a Capability Maturity Model
2. Explain the CMMI process improvement approach development by Carnegie Mellon University (CMU)
3. Describe the structure and levels of the ACMM developed by CMU for the US Department of Commerce
4. Explain the role of Maturity Assessments in the ADM

23.2 Capability Maturity Models

(Syllabus Reference: Unit 26, Learning Outcome 1: You should be able to explain the role of a Capability Maturity Model.)

Organizations that can manage change effectively are generally more successful than those that cannot. Many organizations know that they need to improve their processes in order to successfully manage change, but don't know how. Such organizations typically either spend very little on process improvement, because they are unsure how best to proceed; or spend a lot, on a number of parallel and unfocused efforts with mixed results.

Capability Maturity Models (CMMs) address this problem by providing an effective method for an organization to gradually gain control over and improve its change processes. Benefits of such models include:

- They describe the practices that any organization must perform in order to improve its processes.
- They provide measures for improvement.
- They constitute a proven framework within which to manage the improvement efforts.
- They organize the various practices into levels, each level representing an increased ability to control and manage the development environment.

An evaluation of the organization's practices against the model — called an "assessment" — determines the level at which the organization currently stands. It indicates the organization's ability to execute in the area concerned, and the practices on which the organization needs to focus in order to see the greatest improvement and the highest return on investment. The benefits of CMMs to effectively direct effort are well documented.

The models have been used for assessment in different domains including e-Commerce maturity, process implementation and audit, quality measurements, people competencies, and investment management.

The methods involve using several models, and focus in particular on measuring business benefits and return-on-investment. Another key driver is the increasing use of outsourcing. The CMM is increasingly the standard by which outsourcers are being evaluated.

Capability Maturity Models

The original CMM was developed in the early 1990s by Carnegie Mellon University and is still widely used today. CMMs have also been developed for other areas such as:

- People: the P-CMM (People Capability Maturity Model), and the IDEAL Life Cycle Model for Improvement
- Systems Engineering: the SE-CMM (Systems Engineering Capability Maturity Model)
- Software Acquisition: the SA-CMM (Software Acquisition Capability Maturity Model)
- CMMI: Capability Maturity Model Integration

The increasing interest in applying CMMs to the IT architecture and enterprise architecture fields has resulted in a series of templates which can be used to assess the state of the IT architecture process, the IT architecture, and the organization's buy-in to both.

23.3 Capability Maturity Model Integration (CMMI)

(Syllabus Reference: Unit 26, Learning Outcome 2: You should be able to explain CMMI process improvement approach developed by CMU.)

In recent years, the industry has witnessed significant growth in the area of maturity models. The multiplicity of models available has led to problems of its own, in terms of how to integrate all the different models to produce meaningful measures for overall process maturity. In response to this need, Carnegie Mellon University (CMU) developed a framework called Capability Maturity Model Integration (CMMI), to provide a means of managing the complexity.

According to the developers, the use of the CMMI models improves on the best practices of previous models in many important ways, in particular enabling organizations to:

- More explicitly link management and engineering activities to business objectives
- Expand the scope of and visibility into the product lifecycle and engineering activities to ensure that the product or service meets customer expectations
- Incorporate lessons learned from additional areas of best practice (e.g., measurement, risk management, and supplier management)
- Implement more robust high-maturity practices
- Address additional organizational functions critical to products and services
- More fully comply with relevant ISO standards

23.4 ACMM

(Syllabus Reference: Unit 26, Learning Outcome 3: You should be able to describe the structure and levels of the ACMM developed by CMU for the US Department of Commerce.)

The US Department of Commerce (DoC) has developed an IT Architecture Capability Maturity Model (ACMM) to facilitate internal assessments. The goal is to identify weak areas and provide a way to improve the overall architecture process. The ACMM has three sections:

- The architecture maturity model
- The characteristics of processes at different maturity levels
- The architecture CMM scorecard

The ACMM has six maturity levels:

1. None
2. Initial
3. Under development
4. Defined
5. Managed
6. Measured

The ACMM also has nine architecture characteristics:

1. IT architecture process
2. IT architecture development
3. Business linkage
4. Senior management involvement
5. Operating unit participation
6. Architecture communication
7. IT security
8. Architecture Governance
9. IT investment and acquisition strategy

Two methods are used in the ACMM to calculate a maturity rating. The first method obtains a weighted mean IT architecture maturity level. The second shows the percentage achieved at each maturity level for the nine architecture characteristics.

23.5 Maturity Assessments and the ADM

(Syllabus Reference: Unit 26, Learning Outcome 4: You should be able to explain the role of Maturity Assessments in the ADM.)

Maturity Assessments are referred to in the Preliminary Phase, Phase A, and Phase E of the ADM. The approach to the Preliminary Phase recommends their use as part of developing the Organizational Model for Enterprise Architecture. In Phase A, a maturity assessment is part of the Capability Assessment used to determine the baseline and target capability of the enterprise. This Capability Assessment is also revisited in Phase E, when preparing the Implementation and Migration Plan.

When using CMMs with the ADM, it is recommended that they be customized and discussed in workshops involving the major stakeholders within the organization. The actual levels of maturity can provide a strategic measure of the organization's ability to change, as well as a series of sequential steps to improve that ability.

23.6 Summary

Architecture Maturity Models can be used to assess the maturity of the process of enterprise architecture. The CMMI framework provides a set of models that incorporate best practice for process assessment. A maturity assessment can be used as a business tool and can provide executives with an insight into how to pragmatically move forward when developing an enterprise architecture.

23.7 Exercises

Exercise 23-1
Provide a list of questions which could be used to determine the maturity of the nine architecture characteristics within a particular enterprise architecture. Use the US Department of Commerce ACMM document as a guide.

Exercise 23-2

Provide an assessment of your own organization's enterprise architecture process maturity, on a scale from Level 0 to Level 5 using the templates provided with the US Department of Commerce ACMM document.

23.8 Recommended Reading

The following are recommended sources of further information for this chapter:

- TOGAF 9 Part VII, Chapter 51 (Architecture Maturity Models)

Architecture Skills Framework

24.1 Key Learning Points

This chapter introduces the Architecture Skills Framework. The purpose of this chapter is to help you understand the Architecture Skills Framework, which is a classification model for architect roles.

Key Points Explained

Upon completion of this chapter you should be able to:

1. Explain the purpose of the Architecture Skills Framework and why it is needed

2. Describe the benefits of using the Architecture Skills Framework

3. Describe the structure of the Architecture Skills Framework, including roles, skills, and proficiency levels

---

24.2 Purpose

(Syllabus Reference: Unit 27, Learning Outcome 1: You should be able to explain the purpose of the Architecture Skills Framework and why it is needed.)

The purpose of the TOGAF Architecture Skills Framework is to help organizations seeking to establish an enterprise architecture practice to reduce the time, cost, and risk involved in training, recruiting, and managing enterprise architecture professionals, and at the same time enable and encourage more organizations to institute an internal enterprise architecture practice, based on the role and skill definitions provided.

An enterprise architecture practice is both difficult and costly to establish. To address this, the Architecture Skills Framework provides a standard set of definitions of the architecting skills and proficiency levels required of personnel – internal or external – who are to perform the various architecting roles defined within the TOGAF framework.

24.3 Benefits

(Syllabus Reference: Unit 27, Learning Outcome 2: You should be able to describe the benefits of using the Architecture Skills Framework.)

The benefits of using the Architecture Skills Framework are summarized in Table 25.

Table 25:   Benefits of Using the Architecture Skills Framework

Benefit	Rationale
Reduced time, cost, and risk in training, hiring, and managing architecture professionals, both internal and external	Simplifies communication between recruiting organizations, consultancies, and employment agencies. Avoids wasting resources interviewing staff who may have applied in good faith, but lack the skills and/or experience required by the employer. Avoids staff who are capable of filling architecture roles being overlooked, or not identifying themselves with advertised positions and hence not applying.
Reduced time and cost to set up an internal architecture practice	Many enterprises do not have an internal architecture practice due to the complexity involved in setting one up, preferring instead to simply interview and recruit architecture staff on an *ad hoc* basis. By providing definitions of the architecting skills and proficiency levels required of personnel who are to perform the various architecting roles defined within TOGAF, the Architecture Skills Framework greatly reduces the time, cost, and risk of setting up a practice for the first time, and avoids "re-inventing the wheel". Enterprises that already have an internal architecture practice are able to set enterprise-wide norms, but still experience difficulties as outlined above in recruiting staff, or engaging consultants, from external sources, due to the lack of uniformity between different enterprises. By aligning its existing skills framework with an industry-accepted definition, an enterprise can greatly simplify these problems.
Reduced time, cost, and risk of overall solution development	Enterprises that do not have an internal architecture practice run the risk of unsuitable personnel being employed or engaged. The resultant time and cost penalties far outweigh the time and cost of having an internal architecture practice: • Personnel costs are increased, through the need to rehire or reassign staff. • Even more important is the adverse impact on the time, cost, and quality of operational IT systems, and the projects to deliver them, resulting from poor staff assignments.

24.4 EA Roles, Skills Categories, and Proficiency Levels

(Syllabus Reference: Unit 27, Learning Outcome 3: You should be able to describe the structure of the Architecture Skills Framework, including roles, skills, and proficiency level.)

The TOGAF Architecture Skills Framework defines the competency levels for specific roles within the enterprise architecture team. This includes:
- The roles within an enterprise architecture work area
- The skills required by those roles
- The depth of knowledge required to fulfill each role successfully

This provides value by enabling a rapid means of identifying skills and gaps. Successfully applied, the framework can be used as a measure for:
- Staff development
- Ensuring the right person does the right job

24.4.1 TOGAF Roles

The framework defines the following roles for a team undertaking the development of an enterprise architecture:
- Architecture Board Members
- Architecture Sponsor
- Architecture Manager
- Architects for Enterprise Architecture, Business Architecture, Data Architecture, Application Architecture, and Technology Architecture
- Program and/or Project Managers
- IT Designer

24.4.2 Skills Categories

The framework defines the skills categories for a TOGAF team as shown in Table 26.

Table 26:   Skills Categories

Skill	Description
Generic Skills	Leadership, team-working, inter-personal skills, etc.
Business Skills & Methods	Business cases, business process, strategic planning, etc.
Enterprise Architecture Skills	Modeling, building block design, applications and role design, systems integration, etc.
Program or Project Management Skills	Managing business change, project management methods and tools, etc.
IT General Knowledge Skills	Brokering applications, asset management, migration planning, Service Level Agreements (SLAs), etc.
Technical IT Skills	Software engineering, security, data interchange, data management, etc.
Legal Environment	Data protection laws, contract law, procurement law, fraud, etc.

24.4.3 Proficiency Levels

The framework defines four levels of knowledge or proficiency in any area, as shown in Table 27.

Table 27:   Proficiency Levels

Level	Achievement	Description
1	Background	Not a required skill though should be able to define and manage skill if required.
2	Awareness	Understands the background, issues, and implications sufficiently to be able to understand how to proceed further and advise client accordingly.
3	Knowledge	Detailed knowledge of subject area and capable of providing professional advice and guidance. Ability to integrate capability into architecture design.
4	Expert	Extensive and substantial practical experience and applied knowledge on the subject.

24.4.4 Example Role and Skill Definitions

The framework also includes a number of tables matching roles with skills and proficiency levels within each skill category. A single table is shown in Table 28 as an illustration, showing the definition of enterprise architecture skills by role.

Table 28: Example Role and Skill Definition

Roles / Enterprise Architecture Skills	Architecture Board Member	Architecture Sponsor	Enterprise Architecture Manager	Enterprise Architecture Technology	Enterprise Architecture Data	Enterprise Architecture Applications	Enterprise Architecture Business	Program/Project Manager	IT Designer
Business Modeling	2	2	4	3	3	4	4	2	2
Business Process Design	1	1	4	3	3	4	4	2	2
Role Design	2	2	4	3	3	4	4	2	2
Organization Design	2	2	4	3	3	4	4	2	2
Data Design	1	1	3	3	4	3	3	2	3
Application Design	1	1	3	3	3	4	3	2	3
Systems Integration	1	1	4	4	3	3	3	2	2
IT Industry Standards	1	1	4	4	4	4	3	2	3
Services Design	2	2	4	4	3	4	3	2	2
Architecture Principles Design	2	2	4	4	4	4	4	2	2
Architecture Views & Viewpoints Design	2	2	4	4	4	4	4	2	2
Building Block Design	1	1	4	4	4	4	4	2	3
Solutions Modeling	1	1	4	4	4	4	4	2	3
Benefits Analysis	2	2	4	4	4	4	4	4	2
Business Interworking	3	3	4	3	3	4	4	3	1
Systems Behavior	1	1	4	4	4	4	3	3	2
Project Management	1	1	3	3	3	3	3	4	2

Key: 1 = Background, 2 = Awareness, 3 = Knowledge, 4 = Expert

24.5 Summary

The Architecture Skills Framework is a classification model for architecture roles. It has a number of benefits which have been described in this chapter. The structure of the Architecture Skills Framework stipulates roles, skills, and proficiency levels.

24.6 Exercises

Exercise 24-1

Place yourself within the Architecture Skills Framework and write a brief summary of your role, your skills, and proficiency level.

Exercise 24-2

The director of the human resources department has requested your assistance with recruitment for a new enterprise architecture project. She has asked you to write summary job descriptions for the following roles aligned with the Architecture Skills Framework:

- Enterprise Architecture Manager
- A Project Manager

24.7 Recommended Reading

The following are recommended sources of further information for this chapter:

- TOGAF 9 Part VII, Chapter 52 (Architecture Skills Framework)

PART 7

Bridging from TOGAF 8 Certified to TOGAF 9 Certified

In this Part, we look at the differences between TOGAF 8 and TOGAF 9.

Differences between TOGAF 8 and TOGAF 9

25.1 Key Learning Points

This chapter describes the differences between TOGAF 8 and TOGAF 9. It will be of most use to individuals who have achieved the TOGAF 8 Certified qualification and plan to take the TOGAF 8 – 9 Advanced Bridge Examination.

Key Points Explained

Upon completion of this chapter you should be able to:

1. Describe the new features in TOGAF 9
2. Explain the benefits of the new features
3. Explain the high-level structural changes between TOGAF 8.1.1 and TOGAF 9
4. Describe the key differences between the ADM in TOGAF 8.1.1 and TOGAF 9
5. Discuss approaches to migrate an enterprise from TOGAF 8.1.1 to TOGAF 9

25.2 New Features and Benefits of TOGAF 9

(Syllabus Reference: Unit Bridge 1, Learning Outcome 1: You should be able to describe the new features in TOGAF 9.)

(Syllabus Reference: Unit Bridge 1, Learning Outcome 2: You should be able to explain the benefits of the new features in TOGAF 9.)

TOGAF 9 provides a wide-ranging set of revisions to the TOGAF specification to improve the value of the TOGAF framework. It has been designed as an evolution from TOGAF 8.1.1, adding further detail and clarification.

The major new features of TOGAF 9 are as follows:

Modular Structure: TOGAF 9 has a modular structure. Content that was contained within the TOGAF 8.1.1 Resource Base has been classified and moved into parts that have a defined purpose (as opposed to being generic "resources"). The modular structure supports greater usability as there is a defined purpose for each part; parts can be used in isolation as a standalone set of guidelines which allows incremental adoption of the TOGAF specification.

Content Framework: TOGAF 9 includes a content framework to drive greater consistency in the outputs that are created when following the Architecture Development Method (ADM). The TOGAF content framework provides a detailed model of architectural work products.

Extended Guidance: TOGAF 9 features an extended set of concepts and guidelines to support the establishment of an integrated hierarchy of architectures such as those developed by teams within larger organizations that operate within an overarching architectural governance model. In particular, the following concepts are introduced:

- **Partitioning**: A number of different techniques and considerations of how to partition the various architectures within an enterprise.
- **Architecture Repository**: A logical information model for an Architecture Repository which can be used as an integrated store for all outputs created by executing the ADM.
- **Capability Framework**: A more structured definition of the organization, skills, roles, and responsibilities required to operate an effective enterprise architecture capability. The new TOGAF materials also provide guidance on a process that can be followed to identify and establish an appropriate architecture capability.

Architectural Styles: TOGAF 9, in Part III: ADM Guidelines and Techniques, brings together a set of supporting materials that show in detail how the ADM can be applied to specific situations:

- The varying uses of iteration that are possible within the ADM and when each technique should be applied
- Service Oriented Architecture (SOA) as an architectural style
- The specific considerations required to address security architecture within the ADM

- The various types of architecture development required within an enterprise and how these relate to one another

Additional ADM Detail: TOGAF 9 includes additional detailed information supporting the execution of the ADM. Particular areas of enhancement are:
- The Preliminary Phase features extended guidance on establishing an enterprise Architecture Framework and planning for architecture development.
- The Opportunities & Solutions and Migration Planning phases feature a more detailed and robust method for defining and planning enterprise transformation, based on the principles of capability-based planning.

25.3 Key Differences between TOGAF 8.1.1 and TOGAF 9

(Syllabus Reference: Unit Bridge 1, Learning Outcome 3: You should be able to explain the high-level differences between TOGAF 8.1.1 and TOGAF 9.)

(Syllabus Reference: Unit Bridge 1, Learning Outcome 4: You should be able to explain the key differences between the ADM from TOGAF 8.1.1 to TOGAF 9.)

25.3.1 Changes from a TOGAF 8.1.1 Perspective

Listed below are the Parts of the TOGAF 8.1.1 specification with a description explaining where the TOGAF 8.1.1 content is located within TOGAF 9.

Part I: Introduction

The Introduction from TOGAF 8.1.1 has been used as the basis for creation of Part I: Introduction in TOGAF 9. The introduction to TOGAF 9 reflects the content of TOGAF 9 rather than the content of TOGAF 8.1.1, and also features a number of enhancements to improve accessibility, including a revised executive overview, a new chapter introducing the core concepts within TOGAF, a revised chapter of key terms and definitions, and a chapter containing information about changes in TOGAF 9.

Part II: Architecture Development Method

The essence of the TOGAF 8.1.1 ADM has been retained in TOGAF 9. In TOGAF 9 Part II: Architecture Development Method (ADM) is structured along similar lines to Part II of TOGAF 8.1.1. The "crop circle" diagram is an evolution, with just the single change to rename the "Preliminary Phase: Framework and Principles" to simply the "Preliminary Phase". There is also a double-ended arrow between the Preliminary Phase and Phase A to denote that the Preliminary Phase may be revisited. The TOGAF ADM phase inputs and outputs (Chapter 16 of TOGAF 8.1.1) have been moved from Part II in TOGAF 8.1.1 to Part IV: Architecture Content Framework in TOGAF 9, and renamed "Architecture Deliverables".

The TOGAF 9 ADM features additional content in the majority of ADM phases, which in the most part adds further detail and clarification to the same approach that was described in TOGAF 8.1.1.

Part III: Enterprise Continuum

The TOGAF 8.1.1 Enterprise Continuum has seen a substantial degree of change.

The Enterprise Continuum concept is retained within Part V: Enterprise Continuum and Tools in TOGAF 9. The TOGAF Technical Reference Model (TRM) and Integrated Information Infrastructure Reference Model (III-RM) are extracted and placed within Part VI: TOGAF Reference Models in TOGAF 9. The TRM, rather than having the Detailed Platform Taxonomy as a separate chapter, now includes it as a subsection within the same chapter.

TOGAF 9 adds new material that describes an approach to architecture partitioning and also provides a structured model of an Architecture Repository. These concepts support and elaborate on the original intent of the Enterprise Continuum.

The chapter describing the Standards Information Base in detail has been removed in TOGAF 9. The concept of a Standards Information Base has been maintained within TOGAF, but it was deemed impractical to maintain a current and relevant collection of standards within a specification such as TOGAF. The example SIB remains at The Open Group web site (www.opengroup.org/sib).

Part IV: Resource Base

The Resource Base is not included in TOGAF 9. Some elements of the Resource Base have been deprecated from the specification, but will still be available in White Paper form. Other elements of the Resource Base have been moved to other areas of the specification related to their content matter.

25.3.2 High-Level Structural Changes

This section contains high-level migration information; i.e., a summary description of what is changed from TOGAF 8.1.1 for each chapter of TOGAF 9. Readers are assumed to be familiar with the content of TOGAF 8.1.1.

TOGAF 9 Chapter	Derivation from TOGAF 8.1.1
Part I: Introduction	
1 Introduction	Material revised; based on Chapter 1 This revised chapter describes the structure, an executive overview of enterprise architecture, and the benefits of using TOGAF. Some of the previous contents have been moved to the new Chapters 2 and 4.
2 Core Concepts	New chapter This new chapter introduces the Core Concepts of TOGAF, what it is, what is architecture in the context of TOGAF, what types of architecture does TOGAF deal with, and the ADM. It introduces key concepts such as deliverables, artifacts, and building blocks. It introduces the Enterprise Continuum and the Architecture Repository. It introduces the establishment and operations of an Enterprise Architecture Capability. It describes considerations for using TOGAF with other frameworks.
3 Definitions	Derived from Chapter 36, reworked into formal definitions & abbreviations This revised chapter contains the key terms and definitions. Other supplementary definitions and abbreviations have been moved to separate appendices.
4 Release Notes	New chapter This is a new chapter containing information on this release of the document. It contains an overview of what's new, the benefits of the changes, and summary mappings of the structure of the document from TOGAF 8.1.1 to TOGAF 9 and vice versa. It also includes information on terms and conditions for using TOGAF and where to download it.

TOGAF 9 Chapter	Derivation from TOGAF 8.1.1
Part II: Architecture Development Method	
5 Introduction	Material revised; based on Chapter 3 The changes made in this chapter are to position the ADM with respect to the Architecture Repository, and to Part III: ADM Guidelines and Techniques. The concept of document versioning is introduced with an example. Architecture Levels are described.
6 Preliminary Phase	Material revised; based on Chapter 4 The Approach has been expanded considerably to address in addition the definition of the enterprise, key drivers and elements for the organization, requirements for architecture work, management frameworks and their relationship, as well as enterprise maturity. There are now explicit Steps defined whereas previously there were none.
7 Phase A: Architecture Vision	Material revised; based on Chapter 5 Business Scenarios are now referenced as a separate section in Approach; previously they were included as a subsection to Steps. The Steps have been revised to additionally include an evaluation of Business Capabilities, Readiness for Business Transformation, definition of Target Architecture Value Propositions and Key Performance Indicators (KPIs), and identification of Business Transformation Risks and Mitigation activities. The Inputs and Outputs are reorganized to match the deliverables.
8 Phase B: Business Architecture	Material revised; based on Chapter 6 The Approach is revised to discuss the Architecture Repository rather than the Enterprise Continuum. The description of the Gap Analysis technique is moved to Part III. A revised sequence of Steps is introduced. This same sequence of steps is also used in Phases C and D. Explicit references are made to catalogs, matrices, and diagrams suitable for this phase. The Inputs and Outputs are reorganized to match the deliverables. A key difference is the introduction of two container documents; the Architecture Definition Document and the Architecture Requirements Specification.

TOGAF 9 Chapter		Derivation from TOGAF 8.1.1
9	Phase C: Information Systems Architectures	Material revised; based on Chapter 7 The Inputs and Outputs are reorganized to match the deliverables.
10	Phase C: Data Architecture	Material revised; based on Chapter 8 In Approach, the reference to Enterprise Continuum is replaced with the Architecture Repository. The section on Gap Analysis is removed. A section on Key Considerations for Data Architecture is added. A revised sequence of Steps is introduced. This same sequence is also used in Phases B, C (Application Architecture), and D. Explicit references are made to catalogs, matrices, and diagrams suitable for this phase. The Inputs and Outputs are reorganized to match the deliverables.
11	Phase C: Application Architecture	Material revised; based on Chapter 9 In Approach, the reference to Enterprise Continuum is replaced with the Architecture Repository. The section on Gap Analysis is removed. A revised sequence of Steps is introduced. This same sequence is also used in Phases B, C (Data Architecture), and D. Explicit references are made to catalogs, matrices, and diagrams suitable for this phase. The Inputs and Outputs are reorganized to match the deliverables.
12	Phase D: Technology Architecture	Material revised; based on Chapter 10 In Approach, the reference to Enterprise Continuum is replaced with the Architecture Repository. The Steps have undergone a major reorganization, and now use the same sequence also used in Phases B and C. Explicit references are made to catalogs, matrices, and diagrams suitable for this phase. The Inputs and Outputs are reorganized to match the deliverables.
13	Phase E: Opportunities & Solutions	Material revised; based on Chapter 11 This phase has had a major revision to add extensive detail on an Approach and Steps to move from Target Architectures identified in earlier phases to the implementation and create a draft Implementation and Migration Plan. The Inputs and Outputs are reorganized to match the deliverables.

TOGAF 9 Chapter	Derivation from TOGAF 8.1.1
14 Phase F: Migration Planning	Material revised; based on Chapter 12 This phase has had a major revision to add extensive detail on an Approach and Steps to finalize the Implementation and Migration Plan identified in Phase E. The Inputs and Outputs are reorganized to match the deliverables.
15 Phase G: Implementation Governance	Material revised; based on Chapter 13 The Objectives include rewording and additions to emphasize the governance aspect of the phase. The Approach has been updated to include Business Value Realization. The Steps have had a major revision to include confirmation of scope for deployment with development management, identification of deployment skills and resources, guidance development for solutions deployment, compliance reviews, implementation of operations, and a post-implementation review.
16 Phase H: Architecture Change Management	Material revised; based on Chapter 14 The Objectives have been reworked. The Approach is expanded to additionally include monitoring of the business and capacity management. The Steps have had a major revision, and additionally include establishment of the value realization process, deployment of monitoring tools, management of risks, analysis for change, and development of change requirements to meet performance targets.
17 ADM Architecture Requirements Management	No material change; maps to Chapter 15 The Inputs and Outputs are reorganized to match the deliverables.

Part III: ADM Guidelines and Techniques

18 Introduction	New chapter This new Part is provided to support application of the ADM.
19 Applying Iteration to the ADM	New chapter This chapter describes the concept of iteration and shows potential strategies for applying iterative concepts to the ADM.

TOGAF 9 Chapter	Derivation from TOGAF 8.1.1
20 Applying the ADM across the Architecture Landscape	New chapter This chapter describes the application of the ADM across the Architecture Landscape.
21 Security Architecture and the ADM	New chapter ; derived from the Guide to Security Architecture in TOGAF ADM White Paper This chapter provides specific security considerations for each phase of the ADM.
22 Using TOGAF to Define & Govern SOAs	New chapter This chapter describes how the SOA style of architecture can be supported by TOGAF.
23 Architecture Principles	No material change; maps to Chapter 29 A new example principle of Service Orientation to the Business Principles.
24 Stakeholder Management	New chapter This chapter describes the technique of Stakeholder Management, an important discipline for architecture practitioners.
25 Architecture Patterns	No material change; maps to Chapter 28
26 Business Scenarios	No material change; maps to Chapter 34
27 Gap Analysis	New chapter; derived from Gap Analysis This chapter is introduced to allow the technique to be referenced from the ADM phases, and therefore reduce duplication of text.
28 Migration Planning Techniques	New chapter This chapter describes a number of techniques to support Phases E and F.
29 Interoperability Requirements	New chapter This chapter provides guidelines for developing interoperability requirements.
30 Business Transformation Readiness Assessment	New chapter This chapter describes a technique for identifying business transformation issues.
31 Risk Management	New chapter This chapter describes a technique for managing risk during an architecture or business transformation project.

TOGAF 9 Chapter		**Derivation from TOGAF 8.1.1**
32	Capability-Based Planning	New chapter This chapter describes the technique of capability-based planning.
Part IV: Architecture Content Framework		
33	Introduction	New chapter This new Part of TOGAF addresses content output, providing a framework within which to place major work products.
34	Content Metamodel	New chapter This chapter provides a metamodel definition of all the types of building blocks within an architecture, showing how they can be described and how they relate to one another.
35	Architectural Artifacts	Derived from Chapter 31, plus new material This chapter is revised to address a set of atomic work products created when following the ADM. A diagram to illustrate the concepts from ISO/IEC 42010:2007 is introduced. Classes of viewpoints are defined: catalogs, matrices, diagrams. Additional Architecture Viewpoints are added.
36	Architecture Deliverables	Revised from Chapter 16 A significant revision of the deliverables has been undertaken. A table is provided showing where deliverables are produced and consumed within the ADM cycle. A key difference is the introduction of two container documents: the Architecture Definition Document and the Architecture Requirements Specification.
37	Building Blocks	Revised from Chapter 32 The description of the Building Blocks Specification Process in the ADM has been updated to match the changes to the ADM Steps. The section on Levels of Modeling has been removed.
Part V: Enterprise Continuum and Tools		
38	Introduction	New chapter This chapter introduces this Part.

TOGAF 9 Chapter	Derivation from TOGAF 8.1.1
39 Enterprise Continuum	Derived from Chapters 17 and 18 The explanation of the Enterprise Continuum has been rewritten to better explain its purpose and context, including relationship to enterprise repositories. Organization Architectures has been updated to Organization-Specific Architectures in the diagram of the Architecture Continuum. Organization Solutions has been updated to Organization-Specific Solutions in the diagram of the Solutions Continuum. In the description of the Architecture Continuum, Enterprise Architectures is updated to Organization-Specific Architectures. In the description of the Solutions Continuum, Enterprise Solutions is updated to Organization-Specific Solutions.
40 Architecture Partitioning	New chapter This chapter describes the various characteristics that can be applied to classify and then partition architectures.
41 Architecture Repository	New chapter This chapter describes how the abstract classifications of architecture can be applied to a repository structure.
42 Tools for Architecture Development	This chapter is taken from Chapter 38, but substantially reduced by removing the evaluation criteria and guidelines.

Part VI: TOGAF Reference Models

43 Foundation Architecture: Technical Reference Model	No material change; maps to Chapters 19 and 20 The Detailed Platform Taxonomy is now a section of this chapter rather than being a separate chapter.
44 Integrated Information Infrastructure Reference Model	No material change; maps to Chapter 22

Part VII: Architecture Capability Framework

45 Introduction	New chapter
46 Establishing an Architecture Capability	New chapter This chapter describes how to use the ADM to establish an architecture practice within an organization.

TOGAF 9 Chapter	Derivation from TOGAF 8.1.1
47 Architecture Board	Minimal change; maps to Chapter 23 Changes have been limited to minor editorial updates.
48 Architecture Compliance	Minimal change; maps to Chapter 24 Section 24.3, Project Impact Assessments (Project Slices) has been removed.
49 Architecture Contracts	Minimal change; maps to Chapter 25 Wording is added to tie this chapter more closely to Architecture Governance. Instead of listing the contents of the Statement of Architecture Work, a reference to the definition in Part IV is added.
50 Architecture Governance	Minimal change, maps to Chapter 26 Some editorial rewording has been applied to the section Architecture Governance in Practice.
51 Architecture Maturity Models	Minimal change; maps to Chapter 27 Minor changes have been applied to refer to the latest version of the ACMM.
52 Architecture Skills Framework	Some cosmetic changes; maps to Chapter 30 References to IT Architect have been replaced with Enterprise Architect.
Appendices	
A Glossary of Supplementary Definitions	Derived from Chapter 36 The terms and definitions provided here have been split out from the original glossary as they are not specific to TOGAF.
B Abbreviations	Derived from Chapter 36 This section has been split out from the original glossary.

25.4 Approaches for Migration

(Syllabus Reference: Unit Bridge 1, Learning Outcome 5: You should be able to discuss approaches to migrate an enterprise from TOGAF 8.1.1. to TOGAF 9.)

Approaches to migration will differ from one enterprise to another. There is no single approach to fit all organizations or enterprise architectures. The ADM can be used to determine the best approach to use.

One approach is to treat the migration as an enterprise architecture project and apply the ADM with the specific Architecture Vision to migrate from the current baseline of a TOGAF 8.1.1 enterprise architecture to the target based on TOGAF 9. Such a cycle of the ADM would determine the stakeholders and their concerns in Phase A, demonstrate the business value of the migration in Phase B, determine business process and systems changes through Phases B, C, D, opportunities to migrate in Phase E and so on.

Another approach would be incremental adoption of TOGAF 9, selecting and using individual chapters or parts of the framework. An incremental approach is usually less disruptive, and justification for a migration can often be based on the value of the change. This approach could be introduced by a change request in Phase H.

25.5 Exercises

Exercise 25-1
Identify the likely stakeholders and their concerns for an organization with a mature enterprise architecture practice based on TOGAF 8.1.1 that is considering migrating to TOGAF 9.

25.6 Recommended Reading
The following are recommended sources of further information for this chapter:
- TOGAF 9 Part I, Chapter 4 (Release Notes)

Test Yourself Examination Paper – Section 1

A.1 Introduction

This examination paper is applicable only to candidates who are taking the TOGAF 8 – 9 Advanced Bridge Examination. This Test Yourself paper is for Section 1 of the Advanced Bridge Examination and consists of 20 simple multiple-choice questions.

A.2 Instructions

This Practice Test for Section 1 of the TOGAF 8 – 9 Advanced Bridge Examination is an open-book test. The permitted reference text is the TOGAF 9 specification. After completing this section, please complete the test in Appendix B.

You need to pass both sections in order to pass the test overall.

A.3 Examination – Section 1

There is one correct answer for each question, scoring one (1) point. Please read each question carefully before reading the answer options. Be aware that some questions may seem to have more than one right answer, but you are to look for the one that makes the most sense and is the most correct.

In order to pass this section you need to score at least 14 out of 20.[10]

You should spend no more than 30 minutes on this section.

---

[10]   Note that the pass mark for this practice test may differ from the live examination. Refer to The Open Group website for the latest information on examination pass marks.

Item 1-1

Question:

Which one of the following does the Architecture Content Framework describe as a work product that is contractually specified, formally reviewed, and signed off by the stakeholders?

A. An artifact
B. A building block
C. A catalog
D. A deliverable
E. A matrix

Item 1-2

Question:

In which ADM phase does the initial implementation planning occur?

A. Phase A: Architecture Vision
B. Phase B: Business Architecture
C. Phase C: Information Systems Architectures
D. Phase D: Technology Architecture
E. Phase E: Opportunities and Solutions

Item 1-3

Question:

Which one of the following is described as a view of the Architecture Repository and provides methods for classifying architecture and solution artifacts as they evolve?

A. Architecture Landscape
B. Architecture Governance Repository
C. Enterprise Continuum
D. Governance Log
E. Standards Information Base

Item 1-4

Question:

Complete the sentence: All of the following are technology-related drivers for architecture Change Requests, *except* _____

A. asset management cost reductions
B. new technology reports
C. standards initiatives

D. strategic change

E. technology withdrawal

Item 1-5

Question:

Complete the sentence: In Phase C: Information Systems Architectures, when an existing application is to be replaced, the Data Architecture should

_____

A. be re-factored to align with the technology infrastructure.

B. describe how this change impacts other projects.

C. identify the data migration requirements.

D. include the application interoperability requirements.

E. estimate the effort required to overcome any issues.

Item 1-6

Question:

In which phase of the ADM are the gap analysis results from the four architecture domains taken into account?

A. Phase E

B. Phase F

C. Phase G

D. Phase H

E. Requirements Management

Item 1-7

Question:

In Phase D, which of the following resources from the Architecture Repository should be considered in the development of the Technology Architecture?

A. Architecture Vision

B. Business rules, job descriptions

C. Implementation and Migration Plan

D. Stakeholder Map

E. TOGAF Technical Reference Model

Item 1-8

Question

Complete the sentence: All of the following are part of the approach to the Preliminary Phase, *except* _____

A. defining the enterprise
B. identifying key drivers and elements in the organizational context
C. defining Architecture Contracts
D. defining the framework to be used
E. defining the requirements for architecture work

Item 1-9

Question:

In which phase of the TOGAF ADM do activities include assessing the dependencies, costs, and benefits of the migration projects?

A. Phase E
B. Phase F
C. Phase G
D. Phase H
E. Requirements Management

Item 1-10

Question:

Complete the sentence: Phase A is initiated upon receipt of _____

A. approval from the Chief Information Officer
B. a directive from the Chief Executive Officer
C. a Request for Architecture Work from the sponsoring organization
D. the Requirements Analysis document
E. the Implementation and Migration Plan

Item 1-11

Question:

Complete the sentence: Business Architecture is the first architecture activity undertaken since _____

A. it focuses on identifying and defining the key applications used in the enterprise
B. it provides knowledge that is a prerequisite for undertaking work in the other architecture domains
C. it defines the physical realization of an architectural solution

D. it finalizes the Architecture Vision and Architecture Definition
   Documents
E. it mobilizes supporting operations to support the ongoing architecture
   Development

Item 1-12

Question:

Complete the sentence: According to TOGAF, Capability-Based Planning
is _____

A. a tactical planning technique that enhances system performance
B. focused on business outcomes
C. focused on staffing and human resource management issues
D. focused on technical capabilities
E. relevant to IT architecture

Item 1-13

Question:

In which phase of the ADM is an initial assessment of Business
Transformation Readiness performed?

A. Preliminary Phase
B. Phase A
C. Phase B
D. Phase E
E. Phase F

Item 1-14

Question:

Which of the following is defined as the risk categorization after the
implementation of mitigating actions?

A. Actual Level of Risk
B. Initial Level of Risk
C. Residual Level of Risk
D. Strategic Level of Risk

Item 1-15

Question:

When applying the ADM with the Architecture Vision to establish an Architecture Capability, which phase does TOGAF Part VII recommend define the structure of the organization's Architecture Repository?

A. Application Architecture
B. Business Architecture
C. Data Architecture
D. Preliminary Phase
E. Technology Architecture

Item 1-16

Question:

Stakeholders and their concerns are key concepts in TOGAF. Which one of the following statements is false?

A. Concerns are key interests that are crucially important to stakeholders.
B. Concerns should be SMART and have specific metrics.
C. Stakeholders can be individuals, teams, or organizations.
D. Stakeholders have key roles in, or concerns about, the system.

Item 1-17

Question:

Which of the following is considered by TOGAF an attribute of a good building block?

A. A building block that is re-usable
B. A building block meeting business needs
C. A building block with public interfaces
D. A building block that guides the development of solutions
E. A building block that is product-aware

Item 1-18

Question:

Which one of the following statements does *not* correctly describe architecture deliverables?

A. They are consumed and produced across the ADM cycle.

B. They are defined to avoid tailoring the inputs and outputs of the ADM cycle.

C. They are typically contractual work products of an architecture project.

D. They are usually reviewed and signed off by the stakeholders.

Item 1-19

Question:

What TOGAF deliverable identifies changes that are needed to the current architecture requirements and specification, and also documents the implications of change?

A. Architecture Vision

B. Requirements Impact Assessment

C. Gap Analysis results

D. Architecture Landscape

E. Architecture Roadmap

Item 1-20

Question:

Where does the Integrated Information Infrastructure Reference Model fit in terms of the Enterprise Continuum?

A. Common Systems Architectures

B. Foundation Architectures

C. Industry Architectures

D. Organization-Specific Architectures

Appendix B

Test Yourself Examination Paper – Section 2

B.1 Introduction

This examination paper is applicable both to candidates who are taking the TOGAF 9 Part 2 or TOGAF 8 – 9 Advanced Bridge Examinations.

This is an Open Book examination. You may need to refer to sections of the TOGAF 9 specification in order to answer the questions.

B.2 Instructions

This section consists of eight gradient scored, multiple-choice, single response questions. In order to answer each question you will need to read the related scenario fully. On the basis of the information provided in the scenario, and the guidance in TOGAF 9, which one of the four possible answers is the best answer?

There is a maximum of five (5) points per question.
The CORRECT answer scores five (5) points.
The SECOND BEST answer scores three (3) points.
The THIRD BEST answer scores one (1) point.
The DISTRACTER (the incorrect answer) scores zero (0) points.

In order to pass this section, you must achieve a total of 28 points or more out of a maximum of 40 points (70%).

You should spend no more than 90 minutes on this section.

B.3 Questions

Question 1

SCENARIO 1:

Acme Manufacturing is a multinational conglomerate that operates
production facilities in 24 countries and sells its products in over
100 countries. It has three sectors: Transportation, Energy Systems,
and Automation. Each sector has several business units that operate
independently. An Executive Vice President heads each of the business units.
Traditionally, each business unit has acted independently with few shared
customers or suppliers. They were expected to share financial and human
resource information from the corporate headquarters.

A consultancy firm has recommended a realignment that will enhance
sharing of product information across business units. The implementation
of this strategic realignment will require the development of integrated
customer information systems and product information systems.

Acme has a mature enterprise architecture practice and uses TOGAF 9 for
the basis of the Acme Architecture Framework (method and deliverables).
An architecture development program has been created to address the
development of these capabilities and is about to commence. The enterprise
architecture program is sponsored by the CIO.

At the most recent meeting of the Corporate Board, the Chairman of the
Board expressed a concern about the risk to the business while a potentially
disruptive program is being rolled out across the company. He noted that
several competitors had tried similar initiatives with poor results. The
Corporate Board agreed that this concern must be satisfactorily addressed
before this program can commence.

(Refer to the scenario)

Your role is the Lead Architect.

You have been asked to recommend an approach to address the concerns
raised.

Based on TOGAF 9, which of the following is the best answer?

Answers

A. You recommend that a Risk Aversion Assessment be conducted in the Implementation Governance phase to determine the implementation organization's degree of risk aversion with regard to the proposed business transformation. Based on that, if the Corporate Board is not willing to accept a reasonable amount of risk, then you recommend they put in place a set of parallel systems to mitigate the risks.

B. You recommend that techniques be used throughout the program to manage risk including risk monitoring. This will enable you to identify, classify and mitigate the risks associated with the proposed transformation and ensure suitable business continuity plans are in place. In the Implementation Governance phase, you ensure a residual risk assessment is conducted to determine the best way to manage risks that cannot be mitigated.

C. You recommend classifying the risks in terms of time, cost, and scope during the Architecture Vision phase. This will enable you to ensure that certain risks with certain types of impact are managed by the right individuals. You would then ensure that the Architecture Contracts issued in the Implementation Governance phase address those initial risks and include adequate risk monitoring actions to confirm they have been addressed.

D. You recommend that a risk management framework is used in Phase G, the Implementation Governance phase. This would include a risk classification scheme and completion of worksheets for risk assessment. This will enable you to assess the risks associated with the proposed business transformation. You then ensure that the initial level of risk is well understood before issuing the Architecture Contracts.

Question 2

SCENARIO 2:
Atlas Airlines is a low-cost airline formed in 2002. Its main base is a major international airport on the east coast of North America. It currently serves 65 destinations in 20 US states, and nine countries in the Caribbean, South America and Latin America.

Atlas Airlines has received approval to acquire a smaller regional carrier that will extend the market it reaches and enable it to feed its primary routes with connecting flights from smaller cities.

In order to integrate the new acquisition, an enterprise architecture program has been initiated, using TOGAF 9 as the method and guiding framework. The CIO is the sponsor of the activity. The Chief Architect has indicated that this program should make use of iteration with the ADM.

As the program moves into Phase A within the initial iteration of an Architecture Capability cycle, the CIO has emphasized the need to ensure that the architecture is embraced across the enterprise.

(Refer to the scenario)

Your role is a consultant advising the Chief Architect.

You have been asked to explain how you would identify and engage the stakeholders at this stage of the program.

Based on TOGAF 9, which of the following is the best answer?

Answers

A. You would conduct a series of Business Scenarios with the stakeholders impacted by the acquisition, and determine which stakeholders are likely to block the initiative and which are likely to support it. You would identify the most relevant viewpoints and validate with the stakeholders.

B. You would focus on communications with the stakeholders at the regional carrier as effective communication of targeted information to the right stakeholders at the right time is a critical success factor for such a merger. You would develop a Communications Plan to ensure they are aware of the key features of the architecture and have the opportunity to comment.

C. You would conduct a pilot project in Phase A to demonstrate to the stakeholders the technical feasibility of the approaches that are available from your preferred suppliers. Once the stakeholders confirm the approach meets their requirements you would then complete a Statement of Work and issue an Architecture Contract to your suppliers.

D. You would identify key stakeholders across both Atlas Airlines and the new acquisition. You would classify their positions and influence, recording the results in a Stakeholder Map. You would then focus on key stakeholders ensuring that you identify the most relevant viewpoints for each stakeholder and validate that their concerns are being addressed.

Question 3

SCENARIO 3:

Blue Arrow Bank has been in business for over 60 years, growing through a series of acquisitions with other financial institutions. It has a large IT service department and routinely has over 100 infrastructure and service projects in progress. The Governing Board has decided that a more structured approach to its infrastructure and services is necessary to safeguard the business, especially given the recent turmoil in the financial markets.

As a result, the CIO has sponsored the creation of an Enterprise Architecture group. This group has adopted TOGAF 9 as the basis for its enterprise architecture, developed an Architecture Vision, which has been approved, and defined a set of domain architectures. The time has come to consolidate the domain architectures and review the current initiatives and projects in the corporate portfolio as well as potentially create new projects in order to realize the vision.

The CIO has stated that the implementation approach must accommodate the constantly occurring changes to the technology and business landscapes. Shareholders want to see not just a vision but want to know that there is a flexible, integrated Implementation and Migration Plan that has the best chance of realizing the vision in these uncertain times.

(Refer to the scenario)

Your role is that of the Lead Enterprise Architect, leading a group of domain architects as well as working with the corporate project management office, strategic planners, and operations management planners.

A meeting has been scheduled with the stakeholders and you have been asked to recommend the best approach to address the concerns raised.

Based on TOGAF 9, which of the following is the best answer?

Answers

A. You recommend that the EA team leverage all of the existing projects and their deliverables to address the findings from the Gap Analysis results for the architecture domains. The EA team will request from the stakeholders all of the existing project charters and architectures so that the architects can integrate them together in a coherent manner. They will inform the operations management staff of their plans so that they can prepare to support the deliverables. Each of the domain architects will then come up with specific projects to address their gaps and then consider whether existing projects need to have their scope revised. The sum of the work required in each one of the domains will then be consolidated into the Implementation and Migration Plan. The timeline for progression of the deliverables will be documented in the Architecture Roadmap.

B. You recommend that the domain architectures are implemented immediately and all ongoing projects have their scopes revised to align with the new architectures. In order to save time you will then take the requirements from Phases B through D and create new IT projects for each one of the requirements that will enable the projects to create their individual requirements-based project architectures. The projects will work together through the creation of new point-to-point interfaces following defined interoperability architecture guidelines.

C. You recommend development of a series of Transition Architectures. This can then deliver continuous business value in an incremental manner, achieved by all the projects delivering their increments in a coordinated approach based on capability planning. You will consolidate the Gap Analysis results from each of the domain architectures and analyze the dependencies so as to come up with a work-breakdown structure. You will examine what is achievable and identify logical work packages that can become the basis for projects or the leveraging of existing projects. You will then hold a series of facilitated sessions to seek consensus on the Implementation and Migration Strategy.

D. You recommend that the stakeholders provide input on what has to be done to implement the defined domain architectures. The intent is to ensure that all stakeholders will be allowed to contribute to the EA planning. The joint analysis will then result in a detailed list of work activities that will be rolled into an IT portfolio plan that will eventually give rise to a series of projects. The intent is to create a comprehensive Target Architecture that will include the detailed technology choices for the organization for the next five years. A full report will be completed highlighting what was done including a detailed dependencies and factors assessment.

Question 4

SCENARIO 4:
Brown & Babcock, a major manufacturing firm, has decided to improve the efficiency of its sales force by replacing its legacy fax and paper-based configuration and ordering systems with a hand-held device solution. This will impact both the firm and its suppliers.

Brown & Babcock use TOGAF 9 for their internal Enterprise Architecture and use an iterative approach to applying the ADM. The enterprise architecture team has established the Architecture Capability for this project and also completed the first iteration of the Architecture Development cycle, using a Baseline First approach. The CIO is the sponsor of the Enterprise Architecture program.

The initial iteration has established the approach, the scope, and vision for the project. A set of architecture principles has been established based on TOGAF 9, Chapter 23. The CIO has highlighted the importance of adhering to the following principles:
- Data is an asset.
- Data is shared.
- Data is accessible.

The initial iteration has also established a number of business goals and objectives for the new target system. The principal goal is to give the sales force in the field direct access to the sales process, allowing sales staff to create and verify product configurations, check pricing and availability, and to place an order while still on the client site with the customer.

As part of achieving this goal, the architectures developed will need to address the following stakeholder concerns:

- What changes to existing business processes are needed?
- What data will need to be shared?
- How will distributed data be secured?
- What non-sales applications will need to be integrated with any new sales applications?

(Refer to the scenario)

Your role is that of Lead Enterprise Architect.

You have been asked to identify the most appropriate artifacts (catalogs, matrices, and diagrams) for the second iteration of the Architecture Development cycle.

Based on TOGAF 9, which of the following is the best answer?

Answers

A. Describe the Business Architecture with a Process/Event/Control/Product catalog and Role catalog.
Describe the Data Architecture with a Data Entity/Data Component catalog, Application/Data matrix, and Data Security diagram.
Describe the Application Architecture with an Interface catalog.
Describe the Technology Architecture with a Network Computing/Hardware diagram.

B. Describe the Business Architecture with a Location catalog and Business Interaction matrix.
Describe the Data Architecture with a Data Migration diagram and Data Lifecycle diagram.
Describe the Application Architecture with a Software Engineering diagram.
Describe the Technology Architecture with a Communications Engineering diagram.

C. Describe the Business Architecture with a Location catalog and Business Footprint diagram.
Describe the Data Architecture with a Application/Data matrix, Data Migration diagram, and Data Lifecycle diagram.

Describe the Application Architecture with an Application Communication diagram.
Describe the Technology Architecture with a Network Computing/Hardware diagram.

D. Describe the Business Architecture with a Location catalog and Role catalog.
Describe the Data Architecture with a Data Entity/Business Function matrix, Application/Data matrix, and Data Security diagram.
Describe the Application Architecture with an Application Interaction matrix.
Describe the Technology Architecture with a Network Computing/Hardware diagram.

Question 5

SCENARIO 5:

A European Insurance company has grown substantially over the last 15 years. Due to the many mergers and acquisitions, the application portfolio of the enterprise has grown significantly with little consideration for consolidation or rationalization. Each business unit has managed its own applications, with no coordination between them. In the last two years the competition in the insurance industry has increased with the advent of many Internet-based comparison sites leading to increased pressure to reduce the operational expenses including IT.

The Corporate Board has approved the directive to establish an Enterprise Architecture program within the company to integrate and rationalize the application portfolio and introduce a company-wide customer information management system. The Corporate Board has also given a strategic direction that the company should expand its markets significantly to cover all the member country states of the European Union in the next 24 months.

The company has no existing enterprise architecture. The CIO is the sponsor of the program and has mandated TOGAF 9 for the architecture method and deliverables. The CIO has established an Architecture Board and called the first meeting.

(Refer to the scenario)

Your role is the Lead Architect.

You have been asked how you will establish the Enterprise Architecture program.

Based on TOGAF 9, which of the following is the best answer?

Answers

A. You work with the Architecture Board to develop and tailor TOGAF 9, so it can be integrated with the existing procedures established by the Program Management Office. In addition, you examine the relationship to other processes and frameworks for systems development, operations management, and governance. You then conduct a study to determine the footprint of the enterprise architecture.

B. You issue a Request for Architecture Work so that the necessary resources needed to define an Architecture Vision can be allocated. You then conduct a Business Scenario that addresses the Board's mandate upon expansion. Based on that, you define a Common Systems Architecture that will guide the selection of Solution Building Blocks for integrating the systems across business units.

C. You ensure that there is agreement on the scope of the enterprise architecture, and identify the key business drivers. You document and validate the requirements for architecture work. You develop a set of architecture principles with the Architecture Board to guide the architecture work. You then consider how to best tailor TOGAF 9 for use, and identify tools for supporting the program.

D. You start by conducting an Architecture Maturity Assessment to assess the ability of the organization to undergo change. Using that input you then apply the TOGAF ADM to define the overall requirements for integrating a new company information management system into the enterprise. You then work with the Architecture Board to define the business goals that will drive the enterprise architecture program.

Question 6

SCENARIO 6:

Moon Star Telco Inc. is a telecommunications company that recently formed through the merging of three other telecommunication companies. The business operating model has been unified, and an enterprise architecture program has been put in place as part of the integration of the three organizations.

The company has adopted the TOGAF 9 Architecture Development Method. The Architecture Board has approved the outline Implementation and Migration Plan and they are now at the stage of conducting detailed migration planning. A working group has been formed that involves all the key architects and the stakeholders from the corporate matrix (those who will work on the project).

It is recognized that others outside the enterprise architecture team will have the responsibility to fund, build, support, and use what is put in place based on the enterprise architecture. For the company, getting this right is critical especially as the competition in the marketplace has been fierce and the lines of business have been resistant to implementing any new business model.

The CIO is the sponsor of the program and has mandated an increment approach to rollout the integration program.

(Refer to the scenario)

Your role is the Lead Architect.

You have been asked to describe:
- How you would conduct migration planning
- What you would be implementing
- Who you would involve
- What would be the major deliverable(s)

Based on TOGAF 9, which of the following is the best answer?

Answers

A. Migration planning should be conducted by the Chief Architect, his direct reports and shared with the domain architects. When complete the Implementation and Migration Plan will be sent to the Architecture Board secretariat for circulation before the next meeting. The plan will include a prioritized list of projects, their approximate cost, and the recommended way ahead. Comments from the Board (and their staff) would be incorporated into the plan and then the individual projects would have to go in front of the board to secure approval for project resources for the next project increment. The Implementation and Migration Plan would include a high-level GANT chart that could be used as the Architecture Roadmap.

B. Migration planning should be conducted by the enterprise architecture team. The approach should be confirmed and coordinated with the corporate management frameworks involved. Detailed resource estimates should be created for the work to be completed and the business value identified for all deliverables. A series of Transition Architectures should be planned that take into account the priorities. When this is completed the Implementation and Migration Plan can be finalized. The Business Planning, Portfolio Management, and Operations Management groups should all be involved in the development of the major deliverables. Once the deliverables have been completed, the architecture development cycle should be completed.

C. Migration planning should be conducted by the Project Managers using the Implementation and Migration Strategy from Phase E to create project plans focusing on scope, budget, and time. Project Management best practices can then be used to conduct more detailed analysis and come up with business value on a project by project basis. Project Managers will assign business value and prepare submissions to the IT governance Board for funding. The Chief Architect will sit as a member of the Board and advise members with respect to the criticality of the project and its relative importance. Over time the projects will continuously come forward for renewed funding and approval to proceed. The sum of the project plans and roadmaps will serve as the detailed Implementation and Migration Plan.

D. Migration planning should be conducted by the enterprise architecture team, in particular the domain (Business, Application, Data, Technology, and Security) architects who would look at implementing a series of Transition

Architectures using sound project management techniques. The EA team will then create a prioritized list of activities and place the high-level Architecture Building Blocks in an Implementation and Migration Plan and Architecture Roadmap. These deliverables would be circulated around the organization for comments that would be selectively integrated. The circulation would be to the lines of business and the members of the Executive Board so that they would be ready to fund the proposed EA work.

Question 7

SCENARIO 7:
Freight Logistics, a major business unit of Reading Ltd., has selected a Commercial Off-the-Shelf (COTS) Market Analytics solution in order to improve its capability to respond to market demands for its new rail-based freight delivery service. Freight Logistics has demonstrated that the current system does not provide the required functionality to support the marketing activities. Its performance limitations cause unacceptable delays and missed opportunities to meet market targets. Clearly, the current system is costing the unit in terms of lost revenue.

Reading Ltd. has a mature enterprise architecture capability spanning all of its business units and has recently adopted TOGAF 9 as the basis for its ongoing program. The CIO is the sponsor of the enterprise architecture practice.

The enterprise architecture team initiated a project with Freight Logistics that has defined the business vision and requirements for the new system. It includes a detailed business process analysis. A solution has been proposed that can support the existing applications and technologies currently in place. The proposed solution requires a non-standard operating system platform to support the business application and also requires different web server software to the current supported web server solutions. The Architecture Board has held a review, and it was noted that some of these project requirements were not consistent with the firm's current infrastructure standards.

After discussions with several senior executives, the CIO feels that he must support the business unit's urgent need to deploy the Market Analytics package. He has approved the implementation. A project manager has been chosen, and a feasibility meeting has been held with a decision to move forward. The project is critical and must be completed as quickly as possible; a contract has been signed with the software vendor to implement the solution.

The vendor has provided a statement of work that has passed through the migration planning phase, and major impacts to existing systems and the infrastructure have been documented.

The CIO has asked the enterprise architecture team to prepare for Phase G, ensuring that the Key Performance Indicators for system performance and security are met, and the project remains within budget.

(Refer to the scenario)

Your role is the Chief Enterprise Architect. You have been asked to recommend a plan to implement the direction from the CIO.

Based on TOGAF 9, which of the following is the best answer?

Answers
A. Based on the review held by the Architecture Board, you recommend the vendor modify the web server software and hardware components in the product so they can meet the current infrastructure standards. You recommend development of an in-house prototype of the product to investigate coding change options.

You would then obtain the approval of the development leads for supporting the development effort, develop an Architecture Contract, and provide the project plan to the project manager, emphasizing adherence to schedule. After implementation, you schedule frequent operational reviews to monitor performance of the solution.

B. You review the output from the Architecture Board and recommend the co-existence of a second web server standard, noting the additional hardware and support skills issues. You add this technology to the currently supported inventory of standard products in the company Standards Information Base.

You direct the project architects to construct an Architecture Contract with the development team. You emphasize the importance of using appropriate Architecture Compliance Reviews in addition to the test plans required for performance, and monitor the testing results. You establish agreements with the business unit for Service Level Agreements and delivery dates. After implementation, you identify re-usable objects and procedures.

C. Based on the recommendations of the Architecture Board, you would eliminate the non-standard web server from the solution. You create a revised plan and Architecture Contract for the development of a replacement application and server environment using standard re-usable components and internal development resources.

You would inform the CIO that in the long term the development of this standardized version is the lower-cost option. You ensure that the budget implications to these recommendations are presented to the finance committee. You hold frequent project management meetings to monitor compliance to standards and the revised schedule.

D. You prepare an expanded risk analysis and inform the development team of the required deliverables and the dates. You prepare a detailed impact analysis of the use of a "non-standard" web and hardware solution. You construct an Architecture Contract. You obtain approval from the CIO prior to implementation.

You schedule a test of the solution just prior to implementation according to user performance requirements. You deliver the required artifacts and archive them when implementation is completed.

Question 8

SCENARIO 8:
RealValue Inc. is an online grocer in Los Angeles, California. After several years of continued profitable operations, the Board of Directors has approved a strategic plan to expand operations to major cities in the Southwestern United States.

To realize this strategy, management has an enterprise architecture program in place to plan and implement the rollout which is estimated to take five years to complete. The program needs to consider how to take the current organization, physical plant, and information systems and transform them to support expanded operations.

TOGAF 9 has been adopted as the methodology and framework for the enterprise architecture program. The CIO is the sponsor.

A major concern that must be addressed is how to migrate from a "best-of-breed" logistics system that was built in the early days. It is not expected that this system will be able to scale to support the expanded operations. The CIO recognizes this and has an option to purchase a packaged solution from an industry leader in online sales and fulfillment. One disadvantage of this solution is that the terminology and definitions of its services do not align well to the current enterprise architecture.

This is now being piloted in a major fulfillment center in Southern California. It is a large-scale project and members of your enterprise architecture team have been deeply involved with the pilot program. As part of the pilot program, the Architecture Board has requested a compliance review be held at the fulfillment center to determine the status of the implementation. The timing of the compliance review is such that there is still time to correct any major shortcomings with the proposed solution.

(Refer to the scenario)

Your role is the Chief Architect.

What approach should you adopt to ensure that the compliance reviews are conducted successfully?

Based on TOGAF 9, which of the following is the best answer?

Answers
A. You delegate the review to the lead enterprise architect. You request that she organizes, leads, and conducts the review. Where possible she should involve the appropriate business domain experts. The review should

follow the established 12-step process and deliver an assessment report at completion.

B. You meet with the project architect and check she clearly understands the purpose of the review. You ask her to run a lightweight review process where the architects and team leaders pose a series of questions to themselves highlighting their observations on the performance and scalability of the pilot system. The responses should be aggregated into a report.

C. You assign the enterprise architecture team to manage the review. You request they ensure that the review covers the development methods. You ask them to identify where any modifications are needed to the standards being used in the project. You ask them to document the strategies being used by the implementation team for collaboration with the external supplier.

D. You assign the lead enterprise architect to coordinate the review. You request that she assemble a team of business and domain experts to conduct the interviews for the review. The checklists that the team has prepared for the interviews should be reviewed to ensure they meet the criteria for the program and the business objectives. The responses to the interviews should be compiled into a formal report.

Test Yourself Examination Answers – Section 1

This appendix contains the answers to Section 1 of the Examination Paper in Appendix A.

Item 1-1   D
A deliverable is a work product that is contractually specified and in turn formally reviewed, agreed, and signed off by the stakeholders. Deliverables represent the output of projects and those deliverables that are in documentation form will typically be archived at completion of a project, or transitioned into an Architecture Repository as a reference model, standard, or snapshot of the Architecture Landscape at a point in time.

Item 1-2   E
Phase E: Opportunities & Solutions conducts initial implementation planning and the identification of delivery vehicles for the architecture defined in the previous phases.

Item 1-3   C
The Enterprise Continuum provides a view of the Architecture Repository that shows the evolution of these related architectures from generic to specific, from abstract to concrete, and from logical to physical.

Item 1-4   D
Strategic change is a business driver.

Item 1-5   C
When an existing application is replaced, there will be a critical need to migrate data (master, transactional, and reference) to the new application. The Data Architecture should identify data migration requirements and also provide indicators as to the level of transformation, weeding, and cleansing that will be required to present data in a format that meets the requirements and constraints of the target application.

Item 1-6   A

In Phase E the Gap Analysis results from the previous phases are consolidated and their inter-dependencies closely assessed to derive an initial critical path. The overall intent is to simplify the transformation process by reducing the number of building blocks to be created as well as the administrative overhead associated with portfolio and project management.

Item 1-7   E

The TOGAF TRM should be considered in the development of the Technology Architecture in Phase D.

Item 1-8   C

Architecture Contracts are prepared and issued in Phase G.

Item 1-9   B

Phase F activities include assessing the dependencies, costs, and benefits of the various migration projects. The prioritized list of projects will form the basis of the detailed Implementation and Migration Plan that will supplement the architectures with portfolio and project-level detail assigning tasks to specific resources.

Item 1-10   C

Phase A starts with receipt of a Request for Architecture Work from the sponsoring organization to the architecture organization.

Item 1-11   B

A knowledge of the Business Architecture is a prerequisite for architecture work in any other domain (Data, Application, Technology), and is therefore the first architecture activity that needs to be undertaken, if not catered for already in other organizational processes (enterprise planning, strategic business planning, business process re-engineering, etc.).

Item 1-12   B

Capability-based planning is a business planning technique that focuses on business outcomes. It focuses on the planning, engineering, and delivery of strategic business capabilities to the enterprise. It is business-driven and business-led and combines the requisite efforts of all lines of business to achieve the desired capability. Capability-based planning accommodates most, if not all, of the corporate business models and is especially useful in organizations where a latent capability to respond (e.g., an emergency preparedness unit) is required and the same resources are involved in multiple capabilities.

Item 1-13   B

Business Transformation Readiness is first assessed in Phase A, so actions can be worked into Phases E and F in the Implementation and Migration Plan.

Item 1-14   C

The risk categorization after implementation of mitigating actions is known as "Residual Level of Risk".

Item 1-15   C

TOGAF 9 Part VII (Chapter 46) recommends that the Data Architecture would define the structure of the organization's Enterprise Continuum and Architecture Repository.

Item 1-16   B

"Concerns" are the key interests that are crucially important to the stakeholders in the system, and determine the acceptability of the system. Concerns may pertain to any aspect of the system's functioning, development, or operation, including considerations such as performance, reliability, security, distribution, and evolvability. The terms "concern" and "requirement" are not synonymous. Concerns are the root of the process of decomposition into requirements. Concerns are represented in the architecture by these requirements. Requirements should be SMART (e.g., specific metrics).

Item 1-17   A

TOGAF considers re-usability an attribute of a good building block.

Item 1-18   B

TOGAF provides a typical baseline of architecture deliverables in order to better define the activities required in the ADM and act as a starting point for tailoring within a specific organization.

Item 1-19   B

Throughout the ADM, new information is collected relating to an architecture. As this information is gathered, new facts may come to light that invalidate existing aspects of the architecture. A Requirements Impact Assessment assesses the current architecture requirements and specification to identify changes that should be made and the implications of those changes.

Item 1-20   A

The TOGAF Integrated Information Infrastructure Reference Model (III-RM) is a Common Systems Architecture that focuses on the requirements, building blocks, and standards relating to the vision of Boundaryless Information Flow.

Test Yourself Examination Answers – Section 2

D.1 Question 1

Topic:		TOGAF 9: Risk Assessment
Scenario		1
Subjects		15.4, 31.7-1
Rationale		It is important that the candidate understand how the risks associated with an architecture activity can be identified, categorized, and mitigated.
Most Correct	B	This is the best answer. It summarizes the approach recommended in the TOGAF chapter on Risk Management. It recognizes that risk has to be managed through all phases, and that you need to identify, classify and mitigate risk before starting a transformation. In the Implementation Governance Phase, those residual risks should be understood and managed to the extent possible.
Second Best	D	This choice is less correct since it performs no Risk Assessment prior to the Implementation Governance phase. It provides good guidance on managing the risks using worksheets. However, this answer does not address risk monitoring or the management of residual risks.
Third Best	C	TOGAF does recommend conducting risk classification in Phase A, however the classifications being proposed do not address the concerns being put forward. Also this answer does not address the mitigation of risks or residual risk assessment.
Distracter	A	This answer is incorrect. There is no such thing as a Risk Aversion Assessment in TOGAF. Putting in place a parallel solution would seem excessive and have its own risks.

D.2 Question 2

Topic		TOGAF 9: Stakeholder Analysis
Scenario		2
Subjects		24-1
Rationale		It is important for the candidate to be able to describe the TOGAF approach to Stakeholder Management and recognize that it is a key technique for engaging stakeholders.
Most Correct	D	This is the best answer. Stakeholder analysis and the development of a Stakeholder Map is the technique that TOGAF recommends for identifying and engaging the key stakeholders in Phase A. The Stakeholder Map is a major product output and used to support other outputs in this phase.
Second Best	A	This answer is less correct since it omits the Stakeholder Map approach recommended by TOGAF 9 to explicitly identify stakeholders. Business Scenarios are an appropriate technique to develop the Architecture Vision and can accomplish some of the engagement. This answer also lacks the identification of key players and the active engagement policy of Stakeholder analysis.
Third Best	B	This answer is less correct since it focuses on stakeholders at the regional carrier only, thus omitting key stakeholders that should be involved. The Communications Plan is produced from the work done by the Stakeholder Management approach suggested in answer A.
Distracter	C	This answer is incorrect. TOGAF does not recommend implementing pilot projects in Phase A to assess solution feasibility. This also does not follow the recommended approach for creation and approval of a Statement of Architecture Work.

D.3 Question 3

Topic		TOGAF 9 Level 2: ADM Phases Architecture Definition; Phase E: Opportunities and Solutions
Scenario		3
Subjects		13.*
Rationale		This question determines whether the candidate understands the implications of architecture transformation especially in an existing environment
Most Correct	C	This is the best answer. It recommends the use of transition architectures and capability increments to deliver business value which addresses the concern that the implementation has the ability to accommodate changes to technology and business landscape. It describes the migration planning techniques to deliver Transition Architectures, as well as seeking consensus input on the Implementation and Migration Strategy rather than going straight to an Implementation and Migration Plan.
Second Best	A	This is a less correct approach that addresses the deliverables of the architectures but in an uncoordinated way. It looks at rolling up the work in each domain rather than consolidating the gaps and creating projects as a function of capability management. It also does not directly describe the use of transition architecture. It does describe the role of the Implementation and Migration Plan and the Architecture Roadmap accurately.
Third Best	D	This is less correct as it focuses on a detailed technology-based Implementation and Migration Plan, negating the impact of using Transition Architectures to deliver incremental business value that could absorb technology and business environment change.
Distracter	B	This answer is incorrect. This approach does not address the concerns, nor follow TOGAF guidance. Most likely it would produce IT-centric architectures and plans that ignore proper documentation and coordination with other stakeholders in order to deliver IT infrastructure as soon as possible.

D.4 Question 4

Topic		TOGAF 9: Viewpoint Selection
Scenario		4
Subjects		35, 19
Rationale		This question tests the ability of the candidate to reference TOGAF 9 in order to select appropriate artifacts to address specific concerns.
Most Correct	A	This is the best answer. The Process/Event/Control/Product catalog allows an enterprise to identify the full chain of impacts resulting from changing a high-level process (addressing concern 1). The Data Entity/Data Component catalog and Application/Data matrix address concern 2 (the sharing of data). The Data Security diagram and Network Computing/Hardware diagram would address concern 3 (securing of distributed data). A Role catalog can be used also to support the security definition for the enterprise (addressing concern 3). The Interface catalog allows the interaction between applications to be developed and so will address concern 4.
Second Best	D	This choice is less good since it does not address concern 1 explicitly. The viewpoints selected address the other concerns. Note that the Application Interaction matrix is the matrix equivalent of the Interface catalog.
Third Best	C	This choice as well as not addressing concern 1, falls short on defining roles to aid security (concern 3), Data Sharing (concern 2), and Data Security (concern 3) compared to the most correct answer.
Distracter	B	This answer is incorrect as it does not directly address the concerns.

D.5 Question 5

Topic		TOGAF 9: ADM Preliminary Phase
Scenario		5
Subjects		6.4-1
Rationale		This question checks that the candidate understands that TOGAF has a Preliminary Phase and that they can identify the appropriate procedures and steps given the situation.
Most Correct	C	This is the best answer. It follows the procedures outlined in the Preliminary Phase. As this is establishing the program, these are the key steps for this phase.
Second Best	A	This choice is less correct as it misses out scoping, identifying drivers, and developing principles that would be very much needed in this establishment situation.
Third Best	D	This choice can be performed as part of the Preliminary Phase, but it is not the immediate priority as the scenario is program establishment. This omits key items, such as scoping the enterprise and establishing principles, and moves forward to apply the ADM before that program establishment is completed.
Distracter	B	This answer is incorrect because it skips past the program establishment that would be provided in the Preliminary Phase into Phase A activities, and begins execution of an architecture project focused on the Solution Architecture.

D.6 Question 6

Topic		TOGAF 9 Level 2: ADM Phases Architecture Definition Phase F: Migration Planning
Scenario		6
Subjects		14.*, 28.*
Rationale		This question determines whether the candidate understands the implications of architecture transformation especially in an existing environment in Phase F: Migration Planning.
Most Correct	B	This is the best answer. The answer is concise and complete as per Phase F, with an emphasis on building corporate consensus and ensuring that the Transition Architectures are solidly based upon business value.
Second Best	D	This is a less correct approach, as it is incomplete, missing key steps of Phase F. This also lacks the collaborative planning in close cooperation with the stakeholders within and outside of the organization.
Third Best	A	The approach is also incomplete. Phase F emphasizes collaborative planning in close cooperation with the stakeholders within and outside of the organization, and this lacks that approach.
Distracter	C	This is a wrong answer. The intent of enterprise architecture using TOGAF is to provide detailed guidance to the projects so that they can focus on operational design issues rather than strategic ones.

D.7 Question 7

Topic		TOGAF 9 Level 2 ADM Phases: Governance (Phase G)
Scenario		7
Subjects		Implementation Governance
Rationale		This question deals with the need for Implementation Governance of development projects.
Most Correct	B	This is the best answer. All of the criteria fall within the Phase G. The architect accepts the mandate of the CIO and decides that a second standard is an acceptable compromise, since time is of the essence and a contract has already been signed with the vendor per his product design. The architect then works with the development team to draw up an Architecture Contract. The architect emphasizes use of compliance reviews, the testing of the performance as the solution is developed (a critical user requirement), and gets buy-in and visibility of Service Level Agreements (SLAs) and schedule with the business unit. Finally, after implementation, re-useable artifacts and objects are collected and are available for future projects.
Second Best	A	This answer is less correct as the response (to recommend the vendor change the product) may take time and, as noted in the scenario, this is a time-critical project. Performing a prototype would reduce the risk, but again at the expense of time and perhaps budget. The project plan should be drawn up by the project manager not the architect. Finally, performance is paramount, yet the architect is suggesting monitoring the performance after implementation, rather than testing the product's performance before implementation.
Third Best	D	This approach follows the CIO direction but focuses on risk rather than co-existence. There is no negotiation with the implementation team – just a handover of schedules – or with the business unit regarding service levels. The suggestion to test the solution just prior to implementation is too late, since the solution has already been constructed and any surprises will likely impact schedule and budget. The attention to artifacts is superfluous.
Distracter	C	This answer is incorrect. The scenario states that the decision has already been made, and a contract put in place. This proposed solution does not address the CIO mandate which stated that this is time-critical and approval had been given to move ahead with the selected vendor. The consultation with the finance committee is irrelevant. Holding frequent project management meetings is not the Enterprise Architect's job, but the job of the project manager.

D.8 Question 8

Topic		TOGAF 9: Conducting Compliance Reviews
Scenario		8
Subjects		15.4, 48.6
Rationale		It is important for the candidate to be able to manage the process of conducting compliance reviews that are appropriate to the situation.
Most Correct	D	This is the best answer. It is most appropriate to the situation – it is a large-scale project and the enterprise architects have been heavily involved. In this approach the lead EA coordinates the review and assembles domain experts to manage the reviews. This response includes the mention of checklists and them being reviewed as well as a formal report being produced.
Second Best	A	This answer is less correct. This is a reasonable approach, usually best done when the architects are not involved in the project, however in this case they are. It also omits specific mention of the checklists.
Third Best	B	This answer is less correct. This approach is more suited to smaller-scale projects and the informality is not suitable to such an important project. The aggregation of responses to create the report is incorrect.
Distracter	C	This answer is incorrect. It fails to appoint a specific coordinator, and asks that the review focus on the development methods being used, rather than whether the solution meets any business criteria. It also focuses on collaboration and standards which are not of prime concern.

TOGAF 9 Certified Syllabus

This appendix provides a copy of the Level 2 Learning Units that comprise the Level 2 Syllabus for the TOGAF 9 Certified qualification. Each learning outcome is phrased in terms of what the candidate should have learned. In addition, candidates for Level 2 are assumed to have the knowledge of the Level 1 Syllabus (documented in the TOGAF 9 Foundation Study Guide). The Key Learning Point (KLP) references in the tables can be used to trace the requirements back to sections of the TOGAF 9 document.

E.1 Preliminary Phase

1	Preliminary Phase

Purpose
The purpose of this Learning Unit is to help the Candidate understand how to apply the Preliminary Phase in development of an enterprise architecture.
KLP Reference
6-*, 23-*, 21-3, 36.2
Learning Outcome
The Candidate must be able to:
1. Understand the inputs to the phase (KLP 6.3-1), and be able to explain the following key elements:
   - Architecture Frameworks
   - Business principles, business goals, and business drivers
2. Explain the influence of pre-existing architectural inputs on the phase (KLP 6.3-1)
3. Understand the steps (KLP 6.4-1, 6.4.3), and be able to:
   - Describe how to establish an enterprise architecture team and organization
   - Identify and establish a set of architecture principles for a given scenario (KLP 6.4.4-1, 23.4-1, 23.5-1)
   - Discuss the appropriate considerations for tailoring the framework (KLP 6.4.5-1)
4. Understand the outputs (KLP 6.5-1), and be able to explain the following key elements (KLP 36.2-2):
   - Architecture Principles
   - Architecture Governance Framework
   - Request for Architecture Work
5. Explain how Security Architecture influences this phase (KLP 21-3)

E.2 Architecture Governance (Level 2)

2	Architecture Governance (Level 2)
	Purpose
	The purpose of this Learning Unit is to help the Candidate understand how to apply Architecture Governance in development of an enterprise architecture.
	KLP Reference
	47-*, 50-*
	Learning Outcome
	The Candidate must be able to:
	1. Explain how Architecture Governance fits within the ADM cycle
	2. Discuss the key success factors for putting Architecture Governance into practice (KLP 50.3-1)
	3. Discuss the factors that should be considered when setting up an Architecture Board (KLP 47.3-1)
	4. Explain how to operate an Architecture Board (KLP 47.4-1)
	(There is expected to be some overlap with the Learning Unit covering Phase G.)

E.3 Business Scenarios Technique

3	Business Scenarios Technique
	Purpose
	The purpose of this Learning Unit is to help the Candidate understand how to apply the Business Scenarios technique.
	KLP Reference
	26-*
	Learning Outcome
	The Candidate must be able to
	1. Describe the properties of a good Business Scenario (KLP 26.3-1, KLP 26.7-1, KLP 26.9-1)
	2. Explain how to develop and validate a Business Scenario (KLP 26.3-1, KLP 26.7-1, KLP 26.9-1)

E.4 Phase A: Architecture Vision

4	Phase A: Architecture Vision

	Purpose
	The purpose of this Learning Unit is to help the Candidate understand how to apply Phase A in development of an enterprise architecture.
	KLP Reference
	7-*; 21-4, 30-*, 31-*,36.2
	Learning Outcome
	The Candidate must be able to:
	1. Understand the inputs to the phase (KLP 7.3-1), and be able to:
	    • Describe the typical contents of the Architecture Repository at this point
	2. Understand the steps (KLP 7.4-1), and be able to:
	    • Describe how to identify stakeholders, their concerns, and business requirements
	    • Explain the purpose of a Business Transformation Readiness Assessment
	    • Describe the risk assessment approach taken in this phase
	3. Understand the outputs (KLP 7.5-1), and be able to explain the following key elements including their purpose (KLP 36.2-2):
	    • Statement of Architecture Work
	    • Capability Assessment
	    • Architecture Vision
	    • Communications Plan
	4. Explain the Security Architecture influences on this phase (KLP 21-4)

E.5 Architecture Content Framework

5	Architecture Content Framework
	Purpose The purpose of this Learning Unit is to help the Candidate understand the TOGAF Architecture Content Framework. **KLP Reference** 33-* **Learning Outcome** The Candidate must be able to: 1. Explain the purpose of the Architecture Content Framework (KLP 33.2-1) 2. Describe the main components of the Content Metamodel (KLP 33.2-1) 3. Describe the relationship between the Architecture Content Framework and the TOGAF ADM (KLP 33.3-1)

E.6 Stakeholder Management

6	Stakeholder Management
	Purpose The purpose of this Learning Unit is to help the Candidate understand how to apply the Stakeholder Management technique. **KLP Reference** 35-*; 24-* **Learning Outcome** The Candidate must be able to: 1. Describe the steps in developing a Stakeholder Map (KLP 24-1, 24-2, 24-3, 24-4) 2. Explain the benefits of creating views (KLP 35.2-1) 3. For three example views provided by TOGAF in Chapter 35 (Sections 35.15 ....) (KLP 35.1-3): • Describe the stakeholders and their concerns • Use the example Stakeholder Map (in Section 24.4) provided by TOGAF as a guideline to identify stakeholders

E.7 TOGAF Content Metamodel

7	TOGAF Content Metamodel
	Purpose The purpose of this Learning Unit is to help the Candidate understand the TOGAF Content Metamodel. **KLP Reference** 34.1-*, 34.2-* **Learning Outcome** The Candidate must be able to: 1. Describe the core metamodel concepts (KLP 34.2-1) 2. Explain the purpose of dividing the metamodel into core and extensions (KLP 34.2-1) 3. Describe the key concepts related to the core metamodel entities (KLP 34.2-3)

E.8 Architecture Implementation Support Techniques

8	Architecture Implementation Support Techniques
	Purpose The purpose of this Learning Unit is to help the Candidate understand how to apply different techniques that will assist with the implementation of the architectures defined in the coming phases. **KLP Reference** 7-2, 7-3, 29-* ; 30-*; 32-* **Learning Outcome** The Candidate must be able to: 1. Explain how to reconcile Interoperability Requirements with potential solutions (KLP 29.6-1) 2. Explain the factors that influence Business Transformation Readiness (KLP 30.2-1) 3. Explain how to determine requirements for risk assessments (KLP 31.4-1) 4. Explain how capability-based planning is applied in an enterprise architecture context (KLP 32.4-2) (There is expected to be some overlap with the Phase A Learning Unit.)

E.9 Phase B: Business Architecture

9	Phase B: Business Architecture
	Purpose
	The purpose of this Learning Unit is to help the Candidate understand how to apply Phase B in development of an enterprise architecture.
	KLP Reference
	8-*; 21-5, 27-*
	Learning Outcome
	The Candidate must be able to:
	1. Understand the inputs to the phase (KLP 8.3-1), and explain the following key elements:
	• Business principles, business goals, and business drivers
	2. Understand the steps (KLP 8.4-1), and be able to:
	• Describe three techniques for business modeling
	• Explain the considerations for selecting reference models, viewpoints, and tools (KLP 8.4.1-1)
	• Explain the technique of Gap Analysis (KLP 27.1, 27.2)
	3. Explain how building blocks are used in the development of the Business Architecture (KLP 8.4-1)
	4. Understand the outputs (KLP 8.5-1), and be able to explain the following key elements:
	• Business Architecture components of the Architecture Definition Document
	• Business Architecture components of the Architecture Requirements Specification
	5. Explain the Security Architecture influences on this phase (KLP 21-5)

E.10 Phase C: Information Systems Architectures – Data Architecture

10	Phase C: Information Systems Architectures – Data Architecture

	Purpose
	The purpose of this Learning Unit is to help the Candidate understand how to apply Phase C (Data Architecture) in development of an enterprise architecture.
	KLP Reference
	10-*; 21-6
	Learning Outcome
	The Candidate must be able to:
	1. Explain the considerations for the implementation order of the Data and Application Architectures (KLP 9.2)
	2. Understand the inputs to the phase (KLP 10.3-1), and explain the following key elements:
	  • Data Principles
	3. Understand the steps (KLP 10.4-1), and be able to:
	  • Explain the considerations for selecting reference models, viewpoints, and tools
	4. Understand the outputs (KLP 10.5-1), and be able to explain the following key elements:
	  • Data Architecture components of the Architecture Definition Document
	  • Data Architecture components of the Architecture Requirements Specification
	5. Explain the Security Architecture influences on this phase (KLP 21-6)

E.11 Phase C: Information Systems Architectures – Application Architecture

11	Phase C: Information Systems Architectures – Application Architecture

	Purpose
	The purpose of this Learning Unit is to help the Candidate understand how to apply Phase C (Application Architecture) in development of an enterprise architecture.
	KLP Reference
	11-*, 21-6
	Learning Outcome
	The Candidate must be able to:
	1. Understand the inputs to the phase (KLP 11.3-1), and explain the following key elements:
	  • Application Principles
	2. Understand the steps (KLP 11.4), and be able to:
	  • Explain the considerations for selecting reference models, viewpoints, and tools
	3. Understand the outputs (KLP 11.5-1), and be able to explain the following key elements:
	  • Application Architecture components of the Architecture Definition Document
	  • Application Architecture components of the Architecture Requirements Specification
	4. Explain the Security Architecture influences on this phase (KLP 21-6)

E.12 TOGAF Foundation Architecture: Technical Reference Model (Level 2)

12	TOGAF Foundation Architecture: Technical Reference Model (Level 2)

	Purpose
	The purpose of this Learning Unit is to help the Candidate have a detailed understanding of the TOGAF Technical Reference Model (TRM).
	KLP Reference
	43-*
	Learning Outcome
	The Candidate must be able to:
	1. Explain the TRM graphic, including the following key elements (KLP 43.3-2, 43.3-3, 43.3-4, 43.3-5):
	   • Application Software Categories
	   • Application Platform Interface
	   • Application Platform
	   • Communications Infrastructure Interface
	   • Qualities
	2. Briefly describe the structure of the TRM (KLP 43.1-3, 43.2-1)
	3. Briefly explain the main architecture objectives of using the TRM (KLP 43.2-2)
	4. Explain what the Platform Services Taxonomy is (KLP 43.4-1)
	5. Explain what the Service Quality Taxonomy is (KLP 43.4-2)
	6. Explain how to customize the TRM to meet an organization's specific needs (KLP 43.5-2)

E.13 Integrated Information Infrastructure Reference Model (Level 2)

13	Integrated Information Infrastructure Reference Model (Level 2)

	Purpose
	The purpose of this Learning Unit is to help the Candidate have a detailed understanding of the TOGAF Integrated Information Infrastructure Reference Model (III-RM).
	KLP Reference
	44-*
	Learning Outcome
	The Candidate must be able to:
	1. Describe the business and technical drivers for Boundaryless Information Flow
	2. Explain how the III-RM fulfills the solution space for Boundaryless Information Flow
	3. Briefly describe the high-level structure of the III-RM (KLP 44.2-1)
	4. Explain the III-RM graphic, including the following components (KLP 44.1-3, 44.1-4, 44.2-1, 44.3-1):
	   • Business Applications
	   • Infrastructure Applications
	   • Application Platform
	   • Interfaces
	   • Qualities

E.14 Phase D: Technology Architecture

14	Phase D: Technology Architecture
	Purpose The purpose of this Learning Unit is to help the Candidate understand how to apply Phase D in development of an enterprise architecture. **KLP Reference** 12, 21-7 **Learning Outcome** The Candidate must be able to: 1. Understand the inputs to the phase (KLP 12.3), and explain the following key elements: • Technology Principles 2. Understand the steps (KLP 12.4), and be able to: • Explain how the TRM can be used when developing a Technology Architecture • Explain the role of Architecture Building Blocks (ABBs) 3. Understand the outputs (KLP 12.5), and be able to explain the following key elements: • Technology Architecture components of the Architecture Definition Document • Technology Architecture components of the Architecture Requirements Specification 4. Explain the Security Architecture influences on this phase (KLP 21-7)

E.15 Migration Planning Techniques

15	Migration Planning Techniques
	Purpose The purpose of this Learning Unit is to help the Candidate understand the techniques used in Phase E and F for migration planning. **KLP Reference** 28-* **Learning Outcome** The Candidate must be able to: 1. Describe how the Implementation Factor Assessment and Deduction Matrix can be used to document factors impacting the Architecture Implementation and Migration Plan (KLP 28-1) 2. Explain the purpose of the Consolidated Gaps, Solutions, and Dependencies Matrix (KLP 28-2) 3. Describe the purpose of an Architecture Definition Increments Table (KLP 28-3) 4. Explain how the Transition Architecture State Evolution Table can be used in conjunction with the TRM (KLP 28-4) 5. Explain how the Business Value Assessment Technique can be used in architecture development (KLP 28-5) (There is expected to be overlap with Learning Units on Phase E and F.)

E.16 Phase E: Opportunities & Solutions

16	Phase E: Opportunities & Solutions
	Purpose: The purpose of this Learning Unit is to help the Candidate understand how to apply Phase E in development of an enterprise architecture. **KLP Reference** 13-*, KLP 21-8 **Learning Outcome** The Candidate must be able to: 1. Describe the key stakeholders involved in this phase (KLP 13.3) 2. Explain how migration planning techniques are used in this phase to review and consolidate the Gap Analysis results from earlier phases (KLP 13.4) 3. Describe the steps to create the Implementation and Migration Strategy (KLP 13.4) 4. Describe three basic approaches to implementation (KLP 13.4) 5. Explain how to identify and group work packages (KLP 13.4) 6. Explain how Transition Architectures are created and documented (KLP 13.5) 7. Explain the Security Architecture influences on this phase (KLP 21-8)

E.17 Phase F: Migration Planning

17	Phase F: Migration Planning
	Purpose The purpose of this Learning Unit is to help the Candidate understand how to apply Phase F in development of an enterprise architecture. **KLP Reference** 14-*, 21-9 ;28-* **Learning Outcome** The Candidate must be able to: 1. Describe the management frameworks that have to be coordinated within this phase (KLP 14.3) 2. Explain how business value is assigned to each work package (KLP 14.4) 3. Describe the steps to prioritize the migration projects (KLP 14.4) 4. Describe the steps to confirm the Architecture Roadmap (KLP 14.4) 5. Explain key outputs of this phase (KLP 14.5), specifically: • Implementation and Migration Plan • Architecture Definition Document, including Transition Architectures (if any) 6. Explain the Security Architecture influences on this phase (KLP 21-9)

E.18 Phase G: Implementation Governance

18	Phase G: Implementation Governance
	Purpose The purpose of this Learning Unit is to help the Candidate understand how to apply Phase G in development of an enterprise architecture. **KLP Reference** 15-*, 48-*, 49-*; 21-10; 31-* **Learning Outcome** The Candidate must be able to: 1. Understand the inputs to the phase (KLP 15.3) 2. Understand the steps (KLP 15.4), and be able to describe the following: • Explain how to tailor and conduct an Architecture Compliance Review (KLP 48.6-1) 3. Understand the outputs (KLP 15.5), and be able to explain the following key elements: • The contents of Architecture Contracts (KLP 49.2-1) • Their relationship to Architecture Governance (KLP 49.3-1) 4. Explain the Security Architecture influences on this phase (KLP 21-10) 5. Demonstrate the role that risk monitoring plays in this phase (KLP 31.7-1)

E.19 Phase H: Architecture Change Management

19	Phase H: Architecture Change Management

	Purpose
	The purpose of this Learning Unit is to help the Candidate understand how to apply Phase H in development of an enterprise architecture.
	KLP Reference
	16-*, 46-*, 21-11
	Learning Outcome
	The Candidate must be able to:
	1. Understand the inputs to the phase (KLP 16.3), and be able to explain the following:
	   • Change Requests
	2. Understand the steps (KLP 16.4), and be able to describe the following:
	   • Architecture Board meetings
	3. Understand the outputs (KLP 16.5), and be able to explain when the following might occur:
	   • Updated Architecture Contracts
	   • A new Request for Architecture Work
	4. Explain the Security Architecture influences on this phase (KLP 21-11)

E.20 ADM Architecture Requirements Management

20	ADM Architecture Requirements Management
	Purpose The purpose of this Learning Unit is to help the Candidate understand how to apply the process of managing architecture requirements. **KLP Reference** 17-*; 21-2 **Learning Outcome** The Candidate must be able to: 1. Understand the inputs to the phase (KLP 17.3) 2. Understand the steps and their correspondence to phases (KLP 17.4) 3. Explain how the Requirements Management steps correspond to ADM phases (KLP 17.4) 4. Explain the purpose of the outputs of Requirements Management (KLP 17.5) 5. Explain the Security Architecture influences on the requirements captured (KLP 21-2)

E.21 Architecture Partitioning

21	Architecture Partitioning
	Purpose The purpose of this Learning Unit is to help the Candidate understand how architecture partitioning can be used to simplify the development and maintenance of an enterprise architecture. **KLP Reference** 40.1, 40.2 **Learning Outcome** The Candidate must be able to: 1. Describe the purpose of Architecture Partitioning (KLP 40.1) 2. Describe the classification criteria for solutions and architectures when considering partitioning (KLP 40.2) 3. Describe how Architecture Partitioning can be employed in the Preliminary Phase of the ADM (KLP 40.2-3)

E.22 Architecture Repository

22	Architecture Repository
	Purpose The purpose of this Learning Unit is to help the Candidate understand the purpose of the Architecture Repository, its constituent parts, and its relationship to other parts of TOGAF. **KLP Reference** 41-* **Learning Outcome** The Candidate must be able to: 1. Explain the relationship between the Architecture Repository and the Enterprise IT Repository 2. Describe the purpose of the repository areas that hold output of projects, specifically: • Architecture Landscape (KLP 41.2-1) • Reference Library (KLP 41.3-1) • Standards Information Base (KLP 41.4-2) • Governance Log (KLP 41.5-1)

E.23 Guidelines for Adapting the ADM: Iteration and Levels

23	Guidelines for Adapting the ADM: Iteration and Levels
	Purpose The purpose of this Learning Unit is to help the Candidate understand how to apply iteration and different levels of architecture with the ADM. **KLP Reference** 19-*, KLP 20-* **Learning Outcome** The Candidate must be able to: 1. Describe the concept of iteration and how it applies to TOGAF (KLP 19-2) 2. Describe the factors influencing the use of iteration (KLP 19-3) 3. Describe some suggested iteration cycles (KLP 19-1) 4. Describe how the ADM supports different types of engagements within the organization (KLP 19-2) 5. Explain how to apply iteration cycles to the ADM phases (KLP 19-1, KLP 19-2) 6. Explain how the concepts of levels and the Enterprise Continuum are used to organize the Architecture Landscape (KLP 20-1) 7. Identify the different levels of architecture that exist in an organization (KLP 20-1)

E.24 Guidelines for Adapting the ADM: Security

24	Guidelines for Adapting the ADM: Security
	Purpose The purpose of this Learning Unit is to help the Candidate understand the security considerations that need to be addressed during application of the ADM. **KLP Reference** 21-* **Learning Outcome** The Candidate must be able to: 1. Describe the responsibility that Enterprise Architects have towards Security Architecture (KLP 21-1) 2. Describe the recommended Security adaptations to the ADM (This Learning Unit overlaps with each of the ADM phases.)

E.25 Guidelines for Adapting the ADM: SOA

25	Guidelines for Adapting the ADM: SOA
	Purpose The purpose of this Learning Unit is to help the Candidate understand how the ADM can be adapted for the SOA style of architecture. **KLP Reference** 22-* **Learning Outcome** The Candidate must be able to: 1. Describe SOA as an architectural style (KLP 22-1) 2. Explain how enterprise architecture supports SOA (KLP 22-2) 3. Describe the recommended SOA adaptations to the ADM (KLP 22-3)

E.26 Architecture Maturity Models

26	Architecture Maturity Models
	Purpose The purpose of this Learning Unit is to help the Candidate understand the role of Architecture Capability Maturity Models in enabling an enterprise to determine the state of the enterprise architecture and to evaluate risks and options during the development of the enterprise architecture. **KLP Reference** 51-* **Learning Outcome** The Candidate must be able to: 1. Explain the role of a Capability Maturity Model (KLP 51.1-1) 2. Explain the CMMI process improvement approach development by CMU (KLP 51.2) 3. Describe the structure and levels of the ACMM developed by CMU for the US DoC (KLP 51.3) 4. Explain the role of Maturity Assessments in the ADM (KLP 51.3-2, 51.4-1)

E.27 Architecture Skills Framework

27	Architecture Skills Framework
	Purpose The purpose of this Learning Unit is to help the Candidate understand the Architecture Skills Framework, a classification model for architect roles. **KLP Reference** 52-* **Learning Outcome** The Candidate must be able to: 1. Explain the purpose of the Architecture Skills Framework and why it is needed (KLP 52.2) 2. Describe the benefits of using the Architecture Skills Framework (KLP 52.3) 3. Describe the structure of the Architecture Skills Framework, including roles, skills, and proficiency levels (KLP 52.4)

E.28 Syllabus for Bridging from TOGAF 8 Certified to Level 2

The learning outcome for Candidates bridging from TOGAF 8 Certified to Level 2 is identical to the combination of Level 1 and Level 2, with the following additional Learning Unit:

1	TOGAF 8.1.1 to TOGAF 9 Migration
	Purpose The purpose of this Learning Unit is to help the Candidate understand the differences between TOGAF 8.1.1 and TOGAF 9. **KLP Reference** KLP 4-* **Learning Outcome** The Candidate must be able to: 1. Describe the new features in TOGAF 9 2. Explain the benefits of the new features 3. Explain the high-level structural changes between TOGAF 8.1.1 and TOGAF 9 4. Describe the key differences between the ADM in TOGAF 8.1.1 and TOGAF 9 5. Discuss approaches to migrate an enterprise from TOGAF 8.1.1 to TOGAF 9

Index

Made in the USA
Lexington, KY
23 November 2013